PERSPECTIVES IN PRIMARY EDUCATION

PLAN EUROPE 2000
PUBLISHED UNDER THE AUSPICES OF THE
EUROPEAN CULTURAL FOUNDATION

PROJECT 1
EDUCATING MAN FOR THE
21ST CENTURY

Volume 7
PERSPECTIVES IN PRIMARY EDUCATION

Scientific Committee of Project 1
Chairman: Henri Janne (Brussels).
Members: J. L. Aranguren (Madrid), Raymond Aron (Paris),
Friedrich Edding (Berlin), Alexander King (Paris),
Max Kohnstamm (Brussels), M. J. Langeveld (Utrecht),
J. A. Lauwerys (Halifax), J. Stuart Maclure (London),
Raymond Poignant (Paris), W. Schultze (Frankfurt),
T. Segerstedt (Uppsala), Aldo Visalberghi (Rome).
Director: Ladislav Cerych (Paris).

PERSPECTIVES IN PRIMARY EDUCATION

by

LAMBERTO BORGHI

WITH THE COOPERATION OF

ORNELLA ANDREANI DENTICI
FRANCESCO DE BARTOLOMEIS
ANTONIO SANTONI RUGIU
GASTONE TASSINARI
LYDIA TORNATORE

MARTINUS NIJHOFF / THE HAGUE / 1974

This study has been realised owing to the support of the Shell Group of Companies and the European Cultural Foundation.

© 1972 *European Cultural Foundation, Amsterdam, Netherlands*
© 1974 *English edition by Martinus Nijhoff, The Hague, Netherlands*

All rights reserved, including the right to translate or to reproduce this book or parts thereof in any form.

ISBN 90 247 1643 8

PRINTED IN THE NETHERLANDS

TABLE OF CONTENTS

FOREWORD   VII

I

STRUCTURAL AND EDUCATIONAL DEVELOPMENTS IN THE PRIMARY SCHOOL

1. Aims of Education / by Lamberto Borghi   3

   Why we define educational aims. The current debate on educational aims. The theory of "the cultivation of the intellect" and its social motivation. Definition of the aims of the progressive education movement. The relation between thinking and doing. Educational aims in recent theories of cognitive learning. The study of prejudice in its relation to education. The contribution of psychotherapy. Intergroup education. International education. Education for peace. Education and mass culture. Education for leisure. Education through art. Work in education. Language education. Conclusion.

2. Innovations in the Structures of Primary Education / by Lamberto Borghi   43

   Changes in organisation. The impact of educational democratisation on changing school structures. Compensatory education. The debate on compensatory education. The trend towards integration. Continuity between primary and secondary education. The *Scuola-Quartiere* (School and Neighbourhood) movement. A fresh approach to the educational needs of children from minority groups. Curriculum changes in the light of structural changes in the school. The education of teachers.

3. Progress in Educational Psychology / by Francesco De Bartolomeis   87

   Introduction. Educational psychology and the future of education. Flexibility and planning. Interpersonal relationship and social position. Educational psychology at a turning point. Learning and creativity. Educational psychology and clinical psychology. Laboratory structures. Technology and the future of education. Differential classes and differential treatment. Work as an introduction to technology and the management of social services. Conclusion.

4. Personality, Family and Social Factors of Achievement / by Ornella Andreani Dentici … 123

    Part one – Small sample: Findings
    A. Intellectual operations
    B. Linguistic mediations
    C. The interactions between children, family and school
    Part two – Large sample: Findings
    A. Intelligence and achievement tests
    B. Personality and socialisation
    Drawings of the family and interviews with children and parents. Conclusion.

II

THE CURRICULUM IN THE PRIMARY SCHOOL

5. Mathematics / by Lydia Tornatore … 145

    Introduction. The rôle of mathematics. Research and planning. The development of new mathematics curricula. Mathematics and creativity. Value of play. Discovery method. Open-ended problems and situations. Mathematics in the curriculum. The teacher's rôle. New directions in mathematics education.

6. Social Studies / by Gastone Tassinari … 177

    The educational implications of the term "social studies". Current problems and prospects for social studies. Broadening the field of social studies. Subject approach versus coordinated approach. Criticism of the "expanding environment approach". The cognitive aspect of social studies. Social studies and social education.

7. Artistic and Creative Activity / by Antonio Santoni Rugiu … 213

    Aesthetic activity as play. Creativity, a social necessity of tomorrow? The marginal rôle of art education. Loss of creativity in the ten to twelve age group. The precarious nature of primary education. Art and art education: influences and autonomy. The interaction between art and school. The tendancy to syn-aesthetic forms. Art education as a multilateral process. Creative technology. Artistic and scientific creativity. The rôle of emotivity. The formation of aesthetic taste. Contemplation and its relationship to reality. Artistic creativity and the teacher.

BIOGRAPHICAL NOTES … 246

INDEX … 249

FOREWORD

PURPOSE OF THE STUDY

Primary education in Europe, as in the United States and other continents, is passing through a period of profound change, affecting some of the fundamental educational aims at primary school level and teaching structure, content and methods.

The purpose of this study is to sketch a broad picture of the European educational scene which may be brought about by the impact of innovation in industrialised countries.

We are only too aware of the difficulties inherent in our task. Even when projections and forecasts are firmly rooted in an analysis of existing data, they are liable to be contradicted by the facts. We shall attempt to allow for those alternative situations which may provide the context for the organisation and functioning of primary education. We make no claim to portray the European primary school at the end of the twentieth or at the beginning of the twenty-first century. We shall do no more than analyse existing achievements and experiments based on research in the associated fields of education, psychology and sociology and from this analysis extrapolate a series of forecasts based on objective factors of a social and intellectual nature, offering realistic hypotheses for the future. Our aim is to provide sound guidelines for those who are to build a better future for our children.

The language of our report will be not merely *informative*, in that it will describe the situation in a few of the countries that we have studied – England, France, Germany, Italy, the Soviet Union and Sweden, with the United States in the background – but also *performative*.

This implies that we are involved in and committed towards the achievement of educational conditions that will reflect the ideals of a better social order. One of our primary aims has been to narrow the gap between these two kinds of language, the former describing what is actually happening and the latter formulating plans of action. The success of our endeavour will be measured by our ability to bring the two languages closer.

We will not give a detailed description of the conditions prevailing in the industrialised countries of Europe in the field of primary education, for this would be beyond the scope of our study, although a thorough and up-to-date knowledge of the situation in these countries is implicit in our work.

In our comparative analysis we have provided no more than a general picture of the various contexts in so far as they reflect a common pattern in specific cultural backgrounds. In so doing, we outline certain policy options for the future of primary education in the more advanced European countries which may influence all the developing countries over the next three decades.

Our main effort, however, has been directed towards an investigation of the conceptual frameworks within which we believe the process of change should be interpreted and directed. Our study is essentially an attempt to clarify ideas and to shed light on controversial educational, sociological and psychological issues having a bearing upon primary education.

I

STRUCTURAL AND EDUCATIONAL DEVELOPMENTS IN THE PRIMARY SCHOOL

1. AIMS OF EDUCATION

BY

LAMBERTO BORGHI

WHY WE DEFINE EDUCATIONAL AIMS

Goals and values are not absolute and unchangeable, but must be constantly reviewed in the light of the decisions that men make in a changing society. To discuss educational aims is valuable in that without debate we cannot achieve our stated goals in the field of education; whether we attain these goals will depend upon the attitudes we adopt now and the decisions we make now in planning for the future and in implementing that planning.

Our attempt to define the educational aims of primary education in the 21st century should be viewed in the light of our discussion on the two future alternatives for society, the seeds of which are already contained in the present. The second model of society that we have described is a "participatory democracy", based upon small group activity and face-to-face relationships among individuals who have abolished the oppression that today alienates man from himself and from his fellow human beings. The main agent of his liberation will have been education. This concept has been clearly expressed by Herbert Marcuse in *An Essay on Liberation*. He believes that "the creation of a new reality" depends not only upon the establishment of the "primary, fundamental institutions of liberation" based on "collective ownership, collective control and planning", but also upon the development of a "new sensibility, sensitivity against domination; the feeling, the awareness that the joy of freedom and the need to be free must precede liberation"; a "spontaneous" elan, which can become "a radical and revolutionary force" only "as a result of enlightenment, education, political practice – in this sense, indeed, as a result of organisation".

This "ingression of the future into the present" is made authentic by our new awareness and understanding of the current situation, the prerequisite for its transformation. We manifest our genuine desire to bring about a new social and human condition by the choice we make of the means by which we hope to attain this goal. "If the socialist relationships of production", Marcuse declares, "are to be a new way of life, a new form of life, then their existential quality must show forth, anticipated and demonstrated, in the fight for their realisation", by the objective and subjective relations which will bind the individuals engaged in this process of change to each other. In the common struggle for social change and, most important, in interpersonal relations, there must be no form of "exploitation". "Understanding, tenderness toward each other" will be the key note. "Only thus will the future be lived as if it were already present".[1]

In imparting the type of education appropriate to these societal aims, the stress will be upon the need to maximise human potential to avoid dichotomy between the cultivation of the intellect and the social development of children and young people, factors that are closely related to emotional education.

In deciding on the methods of achieving these goals – and thus forming well-rounded personalities – we will have to translate the model we have chosen for the society of tomorrow, "participatory democracy", into educational terms. Recent research on the future of education has highlighted "the concept of participatory planning", a process that involves teachers, students, administrators, parents and the public in the choice, examination and assessment of alternative paths to the goals "toward which we desire to orient our educative conduct".[2]

THE CURRENT DEBATE ON EDUCATIONAL AIMS

This view of educational aims and of the most suitable method of attaining those aims helps us to understand the substance and implications of recent debates on the purpose of education and the proper choice of educational procedures.

The concept of the school as an institution dedicated to the intellect has played an important role over the past decade. It originated in the anti-pragmatist position taken up by Robert M. Hutchins and a group of educators and writers in the years immediately preceding and fol-

---

[1] Herbert Marcuse, *An Essay on Liberation*, Beacon Press, Boston, 1969, pp. 87-89.
[2] Warren L. Ziegler, "Some Notes on How Educational Planning in the United States Looks at the Future", *Notes on the Future of Education*, Syracuse University Research Corporation, Spring-Summer 1970, p. 18.

lowing the Second World War. The intellectualist trend of this group was well expressed in Mr. Hutchin's words to the effect that "the task of education is to make rational animals more rational", and that the aim of the school is "to teach students to lead the life of reason". "Cultivation of the intellect", which should start from the early stages of education, should culminate at college level with the study of "the one hundred great books".[3]

This rationalistic tendency, disassociated from its Aristotelian and neo-Thomistic aspects, took new shape in the late fifties, following the launching of an artificial satellite by the Soviet Union in 1957. There was bitter reaction against progressive education in the United States when Americans were confronted with the scientific and technological achievements of the Soviet Union, which they saw as jeopardising their military superiority.

To reinforce the intellectual content of education was considered vital in meeting the challenge of international competition.

The new educational trend which gained momentum during those years cannot, however, be attributed solely to political and military factors. Progressive education, in its less carefully thought out applications, was under review during the period that followed the end of the war. Cognitive learning and social learning theories which extended the horizons of education were being developed. What has taken place during the past few years has not been a mere move away from progressive education and a return to traditional educational theory and school practice. Much of the former dichotomy of thought has faded into the background under the impact of experimentation. There has been greater awareness of the contributions of various trends of thought, formerly opposed to each other, to clearer understanding of educational aims and needs.

Traces of former opposition still remain, however, between those who stress "the demand for technically trained students, the demand for training of the intellect only, for scientific proficiency" and those who stand for a more comprehensive and creative development of personality. "One may observe", Rogers went on to say, "an elementary school classroom for hours without recording one instance of individual creativity or free choice, except when the teacher's back is turned".[4]

---

[3] Robert M. Hutchins, *Education for Freedom*, Louisiana University Press, 1944, p. 37.
[4] Carl R. Rogers and Barry Stevens, *Person to Person: The Problem of Being Human, A New Trend in Psychology*, Real People Press, Lafayette, California, 1967, p. 56.

THE THEORY OF "THE CULTIVATION OF THE INTELLECT" AND ITS SOCIAL MOTIVATION

Several other voices have been raised in the United States and in Europe, criticising the type of education whose aim is to accelerate the process of learning through the introduction of efficient educational technology while it neglects those deep-rooted intellectual, social and affective needs of pupils that should be the primary concern of school and educators, linked with the neo-capitalist development of contemporary society.

There are today many teachers and community leaders, as Neil Postman and Charles Weingartner have recently pointed out, who "usually can be relied upon to give unflagging support to educational television, team teaching, green chalk boards, movable chairs, more textbooks, teaching machines, the use of overhead projectors and other innovations that play no role in effective significant learning". Their enthusiasm "for educational innovation" – the authors continue – "is in inverse proportion to its significance to the learning process".[5]

If education of the intellect is viewed out of its social and emotional context, the processes of thought are deprived of all genuine relevance. Critics of the existing curriculum and innovations in contemporary education have pointed out the danger that "the method of intelligence" might be exploited by private and corporate forces, under the impact of vested interest and technological progress, to imbue passive acceptance of society as it stands. The method of learning by enquiry, too, if developed in an environment that does not encourage investigation and if there is no clear understanding of what children should really be learning, can become a tool for the preservation of the establishment. By fostering the process of thought without due regard to real life and the problems of the community, teachers have encouraged pupils to raise convergent rather than divergent questions. One aspect of creative intelligence has been neglected: "the capacity to *generate* questions that learners are not, at first, aware of". Only by associating the "problem-solving method", as John Dewey termed it, or the "hypothetical method", to use Jerome Bruner's expression, with the real issues of genuine concern to the children and their social environment can students be motivated to develop divergent and creative thought – the capacity to formulate "divergent questions" which "are instruments of the expansion of consciousness".[6]

[5] Neil Postman and Charles Weingartner, *Teaching as a Subversive Activity*, Delacorte Press, New York, 1969, p. 57.
[6] *Ibid.*, p. 70.

DEFINITION OF THE AIMS OF THE PROGRESSIVE EDUCATION MOVEMENT

The progressive education movement was primarily concerned with the association between education and the expanding environment. Its main purpose, Paul Goodman explained, was to help overcome the crisis in contemporary society, with its "lack of personal engagement, cultural irrelevance and ineptitude, in conditions of mass industry and mass education".[7]

The Progressive education movement included different trends, but certain of the points which Goodman considered to be common to all are still relevant. These include: "emphasis on individual differences", "tolerance of races, classes and cultures", "minimising authority", "emphasis in the curriculum on real problems of a wider society, with actual participation in the neighbourhood community". These and other points, Goodman affirmed, did not represent "a perfect educational program", but "in a period like ours, of transition, uprootedness, inhuman scale, technical abstractness and conformity no lesser programme is seriously conservative of human resources".[8]

The need to combine the cult of the intellect with the social and emotional aspects of life experience is the basic tenet of Dewey's educational philosophy. Its impact on the effort to determine the aims of education for the future in Europe is worthy of emphasis. The development of intelligence, as Dewey clearly put it, "implies a prior stage of a different kind, a kind variously characterised as social, affective, technological, aesthetic, etc.". The contribution of the intellect is to transform into conscious experience the "non-reflectional" elements of experience. "It is indispensable to note", Dewey said, "that... the intellectual element is set in a context which is non-cognitive and which holds within it in suspense a vast complex of other qualities and things...".[9]

THE RELATION BETWEEN THINKING AND DOING

The moving force of intelligence is the full involvement of the individual in society. Far from devaluing the importance of reflective thought, this idea – central to Dewey's philosophy – attributes the greatest re-

---

[7] Paul Goodman, *Growing Up Absurd*, New York, Random House, 1950, p. 80.
[8] P. Goodman, *Ibid.*, pp. 81-82.
[9] John Dewey, *Essays in Experimental Logic*, Dever Publications, New York, 1916, pp. 1-2, 4.

sponsibility for progress in the human world to reflective thinking. Dewey sees the nature of thought as prospective and forward-looking, believing the development of rationality in children to be the basic prerequisite for the progress of society. Thought is the only instrument available to man to assist him in his attempts to make living conditions less unstable and precarious. The concept of the practical nature of reality, to which Dewey subscribed, admits that thought has a unique and distinctive function closely related to praxis. One of Dewey's most notable contributions to contemporary educational thought is his concept of "the process-oriented perception of knowledge". To "know", one must first become aware of the problematical situations arising in one's individual and social experience, develop ideas as hypotheses to solve the problems that have been identified and then transform those ideas into knowledge after testing their validity in practice. This is the essence of scientific method, formerly restricted to the physical world but now to be extended to the basic concerns of man – social, moral, economic, religious and political. To think is to be able to develop "a *hypothesis* to be employed in directing operations of observation, an idea to be tested or "proved" by the consequences of these operations". Dewey emphasised the idea that experimentation, the core of science, "is a form of doing and making", and also that "no hard and fast line can be drawn between such forms of "practical" activity and those which apply their conclusions to human social ends without involving disastrous consequences to science in its narrowest sense".[10]

We should like to stress the importance of these two concepts when defining educational aims in the broadest of terms: the close connection between the practical (and consequently the social and emotional) and the intellectual aspects of human experience, and the independence – indeed, the purity – of the intellect in its dialectical rapport with the practical. These two points form the substance of Dewey's message, as Dewey himself pointed out in his last remarkable philosophical essay. On the one hand, he stressed the "indissoluble unity" in which "common sense" as it is usually expressed "fuses... senses which when discriminated are called *emotional, intellectual, practical*"; on the other, he pointed out the ultimately practical implications of knowing, both in common sense and in scientific uses. But at the same time he explained that the practical nature of scientific knowing was to be identified in the concern "with the advancement of *knowing* apart

---

[10] John Dewey, *Logic, The Theory of Inquiry*, Henry Holt & Co., New York, 1938, pp. 430 and 439.

from concern with *other* practical affairs". Therefore, he said, "the interests of human living in general, as well as those of scientific inquiry in particular, are best served by keeping such enquiry 'pure', that is, free from interests that would bend the conduct of inquiry to serve concerns alien (and practically sure to be hostile) to the conduct of knowing as its own end and proper terminus".[11] Dewey's recognition of "the liberative outcome of the abstraction that is supremely manifested in scientific activity" was expressed in terms of "the vast return wave of the methods and conclusions of scientific concern with the uses and enjoyments (and sufferings) of everyday affairs; together with an accompanying transformation of judgement and of the emotional affections, preferences and aversions of everyday human beings".[12]

EDUCATIONAL AIMS IN RECENT THEORIES OF COGNITIVE LEARNING

The close connection between intellectual, social and emotional aims in education is recognised by all the leading contemporary exponents of educational, psychological and sociological thought. Although contemporary students of cognitive learning stress that the proper aim of education is "organised knowledge", they nonetheless acknowledge the importance of social and emotional processes.

In his paper on "The Act of Discovery", Jerome S. Bruner, while agreeing with the Jewish philosopher Maimonides that intellectual perfection is the highest of all achievements, considered that children's thought processes are fostered by the "hypothetical mode" rather than by the "expository mode" of teaching. "The hypothetical mode in teaching", Bruner explained, "by encouraging the child to participate in 'speaker's decisions', speeds the process along". "The growth of thought processes" is seen by Bruner, in agreement with Vygotsky, "as starting with a dialogue of speech and gesture between child and parent; autonomous thinking begins at the stage when the child is first able to internalise these conversations and 'run them off' himself".[13] Once the child has been able to assimilate the mature mode of

---

[11] John Dewey and Arthur Bentley, *Knowing and the Known*, The Beacon Press, Boston, 1949, pp. 276, 282-283. Chapter X, "Common Sense and Science", from which these words are quoted, was written by Dewey.
[12] *Ibid.*, p. 282.
[13] Jerome S. Bruner, "The Act of Discovery", *Readings for Social Studies in Elementary Education*, by John Jarolimek and Huber M. Walsh, New York, 1965, pp. 211-212.

thought of adults who are important to him – parents and teachers – he is capable of extending thought beyond the information he has received and using ideas as "a basis for formulating reasonable hypotheses". Even more important, he can "carry out his learning activities with the autonomy of self-reward".[14]

The origin of thought processes is thus closely related to the origin of social processes. Social identification of the child with his parents and teachers is fundamental in developing his capacity for knowing. The reciprocal nature of a child's personal relationships, acquired through his contacts with adults who play a leading part in his development, is of great assistance to him in organising his thinking within a framework of a reciprocal dialogue, the prerequisite for rational thought. The intrinsic motive in learning is not merely social but also emotional in character for, in Bruner's words, "it involves a deep human need to respond to others", a response that is "probably... the basis of human society". Bruner complained that since "the corpus of learning, using the word now as synonymous with knowledge, is reciprocal, the conduct of our educational system has been curiously blind to this interdependent nature of knowledge".[15]

Students of cognitive knowledge in Europe had already stressed this close connection between the intellectual and the social growth of personality. The best known, Jean Piaget, made this point very clear in his view that the child develops the capacity for rational thought at the same time as he becomes able to establish relationships based on reciprocity with his peers. Thus genuine communication and abstract logical thinking are two inseparable aspects of a mature person. "The full development of personality", Piaget stated, "in its distinctive intellectual aspect, is inseparable from the affective, social and moral relations which form the life of the school".[16]

Although Piaget, Bruner and Montessori were mainly concerned with learning problems, they were well aware of the social and emotional aspects of learning. Their concern for these aspects of the maturing personality and their educational implications was, nonetheless, incidental. Both cognitive learning and social learning theorists "have neglected the emotional side of human relations until recently".[17] Even

---

[14] *Ibid.*, p. 210.
[15] Jerome S. Bruner, *Toward a Theory of Instruction*, Cambridge, Mass., 1967, pp. 125-126.
[16] J. Piaget, *The Right to Education in Modern World* (Italian translation, Edizioni di Comunità, Milano, 1951, p. 60: *Il diritto all'educazione nel mondo attuale*).
[17] Robert D. Singer and Anne Singer, *Psychological Development in Children*, W. B. Saundern Company, Philadelphia, 1969, p. 181.

Aims of Education

Dewey did not pay sufficient attention to the affective implications of his educational philosophy, although he linked the intellectual and social processes very closely.

THE STUDY OF PREJUDICE IN ITS RELATION TO EDUCATION

Those psychologists and sociologists – the majority being influenced by psychoanalysis – who have made a special study of prejudice have contributed greatly to an understanding of the emotional basis of the intellectual and social formation of personality over the past few decades. Prejudice is widespread and is a factor that must be taken into account when we evaluate the obstacles to achieving the aims of education in 21st century society. In a conceptual analysis of the phenomenon, John Harding has described prejudiced behaviour as infringing three ideal norms: prejudice signifies a departure from the norm of rationality, from the norm of justice and from the norm of human-heartedness.[18] Individuals prone to prejudice suffer from severe lesions in the intellectual, social and emotional areas of their personality. The task of education is to forestall and eliminate prejudice, as shown by the leading exponents of European Enlightenment in the 18th century.

Recent research has revealed the magnitude of the phenomenon of prejudice in most European countries. A study conducted by Professor Melvin M. Tumin in Germany, France and England in the early sixties indicated that the average rate of rejection of out-groups in a sample of adults amounted to 28% in Germany, 23% in England and 24% in France; the corresponding figures for young people were 26%, 23% and 21%.[19] Another survey conducted in certain communities in Northern, Central and Southern Italy in 1966 showed the average percentage rejection to be approximately 33% for adults and 21% for children aged 10 to 15 in the selected sample. Of the total sample in the Southern community, 50.2% were found to reject Jews. In their replies to a questionnaire and in interviews, the members of the Southern community proved to be far more exclusive than those in the Centre and the North of Italy.[20] This appears to confirm Gordon

---

[18] John Harding, *The Conceptualization and Measurement of Prejudice*, August 1962, pp. 3-4 (mimeographed).
[19] Melvin Tumin, *International and Inter-Generational Patterns of Ethnocentrism*, A Study of Youth and Adults in England, France and Germany, Princeton University, 1961, pp. 19-20 (mimeographed).
[20] L. Borghi, A. Carbonaro, F. Lumachi, "Pregiudizio e comunicazione sociale", *Scuola e Città*, September 1967, pp. 474-476.

W. Allport's observation that "prejudice is greater whenever there are severe barriers to communication between groups".[21]

In his study of the nature of prejudice, Allport points out that "this syndrome, originally established in adults, has been found to reach down into the middle years of childhood... But we do not know for certain – though these studies strongly imply it – that early childhood training is responsible. Indications are that harsh and capricious discipline, deprivation of affection, feelings of rejection, may underline the character-structure thus formed".[22]

The importance of the affective (psychological) factor in the aetiology of prejudice, which Allport has repeatedly emphasised[23], was also stressed by the authors of *The Authoritarian Personality*[24] – Theodor Adorno being the author of its fourth section dealing with the "qualitative studies of ideology". M. Horkheimer and T. Adorno wrote in their summary of this major study about 16 years after its publication, that "it has been seen that totalitarian characters have often suffered grave wounds in their infancy, both owing to a rigid father and to lack of affection in general, and that they repeat what they had to suffer in the past, in order to be able to survive morally".[25] The same authors also stressed, however, the social origin of prejudice, which they attributed to the "cultural climate", whose roots, they declared, "lie in factual conditions largely independent of the will of the single individual, whose power greatly exceeds his own".[26]

In the course of research on prejudice in children in the late forties, Else Frenkel-Brunswik gathered evidence of the influence of ethnocentric parents on the growth of hostility feelings in their children. Characteristic features of their attitudes were rejection of out-groups and approval of authoritarian modes of behaviour in their parents and teachers. This author's most notable finding was that the intellectual horizon of children of authoritarian parents is far narrower

---

[21] Gordon W. Allport, *Personality and Social Encounter*, Boston, Beacon Press, 1960, p. 232.

[22] Gordon W. Allport, "Prejudice: A Problem in Psychological and Social Causation", *The Journal of the Social Issues*, November 1950, p. 14.

[23] G. W. Allport, *The Nature of Prejudice*, The Beacon Press, Boston, 1954, pp. 206-218, chapter 13: "Theories of Prejudice". See another work by Allport, "Prejudice: Is It Societal or Personal?", *The Journal of the Social Issues*, 1963, pp. 120-134.

[24] T. W. Adorno, Else Frenkel-Brunswik, Daniel J. Levinson, R. Nevitt Sanford, *The Authoritarian Personality*, Harper, New York, 1950, p. 337, from chapter X by E. Frenkel-Brunswik, "Parents and Childhood as seen through the Interviews".

[25] Max Horkheimer and Theodor W. Adorno, *Soziologische Exkurse* (1956) chapter XI dealing with "Prejudice"; Italian Translation, Einaudi, Torino, 1966, p. 199.

[26] *Ibid.*, p. 201.

Aims of Education

than the broader interests of "liberal" children brought up in a permissive, democratic family atmosphere.[27]

Frenkel-Brunswik's empirical investigation of stereotyped behaviour in children revealed that one effect of the over-rigid personality was to extend "intolerance of ambiguity" from the emotional to the perceptual sphere. Underlying anxiety originating from the irrational authoritarian behaviour of one's parents and a confused self-image and concept of one's own identity, the author remarks, "hampers individuals in groups in facing even the purely cognitive types of ambiguity". In support of her findings, Frenkel-Brunswik quotes the findings reported by M. Rokeach in his study of "generalised mental rigidity as a factor of ethnocentrism", indicating that "children scoring extremely high on ethnic prejudice solve new problems more rigidly than those extremely low on prejudice".[28]

The dissemination of prejudice in our time is a major problem in education and constitutes an important urgent task that must be tackled by teachers and educators. Teachers must be aware that the handling of interpersonal relationships within the family situation has a profound influence upon the future of the child. It is imperative that the school, especially at nursery and primary levels, realises that its success in eliminating prejudice will depend very much upon the family experience of its pupils. A two-way channel of communication must be set up between the family and the school, allowing the parents to have a role in the running of the school. The school must establish closer contacts with families and become community-oriented in the structure and curriculum along the lines described in the preceding chapter.

THE CONTRIBUTION OF PSYCHOTHERAPY

Parents are undisputably responsible for preliminary education of the emotions. The school must expand to embrace the community by the creation of psychological services which will encourage parents to adopt the necessary line of behaviour towards their children. These community services have such far-reaching educational implications that they must be closely linked to the schools.

---

[27] E. Frenkel-Brunswik, "A Study of Prejudice in Children", *Human Relations*, 1948, I, pp. 295-306.
[28] E. Frenkel-Brunswik, "Intolerance of Ambiguity as an Emotional and Perceptual Personality Variable", *Journal of Personality*, 1949, 18, pp. 128-130.

The foundations of a small child's feeling of security and confidence to seek broader experience is built up not merely by establishing a relationship between himself and his mother, but by the quality of this relationship. When discussing education in early childhood, it has been pointed out that in the long run the important factor in child-rearing is "how the mother does it and the reason *why* she does it".[29] The type of relationship which will provide the proper ground for healthy development of the child is, it is believed, a relationship of "reciprocity", in other words a social method of "mutual regulation" within "a general aura of warmth and mutuality".[30] Satisfaction of the need for "audience response", which manifests itself at a very early age in life, has also been regarded as important in the intellectual development of the child as it provides "the rewards which encourage learning in the very young".[31]

This two-way communication must continue throughout the school. The trust which students must develop through the climate created by their teachers is a continuation of the "basic trust" which forms the foundation of personality growth in the early stages of life. Carl Rogers stressed the importance of the teacher's "empathy" toward his students and the need to foster a climate of "personal closeness" among students, two prerequisites of what he calls "the process of learning to be free". Schools have devoted too little attention to this emotional basis of intellectual growth in children, which will create the proper climate for independent study and for their "self-initiated learning" with which educational theorists are so concerned today. Rogers complains that the "ability to understand the student's reactions from the inside" (empathy) which in his experience "adds an extremely potent aspect to the classroom climate", "is a kind of understanding almost never exhibited in the classroom". He says it is "the tragedy of education in our time" that "student after student" reported a classroom atmosphere brought about by an empathetic teacher and by personal closeness of pupils toward each other, "to be his first experience".[32] To transfer this concern for personal relations from individual and group therapy to normal everyday school life will be very important in the education of the future.

It is of course too much to expect of schools that they should cope by

---

[29] Singer and Singer, *Ibid.*, p. 181.
[30] Erik Erikson, *Childhood and Society*, 2nd edition, New York, 1963, pp. 76-79.
[31] Harry Stack Sullivan, *The Interpersonal Theory of Psychiatry*, New York, 1953, p. 155.
[32] Carl R. Rogers, "Learning to be Free", in: Carl R. Rogers and Barry Stevens, *Person to Person*, Lafayette, California, 1967, pp. 60, 63, 65.

themselves with the economic, social and political problems faced by the family. They may, however, help to solve these problems in close cooperation with other forces, thus bringing about a transformation of present day society in the political and social spheres.

An awareness of the close relationship between the intellectual, social and emotional aspects of education means that it is important for the school over the next few decades to pursue those goals whose relevance has been stressed in recent educational theories.

A child finds his identity in "interpersonal situations", largely responsible for creating a climate that will induce students to embark upon self-initiated learning. While one of the goals of the individualised school must be independent study, educators must also be acutely aware of the need for producing a social atmosphere in which children can feel themselves to be participating in a common process, their freedom to investigate and their mutual respect being essential factors in the success of the overall educational process.

INTERGROUP EDUCATION

Concern for and respect of each child in the school community imply concern for and respect of the child's culture or subculture in his own environment. The school must orchestrate the varying cultures of which its pupils are the carriers; *intercultural education* is, therefore, vital in individualised teaching in a genuinely democratic setting. The notion that the school milieu should be homogenised by imposing the culture pattern of the prevailing majority group upon all is highly detrimental to the success of education. This also applies to the use of dialect by children from different districts, regions or ethnic groups. Pupils must never feel that the prevailing national language is a structure forced upon them, restricting their powers of original expression and alienating them from their home background. As John Dewey wrote in his late years, "narrowing of the medium is the direct source of all unnecessary impoverishment in human living; the only sense in which 'social' is an honorific term is that in which the medium in which human living goes on is one by which life is enriched".[33]

The ideas evolved a few decades ago in the United States by John Dewey, William H. Kilpatrick and Horace Kallen on "the way to deal with hyphenism", welcoming it "in the sense of extracting from it its

---

[33] J. Dewey, "Common Sense and Science", in the book by J. Dewey and Arthur F. Bentley, *Knowing and the Known*, The Beacon Press, Boston, 1949, p. 272.

special good, so that it shall surrender into a common fund of wisdom and experience what it especially has to contribute",[34] were later experimented in the project carried out by the "Committee on Intergroup Education in Cooperating Schools" under the sponsorship of the American Council of Education. Some of the issues raised and the problems examined during the three and a half years that the project lasted are relevant to the situation which still exists in many European countries. Ideas on the determining effects of community culture on individual thought and behaviour, inter- and intra-community divergences, school and community relations, worked out by the committee (of which Kurt Lewin was a member) may still be effective on the European scene. In this social and educational perspective, teachers should be trained to relate programmes to children's needs arising from their cultural and social differences, to understand differing patterns of interpersonal relations and different behaviours originating in children's experiences within their homes and their community. The effects of these situations and new perspectives on the reorganisation of school structures and curriculum have already been discussed in detail in a previous chapter.[35]

INTERNATIONAL EDUCATION

Intercultural education is closely connected with international education. Ethnocentrism in children, as in adults, implies the rejection not only of racial and religious out-groups, but also of national aliens.

Stereotyped ideas on people from different countries are formed in children's minds by various agencies: text books (particularly history and religion), teachers, parents and the mass media. Children should be helped to react against these influences for two basic reasons. First of all, it is vital for their healthy development that they acquire a capacity for emotional and intellectual coordination by which they can extend their sympathy to people of countries other than their own, while the same time they acquire an intellectual understanding of national realities, differences between nations and correlations be-

---

[34] Horace M. Kallen's ideas on this point, which is fundamental to his thought, are expounded in *The Education of Free Men* (1949). William H. Kilpatrick was the editor of "*Intercultural Attitudes in the Making*" (1947). John Dewey's words, quoted in the text, are from the article, "Nationalizing Education", 1916, *Education Today*, New York, 1940, p. 115.

[35] The books setting out the results of the studies conducted from 1945 to 1948 were published by the American Council on Education; those which have a direct bearing on our study are: *Elementary Curriculum in Intergroup Relations*, Washington, DC, 1951; Hilda Taba, *Leadership Training in Intergroup Education*, Washington, DC, 1953.

tween nations in the world today. Secondly, children must be able to counteract ethnocentric influences so that they can combat the dissemination of national prejudice – the psychological root of international tension.

In an essay on the development in children of the idea of nationhood (*patrie*) and relations with foreigners, Piaget emphasised how lengthy and arduous is the process that children undergo in forging "an instrument of coordination, intellectual as well as emotional", through which they can "gradually discover their own nation and other children's nations" and reach the stage in which they can develop "that intellectual and affective reciprocity that will enable them to overcome the phase when they have an absolute concept of a foreigner". The difficulty is not merely that their logical powers have not yet fully developed; there is also "a profound mental attitude", amounting to "an egocentric motivation in values", corresponding to their "intellectual incomprehension of reciprocity".[36]

Schools can exert a profound and lasting influence on children by making them more aware of the true nature of the international situation and the obstacles to international cooperation as well as the urgent need to go beyond their own national horizons in their intellectual and emotional attitudes. Teachers must realise that an attitude of reciprocity is an essential factor in the maturation of the personality as a whole. Therefore, education and international understanding are essentially the same thing. To provide an international education is not a question merely of choice of subjects to be taught, but of developing certain attitudes in the child or, as Piaget has expressed it, of "intellectual structuring" in the direction of reciprocity. Piaget believed that only during the third stage of mental development, towards the age of 12 or 13, could children acquire "a true comprehension of the reciprocity of points of view". Recently this belief has been disputed on the grounds of evidence gathered in experimental studies showing that children can develop the power of abstract logical thought at an earlier

[36] Jean Piaget and Anne-Marie Weil, "Le devéloppement, chez l'enfant, de l'idée de patrie et des relations avec l'étranger", *Bulletin International de Sociologie*, 1951, pp. 605-621. Piaget's final remarks in his book *The Right to Education in Modern World* suggest that international education must be developed by making "the whole of teaching... international", thus internationalising all subjects and school activities, not merely few subjects such as history, geography, civics and modern languages, as is the current practice. Piaget stated that "only if one starts with a variety of activity methods which stress group work and self-government of pupils will the study of their national and international attitudes as well as of the difficulties of their coordination take a concrete form". Thus he emphasised the need for reshaping the school curriculum and transforming the training of teachers, starting from the primary grades, to bring out and foster international attitudes in children.

age. Piaget himself, however, in his comments on the 26th article of the Universal Declaration of Human Rights, stated that awareness of the logical and time sequence of the phases of intellectual development must not discourage teachers from initiating didactic procedures and action that might foster an international attitude in children at an earlier age.

EDUCATION FOR PEACE

This also applies to the educational implications of the Piaget theory on "child psychology of war and peace". Research on the concepts of war held by English and Japanese schoolchildren has revealed that, following "a stage of social egocentricity" up to the age of 11, there begins a stage of "social identification... where the child links his own fate with that of his fellows". This attitude does not amount to a rejection of war, but as the author of the studies remarks, "the child appears to overcome ideas about a natural order and to reach a form of reciprocity after the age of 10-12". The author adds that "what we cannot optimistically assume is that the child (or teenager) would implicitly or otherwise examine the nature of war and come to a peace-loving conclusion". Education, however, can help children towards this conclusion. Children are affected by the teaching of history, geography and other subjects. A comparative examination of text books and a realisation of "the fact that there is inevitable bias" can have an influence on the formation of a "child's patriotism". More information and communication may prove to be a source of positive motivation for peaceful attitudes, as Piaget pointed out. "This problem of the amount of communication or information, quite apart from its content, is a fascinating topic for research in conflict resolution".[37] In a further discussion of child psychology of war and peace, the author stressed the importance already perceived in the previous study on the introduction of "role-reversal" and "role-inspection" in the classroom as educational devices for "preparing the child for inter-cultural experience" and for creating the conditions of "the beginning of insight and reconciliation".[38] A few years earlier, Bertrand Russell, in the final pages of his book *Has Man a Future?* advocated similar educational innovations

---

[37] Peter Cooper, "The Development of the Concept of War", *Journal of Peace Research*, 1965, 1, pp. 1-17.
[38] *Ibid.*, p. 16, note 18; and more extensively in "Child Psychology of War and Peace", *War Resistance*, 3rd Quarter 1967/Vol. 2/No. 22, pp. 19-25.

in school teaching "in a stable world such as we are envisaging". "A much greater freedom in education than there is at present" and "the whole emphasis, in all teaching of history or social subjects" to be placed "on Man and not on separate nations or groups of nations" were his major demands. "It should be one of the aims of education", Russell went on, "to make young people aware of the possibilities of world-wide cooperation and to generate the habit of thinking about the interests of mankind as a whole".[39]

The core of the pacifist argument today is its insistence on the fact that education for peace rests primarily on developing the habit of critical thought in individuals from early childhood. Critical analysis and examination of different versions of the same fact or different interpretations of the same idea are essential elements in future-oriented attitudes, for they foster refusal of mere acquiescence to given facts and notions and encourage further examination. This is why peace research is now considered to be the proper basis of effective peace movements, as it carries peace-loving persons far beyond the rejection of, and opposition to, outward forms of direct violence, which in some cases has amounted to an "unquestioned" acceptance of the existing social order. Peace research becomes "future-oriented" in so far as its task is "to try to bring values and hypotheses together so as to work out blueprints of future worlds that are closer to the double goals of eliminating direct and structural violence".[40] This position supports the idea advanced by Horkheimer and Adorno that the objective processes of mechanisation and bureaucratisation which have become so pervasive in our society are mainly responsible for creating a "cultural climate" which makes men's minds vulnerable to prejudice through the "homogenisation of thought".

[39] Bertrand Russell, *Has Man a Future?*, Penguin Books, London, 1961, p. 124. Taking up a concept already developed by William James in the essay "The Moral Equivalent of War", written in 1910 for the Assocation for International Conciliation, (W. James, *Essays on Faith and Morals*, Longmans, Green & Co., New York, 1949), Russell expresses the belief that in a "transition period during which men's thoughts and emotions were still moulded by the turbulent past, there would still be an excess of competitive feeling", and a "work of reorientation" should take place "to bring about the necessary adaptation". James' idea that a "Gospel of relaxation" was needed in the present time for young people now so greatly concerned with individual feelings, was echoed by Alfred North Whitehead in the pages devoted to peace in *Adventures of Ideas* (1933). According to Whitehead, peace conveys "the notion of a Harmony of Harmonies", which is necessary "to exclude restless egotism from our notion of civilisation". He describes peace as "a broadening of feeling", whose "first effect is the removal of the stress of acquisitive feelings arising from the soul's preoccupation with itself". (A. N. Whitehead, *Adventures of Ideas*, Pelican Books, London, 1942, p. 271).

[40] Johan Galtung, "Peace Research and Pacifism", *War Resistance*, 4th quarter 1970, Volume 2, No. 34, pp. 9-10.

The "bureaucratic *ethos*", which has become one of the dominant forces in our society, demands of education, as C. Wright Mills has pointed out, that individuals and the public be given "confidence in their own capacities to reason and, by individual criticism, study and practice, to enlarge its scope and improve its quality".[41]

The educational difficulty in achieving this goal is that the influence of those agencies which endanger man's autonomy is much greater than the influence of education itself. The trend toward "other-direction" operates through various channels in all social activities and its impact is felt even in the schools. David Riesman described "the other-directed person" as one who is able "to receive signals from far and near" and to assimilate not so much "a code of behaviour", as is the aim of the inner-directed person, but "the elaborate equipment needed to attend to such messages and occasionally to participate in their circulation".[42]

In these circumstances, one of the primary aims of education is to develop in individuals the power to control information conveyed to them by the mass media.

EDUCATION AND MASS CULTURE

The school is ill-equipped today to compete with the counter-attractions of the mass media. In its effects upon education, the mass media counteract the school's work of helping children to develop non-conformity, a reasonable attitude towards the world and society, respect for others and an integrated personality. Mass indoctrination is to a large extent replacing the training of children in the habit of independent thought. In Paul Goodman's words, children become accustomed to seeing men and women in TV advertising as "clowns and mannequins, in grimace, speech and action".[43] Of even greater danger to education is the control of opinion through television programmes by governments or government-controlled agencies: this is a one-way communication which deprives children and adults of any right to question or to participate. Television is important in that it provides information on events both at home and in distant places – one of the main sources of its popularity. Its usefulness is, however, often cancelled out

---

[41] C. Wright Mills, *The Sociological Imagination*, Oxford University Press, New York, 1959, p. 189.
[42] David Riesman, *The Lonely Crowd*, Yale University Press, New Haven, 1950, p. 26.
[43] P. Goodman, *Growing Up Absurd*, p. 25.

by the fact that the message is being controlled from above, so that "technical developments in communication become devices for the distortion of reality rather than for its transmission".[44]

Under these circumstances, schools can and must do all in their power to counteract the evil of the "imperative", authoritarian character of mass communications by joining forces with the public in an attempt to exercise control over the channels of information. To re-organise television services under local bodies and to set up competitive and alternative programmes on a regional and local scale are valuable ways of countering any authoritarian attempt to control education. Some of the educational activities that foster genuine communication are to teach communications technology to children from an early age, allowing them to make their own films in classroom projects and training student teachers to organise independent closed circuit programmes, jointly sponsored by their university or teacher training college and the community.

In the long run, this may also prove to be beneficial where parents use television to keep their children quiet and out of misschief or to tie their children to the home.

EDUCATION FOR LEISURE

If children develop control of the mass media, this will help to diminish the negative aspects of the revolution for which technological developments in the field of information and communication have been responsible, and induce children to make more reasonable use of their free time. Children will become more spontaneously sociable once they are able to devote more of their time, both inside and outside the school, to play and work activities that they have freely chosen. Away from the control of parents and teachers, they will make creative use of their imaginative, emotional and intellectual energies. This will also help parents and teachers to gain a clearer insight into their child's inner emotional life.

Although the role of play in education has been stressed in educational theories, teachers and administrators in many countries have not given enough attention to the formative value of such activity. Education for leisure must be one of the most important aims of education.

The liberating effect of removing outside control and direction of

---

[44] G. H. Bantock, *Culture, Industrialisation and Education*, Routledge and Kegan Paul, London, 1968, p. 52.

children's emotional, social and intellectual activities will also be apparent in the greater time which they are able to devote to artistic expression. When the alienating influence of the mass media is reduced, when feelings and thoughts are no longer directed from above and made to conform, they will direct their imaginations to new creative human experience.

EDUCATION THROUGH ART

Experts in children's art generally agree that its aim is to foster personal growth, provide the means of self-expression and help them adapt to reality. By the development of imagination, inherent in expression through art, children can evade the immediate control exercised by their environment and acquire a personal life style. This is why cultivation of the intellect – a need so widely felt in contemporary education – must not be divorced from the encouragement of artistic expression, for it has far-reaching social and emotional effects upon the overall formation of the child's personality.

The progress achieved over the past few decades in introducing art into the educational curriculum has been mainly the merit of the progressive education movement. As early as 1897, Dewey wrote in *My Pedagogic Creed* that "the image is the great instrument of instruction". He added that "the work of instruction would be indefinitely facilitated if nine tenths of the energy at present directed toward making the child learn certain things were spent in seeing to it that the child was forming proper images". He went on to say that "much of the time and attention now given to the preparation and presentation of lessons would be more widely and profitably expended in training the child's power of imagery". In 1934, when he wrote the final remarks of his book on art, Dewey pointed out that there was still much opposition to the tendency "to connect art to education and learning". He explained this fact by saying that "our rebellion is actually the outcome of an education which proceeds with such formal methods as to exclude imagination, and which does not touch men's desires and emotions".[45]

We are now in a happier position, for there is widespread recognition of the importance of imagination and emotion in personality development. Former restraints on these two essential aspects of human life have been shaken off. The revolution of the young has erased the last

---

[45] J. Dewey, "My Pedagogic Creed", in *Education Today*, New York, 1940, p. 13; and *Art as Experience*, New York, 1934.

traces of the Victorian era in western society. In most countries, the best schools place great emphasis on developing powers of expression. In England, art and craft subjects have won an important place in schools, and this is also true of schools in other countries in West and East Europe. Yet integration of art into the curriculum, not as a minor subject but as a functional part of what used to be the traditional curriculum, is still far from universal.

The recent accusation that in many parts of the United States the behaviour demanded in the school environment is a "pervasiveness of dogmatism and intellectual timidity"[46] could also be levelled at most schools in Europe, where the stress on disciplinary methods in education is still very strong. Teachers and administrators are consciously or unconsciously afraid of the instincts and emotions which they believe to be the sources of unrest, indisicipline, unruliness and a threat to the social order; their attitude is shared by government authorities and politicians. There is still a widespread concept that imagination is an obstacle to reason. In certain countries such as Italy, the platonic idea that the intellect and the imagination are irreconcilable has been inherited by irrationalistic and idealistic trends of thought which regarded children as being endowed with instinct and imagination but without reason or willpower. The belief that religious teaching should be the "foundation and crown" of the school curriculum was based on the idea that external control of children's minds was an essential factor in their education.

The concept of art as a "dialectical activity" capable of developing a synthesis of reason and imagination, in Herbert Read's words,[47] is still slow in gaining full acceptance in our schools, notwithstanding the emphasis placed by Dewey on the imaginative roots of the creative power of intelligence.

We believe that the most significant educational implications of contemporary theories of art are those which stress the impact of art in deflating the authoritarianism of our times. Hegel's "Aesthetics" is enjoying fresh critical esteem for its contribution to the appreciation of art as a powerful force in the reconstruction of society, and Hegel's point has been taken up by Herbert Marcuse. Hegel stated that "art is able to reduce the apparatus which external appearance requires in order to preserve itself, to reduce it to the limits in which the external

---

[46] N. Postman and C. Weingartner, *Teaching as a Subversive Activity*, p. 24.
[47] Herbert Read, *Art and Society*, London, 1950.

can become the manifestation of spirit and freedom".[48] Marcuse interprets this theory of aesthetic "reduction" in the light of Schiller's romantic ideas. In the work of art, "the actual circumstances are placed in another dimension, where the given reality shows itself as that which it is". "In various forms of mask and silence, the artistic universe is organised by the images of a life without fear". The appearance, the "*Schein*", the illusion of art have "resemblance to a reality which exists as the threat and promise of the established reality".[49]

Education through art is conceived as education in liberty, as a training of the mind to forms of experience whose components and participants have experienced genuine communication. The effects of this type of education are to increase awareness of the need to achieve natural and human truth, eliminating its existing contradictions through vivid perception of these very contradictions. In this way, art education is universal in its scope and in its formative value. Experience of art is fundamental for all children in the school of tomorrow.

Deferring a broader analysis of the subject to a specific chapter in this report, we must emphasise here that aesthetic education should not be linked with one specific subject but should be an integral part of the whole process of education, since it develops the imaginative and emotional aspects of children's personality, helps them achieve harmony and completion in their expression of the physical and practical, as well as in the intellectual and artistic, needs which arise in their daily life.

Aesthetic education helps children to develop a creative attitude toward reality by making constructive use of the materials at their disposal. To link fantasy with reality is a primary goal of art education. In the practice of art, children learn that reality is not beyond their grasp but that they can, through imagination and craftsmanship, impress their own inner world upon it. All the different realms of expression help children to come to terms both with themselves and with reality: drawing and painting, dancing and music, modelling and drama. Certain authors have pointed out the contribution of puppets and of children's play-acting in general upon the emotional education and socialisation of the young. "Role reversal" and "role inspection" are valid instruments in training children to understand other people and to "decentralise". Walter Benjamin defined children's theatre as

---

[48] Hegel, *Vorlesungen über die Aesthetik*, Sämtliche Werke, Stuttgart, 1929, vol. 2, p. 217, quoted by H. Marcuse, *One-Dimensional Man*, Beacon Press, Boston, 1964, p. 239.
[49] *Ibid.*, p. 62, p. 238.

Aims of Education

"the great creative pause in their educational work", especially when it involves improvisation. For children, Benjamin remarked, "it represents what the carnival did in ancient cultures. What is high is lowered and, as in the Roman Saturnalia, when the master served the slave, children during a show hold the stage and teach and educate their educators". During a play, "new forces and connections come to light of which instructors had no idea during the phase of training". Even more important is the ability which children develop to identify with the characters and persons they represent. With their ability to combine play and reality, "represented sufferings may become for them real and authentic sufferings". In this process they become aware of the conditions in which other people live and of the need for social change. Here lies the revolutionary import of children's theatre. There is no question of making it an instrument of propaganda. What is "truly revolutionary is the *secret signal* of the future, which speaks out of the children's gestures".[50]

WORK IN EDUCATION

We have already mentioned the close connection between what has been called the "play attitude" and the "work attitude" in children, when they are involved in expressive activities sometimes bordering upon the realm of art. Most of these activities involve the use of materials and direct experience in the physical milieu.

Manual and technical work in primary schools is also important, in that it satisfies the children's need for self-expression and also their need to adapt to reality, to get to know things by handling them and by producing them. Describing the period at which the child "enters into life" at the start of latency, Erik Erikson remarked that the child "develops a sense of industry – i.e. he adjusts himself to the inorganic laws of the tool world... his ego boundaries include his tools and skills: the work principle (Ivor Hendrick) teaches him the pleasure of work completion... Thus the *fundamentals of technology* are developed as the child becomes ready to handle the utensils, the tools and the weapons handled by adults". This is the time, Erikson added, when the child develops "a sense of the *technological ethos* of a culture".[51]

---

[50] Walter Benjamin, "Programme for a proletarian theatre for children", *Quaderni Piacentini*, n. 38, July 1968, pp. 147-150.
[51] Erik Erikson, *Childhood and Society*, W. W. Norton & Co., New York, 2nd edition, 1963 (1950), pp. 258-260.

The introduction of workshop activities into schools is, therefore, an essential means of helping children to meet both their personal and their culture demands.

Even in its earliest phase, the progressive education movement pointed out the beneficial effect on the social development of children obtained by introducing work occupations. Outlining the importance of these occupations in the development of "the intellectual and emotional interpretation of nature" and their significance in the child's approach to science, Dewey stressed their contribution to "the development of social power and insight". He added that, in educational terms, these occupations were to be considered "active centres of scientific insight into natural materials and processes, points of departure whence children shall be led out into a realision of the historic development of man".[52] It is not their immediate "economic value" which renders these practical activities educationally important, but their contribution to the social and intellectual growth of children, their introduction to the fundamental patterns of their culture. Hence they also have a bearing on emotional development. They are important in the contribution they make to the education of emotions. Contact with the materials he uses helps a child to gain a sense of security. His growing capacity to give shape to these materials, to express his ideas and to produce objects is instrumental in attaining self-confidence. But, even more, the emotional impact of these activities lies in the fact that they help the child to experience a feeling of participation in his own culture and in being able to play a meaningful role "in its technology and economy" (Erikson).

It would be interesting to trace the historic roots of these concepts in Marxian theory, to evaluate the place that "useful social work" occupies in the curriculum in the Soviet Union and other Communist countries. Marx believed that work helps man to achieve self-awareness as "one of the powers of nature, opposed to its material character", and to develop and change his own nature "while changing nature outside". In his definition, Marx considered work "in a form in which it belongs exclusively to man". The aspect of "necessity" in work, according to Marxian theory, is therefore related to the persistance of a residue of "control of natural necessity in all forms of society and in all possible forms of production". This element of necessity remains, notwithstanding all the efforts made by "associated producers" to "sub-

---

[52] John Dewey, *School and Society*, The University of Chicago Press, Chicago, Ill., 1900, pp. 32-33.

ject nature to their control" and to introduce freedom into the sphere of economic production through the abolition of private ownership of the means of production.

Marx considered that education through work was man's way of obtaining mastery of himself (self-appropriation) and his initiation into the realms of freedom; but at the same time it was a recognition of the aspect of necessity inseparable from work. Here lies the root of the dialectics of freedom and necessity which Marx considered to be inherent in work.[53]

The Marxian concept of work as an activity involving society as a whole in the struggle against nature and in the attempt to "secure rational control of the exchange between man and nature" is at the root of the role assigned to work in education in Communist countries. Stress is laid upon the need for society to control production through science and technology, a concept that has three important educational implications. Education for work is closely linked with study of the scientific basis of all types of productive activity. The intellectual and practical training of students is considered to be inseparable. Students learn about the technical applications of science in all branches of industry and agriculture. Education incorporates both the theory and practice of production as it is organised and as it functions in real life. Finally, the enjoyment of leisure – which Marx called "free disposable time " – can start only when work has been done and efforts have been made to free it from the aspects of necessity that are not inherent in work. The connection between work and leisure, between "time for work" and "time for leisure", is very strong.

These principles of "polytechnical education" are at the core of Communist educational theory and have been applied in many different ways at various periods of the development of Communist countries. They help us to understand the basic differences between education in the West and the East of Europe. The stress on the collective aspects of teaching and learning in the latter, in contrast to the emphasis on individual learning in the former, may be traced to the concept of work and its place in education. The overshadowing of the "personal" by the "social" in the educational process is rooted in the polytechnical concept of education, although it may have been influenced by many other historical events.

There have been certain changes in the practical application of

---

[53] K. Marx, *Das Kapital*, Book 1st, pp. 211-212 (Italian Translation, Editori Riuniti, Roma, 1964), and Book III, pp. 231-232 (Italian Translation, Editori Riuniti, Rome, 1970).

these concepts over the past few years. In the Soviet Union, the elementary education cycle has been shortened to three years, accelerating intellectual learning and introducing the systematic approach to subject matter at an earlier age. In consequence, the time devoted to work at school has decreased. China, on the contrary, has adhered "firmly to the European Marxist tradition", productive labour being seen as an essential instrument of education.[54]

Although great emphasis has been placed on cognitive learning in Western countries during recent years, some have come to recognise the value of practical activities in the school curriculum. In West Germany, the German Council of Education's recent plan for the structure of education stated that "in the educational system of the future there will be no separation between purely theoretical and practical education". The report stressed that "the integration of theory and practice will be the central factor in education".[55]

This wider view of the education of tomorrow has also been adopted by the State Committee on Public Education in California, whose report pointed out the need to build "a suitable and realistic educational programme", in which attention would be paid not only to subject matter but also to the child and society. The intellectual development of pupils should be fostered by adopting "a process-centered approach to learning" a discipline and by employing "methods and materials which are intended 1) to help children understand its structure and 2) to learn a subject by "doing", through laboratory enquiry-centered procedures". This closely links the social and practical aspects of education with its intellectual function. The report argues that human communities can

---

[54] R. F. Price, *Education in Communist China*, Routledge and Kegan Paul, London, 1970, pp. 27, 35. Current changes in primary and secondary schools in China are being introduced in an attempt to create close links between factories and schools. The factory itself is taking over responsibility for running the school. This, according to a recent report, has benefited both students and workers and contributed considerably to improving learning processes. An article published in Hung Ch'i 1969, n. 2, pp. 30-35, under the title "A Factory Runs a School and the School Makes Two Links", while describing the experience, remarks that "the working class... has helped the students towards balanced development in moral, intellectual and physical education". It adds that "the working class has completely corrected the abnormal situation in which education was divorced... from productive work", *Chinese Education, A Journal of Translations*, vol. II, n. 4, Winter 1969/70, pp. 10-11. An article reproduced in the same issue from "Jen-min Jih-pao", May 12, 1969, on "Educational programme for rural middle and primary schools (draft for discussion)", issued by the revolutionary committee of Li-Shi Hsien, Kirin Province, expresses the view that "rural middle and primary schools are a new form of socialist school under the leadership of the Chinese Socialist Party, directly managed by the poor and lower-middle class peasants". Their purpose is to "firmly implement Chairman Mao's policy that education must serve proletarian politics and be coordinated with productive work" (pp. 54-55).

[55] Deutscher Bildungsrat, *Empfehlungen der Bildungskommission, Strukturplan für das Bildungswesen*, Bonn, 1970, p. 35.

be reconstructed only with the help of a type of education that develops the whole of the child's personality, not merely certain facets, that treats all three foci – the child, the subject and society – as inseparable.[56]

LANGUAGE EDUCATION

Language plays a fundamental role in the education of children, both during their first few years of life in the home and during their nursery and primary school years. This subject is discussed in the section devoted to educational aims, for the development of language ability in children is intimately associated with the satisfaction of their social and emotional needs while it lays the foundation for, and is an intrinsic aspect of, their intellectual maturation. Like other forms of expression and aesthetics, language is an integral part of children's total behaviour pattern. Language is not the only vehicle of expression for children. They are, indeed, endowed with expressive non verbal powers which in some instances represent for them a more important instrument of communication both of their inner self and of their relationship with the outer world. However, language progresses beyond "sign-significance" to symbol-significance" and is therefore of the utmost importance in their life cycle. As John Dewey expounds in his *Logic*, language or "the meaning system" makes men "capable of entering into relations with any number of other meanings, independently of the actual presence at any given time of the object table".[57]

In connection with the origin of language in children, psycho-analysts concur with Ernst Cassirer and O. Jespersen in their concept of the "playful" origin of language and its connection with "the infantile

---

[56] *Citizens for the 21st Century, Long-Range Considerations for California Elementary and Secondary Education.* A Report from the State Committee on Public Education to the California State Board of Education, Sacramento, State Committee on Public Education, 1969, pp. 349-350. It should be pointed out that the California State Committee Report tries to strike a balance between the individual and social aspects of education, while emphasising concern for the individual. The Report adopts the view – developed by the pragmatist philosophers, Pierce, James and Dewey – that education is "geared to the emerging interests and capacities of a unique human being living through a unique environment". It sponsors the child-centered rather than the society-centered approach to education. It states that "the society-centered approach sacrifices the unique capacity of the child for social adaptation, thus limiting the contribution to society that the individual is capable of making". This approach, which gives place to the "emotional" as well as the "aesthetic" aspects of education, is considered to be closely connected with a future-oriented educational outlook. "The child *cannot* be prepared for a distant future except by helping him cope with problems that concern him in the present" (*Ibid.*, pp. 347-348).

[57] J. Dewey, *Logic, The Theory of Inquiry*, New York, 1938, p. 54.

life of play, pleasure and love which centres around the mother",[58] i.e. its affective and social roots.

Language ability, however, is not merely transmitted by the means common to every culture but also by the purposive process of acquisition, for which education alone is responsible. In this sense, as Bruner has expressed it, "the educational system is... the sole agent of evolution".[59]

In modern linguistic psychology, consistent emphasis has been laid upon the emotional and social forces which accelerate, although they do not originate, the language ability of children. Jean Piaget made a distinction between the "egocentric" type of language which prevails in children up to the age of 7 or 8 during the period of subordination to parents and adults, and the "socialised" type of language that they develop as they acquire the ability to communicate with peer-groups. Adults in fact can help the child to move from egocentric to socialised language by establishing a relationship in which they are on an equal footing, rather than holding themselves aloof in a status of authority.[60]

Cameron and Magaret, in the chapter of their *Behaviour Pathology* which deals with the origin of the human word, state that the "biological beginnings", the immediate antecedents of "communicative word" lie in the "first social interaction" between the infant and its mother. Language learning is stimulated by those "situations of social participation" which unite infant and mother, starting with feeding and bodily care.[61] The converging responsibility of the family and school for language education needs no theoretical justification; it is vital that the school and family cooperate in their educational role. The school has a dual task: its primary function is to offset the deficits in family education if the family has provided little or no stimulus due to its low level of education or to the lack of communication between parents and children. Properly planned and conducted action on the part of the school and associated agencies is required when there has been deprivation of family care due to broken marriage or the death of one or both parents, or long absence of the parents from home – situations from which so many children suffer in our time. Educators have been universal in their concern for the social background of their pupils. It is now a known fact that the "structure of the language system which

---

[58] N. Brown, *Life against Death*, London, 1970 (first published in 1959).
[59] J. S. Bruner, *Toward a Theory of Instruction*, p. 26.
[60] J. Piaget, *Le langage et la pensée chez l'enfant*, Neuchâtel, 1948, pp. 58-67.
[61] N. Cameron, A. Magaret, *Behavior Pathology*, Chapter IV (Italian Translation, Florence 1962, p. 114).

Aims of Education 31

an individual acquires is related to background features associated with social class".[62] A tremendous amount of educational research still remains to be done in connection with both aspects of this point. The school must take on increasing responsibility for countering what has been termed the "illiterate culture"[63] or, in a different social context, "the culture of silence".[64]

Educators involved with action programmes directed at groups formerly excluded from an equal share in political, social and cultural life consider language education to be of paramount importance. This idea is vigorously expressed by Paolo Freire when discussing the downtrodden Brazilian peasants and minority groups who are still exploited on colonial lines. The conquest of "thought-language", i.e. of language closely linked with the capacity to reason or for reflective thought, is the principal task of "pedagogy of the oppressed" whose aim is to help those isolated in the silence of "non-culture" to acquire a critical awareness of their condition.[65] In a similar vein, the disciples of Don Milani, authors of *A Letter to a Teacher*, have denounced educational discrimination against working class children, especially peasant children, in Italy. Before the peasants can be emancipated they must emancipate themselves.

The political parties are little concerned with anyone who is unable to make his voice heard on the political scene. "They who are unable to speak are far removed from us. We are in need of language, today's language, not yesterday's language. Because language alone makes men equal. A man is equal when he knows how to express himself and to understand what others say". "Mastery of the word" is regarded as the only worthwhile aim in the education of the poor. The better educated, higher class young should give up all privileges, contacts with parents, university, political parties, careers and "start teaching at once: language alone, nothing else".[66]

According to this view, language education is the essential instrument of change, of liberation from subordination and inequality of the achievement of coordination and reciprocity. This attitude leads us to the second task of language education in all types of schools. Depending

---

[62] M. Deutsch et al., *The Disadvantaged Child*, New York, 1967, p. 177 in Ch. Ten: "Communication and Information in the Elementary School Classroom".
[63] G. Harrison and M. Callari Galli, *Né leggere né scrivere*, Milan, 1971.
[64] P. Freire, *Pedagogia do oprimido*, English transl.: *Pedagogy of the Oppressed*, 1970; Italian transl.: *La pedagogia degli oppressi*, Milan, 1971.
[65] P. Freire, *op. cit.*
[66] Scuola di Barbiana, *Lettera a una professoressa*, Florence, 1967, pp. 96-97.

on the child's age and ability, language learning gradually increases his power of thought; in Jerome Bruner's words, it is "the ideal example of one such powerful technology, with its power... for representing matters remote as well as immediate... according to rules that permit us both to represent reality and to transform it...".[67] The use of language not only as a vehicle of expression but also as a tool for developing the capacity for research and problem-solving in children was stressed by John Dewey in his distinction between "language in common use" and "scientific language". While the meanings conveyed by the former are deeply embedded in "cultural habits and expectation", scientific language goes far beyond this realm of set and established values and "is subject to a test over and above this criterion", in which "the customs, the *ethos* of the group is a decisive factor in determining the system of meanings in use". Each meaning that enters scientific language obeys a logical criterion and "is expressly determined in its relation to other members of the language system", thus enabling its users to obtain "intelligent control of activity".[68] Seen in this perspective, language learning has a unique role in the work of the school and in education in general. If the aim of education is not only to transmit our heritage of culture but also to develop those creative powers needed to expand our culture beyond its bounds and to add something new to what has already been created, then we need language. As we have explained in the previous chapter, language education in the nursery school years must retain a respect for the vernacular idiom or the dialect familiar to the child. Basic confidence in the school – a prerequisite of a child's willingness to learn – will be created by eliminating any situation that may give rise to a feeling or rootlessness in the school, making him aware of the continuity between home and school.

A classroom full of children from different cultures offers the teacher a stimulating opportunity to create a rich environment which will encourage the interchange of experiences, broadening the horizons of all concerned. The Babel which certain teachers fear as the result of this cultural open-mindedness will not be overcome by indoctrination or the imposition of a national language with which children are not already familiar. In Dewey's words, "genuine community of language or symbols can be achieved only through efforts that bring about community of activities".[69]

[67] J. S. Bruner, *Toward a Theory of Instruction*, p. 26.
[68] J. Dewey, *Logic*, p. 50.
[69] *Ibid.*

Aims of Education 33

Mass media exert tremendous pressure upon both children and adults today to adopt a *lingua franca* that destroys rather than promotes the natural evolution of a common instrument of language or effective communication. Dialect and the vernacular used in different parts of the same country may well be abolished by the levelling policy of official bodies wielding power through mass communications. In its effort to combine unity and differentiation, education for the future will also foster an "orchestration of diversities" in the realm of language, so that a community of symbols will gradually be formed.

This is a criterion that applies not only to the relationships between dialect and national language but also to the relation between the learning of the national language and the learning of other languages. Language learning has a prominent role both in intercultural and in international education. Just as the conferring of full "citizenship" to dialect in the classroom may be of value in overcoming ethnic prejudice derived by the children from their environment, if children are introduced to a foreign language in the primary school or, if feasible, in the nursery school and later embark upon other foreign languages, this may prove to be an effective means of promoting international understanding in them.

The study of language provides a tremendous stimulus to intellectual education, as well as to social and emotional education. A language is only truly learned, both through spontaneous family groups and through formal school teaching, when advanced methods of learning are applied. There is a generally felt need, especially when teaching a new language to young children, to link their gradual introduction to the conceptual framework, basic ideas and structures of that language with concrete experience of the way of life of the people whose language is being studied. Direct contact with children from that people, when they happen to live in the same town, or indirect contact through correspondence or drama, have been tested as devices to reinforce learning. Communication is closely linked with symbolisation and the overcoming of language deficiencies, very often the effect of impoverished personal relationships in their families and social groups. In a similar way, as children become proficient in art, mathematics, social studies and all branches of learning in general, they develop linguistic ability. In other chapters, this Report will examine the subject of language education in more concrete ways.

We should like to end these short introductory remarks on language education by highlighting two different aspects of this enormously complex problem, rendered even more so by the rapid advances in contemporary linguistics. The first consideration is the problem of providing language education for underprivileged children, a field to which particular attention has been paid in compensatory education projects. Basil Bernstein's contribution to a proper understanding and solution of this problem has already been discussed in the previous chapter, but we should like to mention his observations on the differences between the symbolic skills of children of a lower status in a linguistic environment limited to public language, and middle and upper class children living in an environment in which both public and formal language is used. According to Bernstein's theory, reminiscent of a theory advanced by John Dewey when distinguishing between language "in common use" and "scientific" language, public language is the speech used by individuals who operate "within a speech mode in which individual selection and permutation are severely restricted" and is subjected to severe social conditioning; formal language, on the contrary, is employed by speakers who are "able to make a highly individual selection and permutation". It is a kind of language "where speech becomes an object of special perceptual activity and one where a theoretical attitude is developed toward the structural possibilities of sentence organisation". Public language is the carrier of tradition; formal language is the instrument of innovation.[70] The best type of assistance that the school can offer the socially disadvantaged child in developing individual perception and the selective use of symbols is to minimise the "impersonal authoritarian methods of class control" and to maximise individual and small-group teaching and learning methods. The author states that "in order for the pupil to participate actively and to learn to create appropriate speech, the relationship between teacher and pupils needs to be one of mutual respect and concern. This requires a sensitive understanding on the part of the teacher, an awareness of the emotional and cognitive difficulties for the child and the ability to allay the pupil's anxiety and tension".[71]

Similar educational proposals are implied in the research conducted by Martin Deutsch and co-workers. They clearly state that "it is, after all, experience that largely determines a child's language development, including his skill in using language for different purposes. The extent

---

[70] B. Bernstein, "Social Class and Linguistic Development: A Theory of Social Learning", in *Education, Economy and Society*, edited by A. H. Halsey, Jean Floud and C. Arnold Anderson, The Free Press, New York, 1961, pp. 288-310.
[71] *Ibid.*

Aims of Education 35

to which the child can manipulate ideas, even when he possesses the language skills to reflect on those ideas, depends on his background. Since the child's culture, including his social class membership, provides him with the basic model from which to learn, differences in culture can be expected to produce differences in behaviour, including language behaviour".[72]

The educational implications of these findings are summarised in the necessity "to emphasise language development at an early an age as possible" and to provide "children disadvantaged by conditions related to social class status and/or minority group memberschip... with... special training in such language areas as vocabulary development, general ease in self-expression leading to lengthy but meaningful verbalisation, greater exactness in sound discrimination and precision in the use of language".[73]

In the "Early Childhood Project", directed by Martin Deutsch since 1964 in New York City for the benefit of disadvantaged pre-schoolers with 17 classes in public schools, both in pre-kindergarten and kindergarten classes, great attention has been paid to changing the atmosphere of the school, since "the traditional school can be an alien, frightening, hostile world, difficult to understand and filled with failure".[74]

The stress of the Project was on "early intervention" through a programme "founded on the abilities of the individual child rather than on stringent goals for each grade level". The Project Report underlined the fact that "the primary objective for each child was to learn to cope successfully with the classroom environment as a means of establishing a feeling of competence which in turn would lead to enhancement of the child's self-image". This objective was also pursued through a series of devices introduced to instill in children from the Harlem Negro community "a sense of pride in the community of Harlem and similar communities". Meetings with parents of the children were also held regularly. Creative drama was widely used to foster learning in different subjects. Language development was promoted through the use of various technological devices such as listening centres equiped with tape recorders, padded earphones and telephones designed to enable children to proceed at their own speed and to establish

---

[72] M. Deutsch et al., *The Disadvantaged Child*, p. 216.
[73] *Ibid.*, pp. 227-228.
[74] Early Childhood Project, *New York Pre-school Programme in Compensatory Education*, 1; US Department of Health, Education and Welfare, Office of Education, Washington, 1969, p. 3.

personal relations with one another and with speakers at a distance at will. The programme was organised in such a way as to provide for the cognitive growth of children by an advanced set of methods and by the use of teaching technology within a socially and emotionally stimulating environment.

The study on "Personality, Family, and Social Factors of Achievement" by Prof. O. Adreani in this Report, investigating groups of under-achievers and over-achievers in the Milan area, has developed hypotheses put forward by Basil Bernstein and Martin Deutsch. Great emphasis is placed on the importance of the "linguistic mediator" in the total behaviour of children. The need is expressed for "the planning of an extensive enrichment programme for early infancy and nursery school" for children of low intelligence. Discarding an over-clinical approach, the author emphasises the need "to direct attention to personality patterns which occur so frequently as to require social and educational intervention" owing to the existence of a great variety of cases which "result from an intricate combination of intellectual, emotional and social factors".[75]

The second consideration concerns the growing interest in the teaching of foreign languages in the primary and also in the pre-primary school of many European countries. In the Soviet Union the study of the first foreign language begins with the fifth grade, according to 1970/1971 syllabus. English is included in the programme of the nursery schools in several places for five and six year olds. In recent years, however, there has been a decline in language study, owing to a shortage of trained teachers. At the primary level, especially in the big cities, various special schools teach one specific foreign language – English, French or German – from the second grade on. For example, Italian is taught in Special School No. 318 in Leningrad. In these cases, an appropriate linguistic atmosphere is created to familiarise children with the culture of the country whose language is being studied.[76]

Television courses have been organised in Leningrad and Moscow both for individual children and for pre-primary and regular primary classes.

In Germany, Education Ministers attending the Hamburg Meeting of September 1964 declared foreign language teaching to be compulsory in *Hauptschulen* (senior classes of the primary school), starting with

---

[75] See p. 134 of this Report.
[76] USSR Ministry of Education, *Programmes for the Compulsory School*, Part I, Moscow, 1968.

Aims of Education

the fifth grade.[77] More recently, the Structural Plan for the Educational System, issued by the German Council of Education in 1970, envisaged "the introduction of new areas of learning, like a foreign language" in the *Grundschule*.[78] In its structural plan the Council has, however, recommended that one compulsory foreign language be taught in classes 5-10 and a second one be provided only as an option.

A serious obstacle to the teaching of foreign languages is the lack of teacher training, a factor also experienced in the Soviet Union. "Some years passed before the teacher situation made it possible to implement the agreement" reached by the Education Ministers in 1964.[79] Conditions have now improved and recent reports reveal that "pupils at *Hauptschulen* are in many ways better off than pupils at *Realschulen* and *Gymnasien*. Now that three and sometimes four courses catering for different demands have been created, better provision is made for the performance of individual pupils".[80] The teaching of foreign languages in the first few years of the *Grundschule* and kindergarten is still in an experimental phase.

In England, a country where there is a wide range of organisational and curricular structures, since powers are delegated to Local Education Authorities, there have been many new approaches to the study and teaching of foreign languages at primary school and other levels. Children usually start to study foreign languages at the age of 11 but, since 1962, there has been a tendency to lower this age. Before 1962, as the Plowden Report stated, "the majority of primary school teachers were not qualified to teach a modern language". This was the reason why for a long time teaching was "confined to the most able children in the fourth year" and was limited to French. In 1962 the Nuffield Foundation sponsored "the production of materials for experimental teaching of French in primary schools" and "the Department of Education and Science undertook responsibility for organising the necessary teacher training". As the result of these two measures, the study of French was first introduced for eight year olds in the school year 1964-65. The Plowden Report stated that "the experiment was still in progress" in 1966-67; it emphasised that "the introduction of a modern language in primary schools acutely raises the question of specialisation. It will

---

[77] *Education in Germany*, 1971, 8, p. 3.
[78] *Strukturplan für das Bildungswesen*, Bonn, 1970, p. 139.
[79] *Education in Germany*, 1971, 8, p. 3.
[80] *Ibid.*, p. 8.

be easier when many more teachers are qualified to teach French, but that time is a long way off".[81]

A recent report on progress in the teaching of French to eight year olds in East Sussex primary schools underlined the organisational and teaching problems still unsolved by that progressive county. Whether the experiment was successful, the report stated, depended on the experience of the teacher and his command of the language. The teacher bears the main responsibility for motivating the child's involvement in the venture. Less experienced teachers tended to make too much use of the course book, the tape recorder and audio-visual courses. Teachers more familiar with the language introduced a freer approach. It was expected that language learning would be reinforced as "one third of all primary schools in the country would be taking a group of pupils to a French-speaking country for an educational visit".[82]

In France, a major impetus to systematic early initiation of children to foreign languages is derived from agreements between the French authorities, the German government and the British Council. About thirteen years ago, German was first taught in French nursery schools on an experimental basis, although the scope was limited. A cultural agreement was reached between the two countries in October 1967, known as the Peyrefitte-Goppel Agreement. This transformed what had previously been experiments into a formal programme. In the school year 1967-68, twenty French nursery school teachers went to nursery schools in Bavaria to teach their language, while an equivalent number of German teachers taught German in French nursery schools. Under the cultural agreement, the exchange programme was intended to expand every year, with twenty more teachers in each of the two countries. It was decided that teachers would be selected from students having studied the other country's language during their teacher training period. This would mean that when they returned to their own country they could continue to teach the foreign language in the primary schools to children who had first studied that language in the nursery school with a foreign teacher. It was also planned that pupils who had started the programme in the nursery schools would, after reaching the elementary level, spend a few weeks in schools in the other country following their regular courses, so that they could become fully integrated with the other children. By 1968-69 bilingual

---

[81] *Plowden Report*, Vol. I, 1969, pp. 223-225.
[82] A. D. Russell, *French in the Primary School: A Progress Report* (Author's personal communication).

nursery schools had been set up in 37 French *Départements*. Statistics for 1969-70, though as yet incomplete reveal that "about 550 English classes and 250 German classes were operating, in 21 *Départements* for German and in 36 for English". Teachers have been exchanged between England and France for some time, but the lack of formal agreement between the governments has meant that the system has encountered some difficulty and has not developed on so wide a scale. With the official agreement, however, the exchange of teachers between Germany and France has proved beneficial for both countries. When the agreement was renewed in October, 1969, it became "possible to extend the early study of French to Rhein-Westphalen, where about 90 new classes were set up in October, 1970".[83]

A realisation of the importance of inter-governmental agreement upon the expansion of foreign language teaching to young children, in the light of the French-German experience, has resulted in efforts on the part of the British Council and the French Ministry of National Education towards developing a closer and more systematic pattern of exchange between France and England.[84]

In Sweden, under the new school plan, the study of English begins at the age of 11, in the fourth grade of the comprehensive school. A government-sponsored experiment is being conducted to develop a methodological system to enable children to learn a foreign language from the first grade (at the age of 7). In 1962, when the comprehensive school reform was introduced, the Minister of Education expressed the view that an attempt should be made to teach English to children at less than 11. He was supported by professional associations and educational experts on the grounds that the younger the child, the easier it is for him to gain an insight into the structure of a language. At an educational conference held in 1956, the statement was made that "the optimum age for beginning the continuous learning of a second language seems to fall within the span of ages four to eight, with higher performances to be expected at the ages 8, 9 and 10".[85] In the absence of clear evidence, the Scandinavian Cultural Commission insisted upon a research project in 1968 to assess "the optimum time for the commencement of language learning... by an assessment of how the objectives

---

[83] Alice Delaunay (General Inspector of Public Education), *L'acquisition précoce des langues vivantes par la méthode naturelle* (mimeographed; kindly transmitted by the author): VII: L'initiation précoce aux langues vivantes en milieu scolaire, pp. 2-3.
[84] *Ibid.*, p. 3.
[85] School Research, 1969, 5: "English in the Lower Department of the Comprehensive School. Planning for a FOU Project extending from 1970 to 1979".

aimed at, both the cognitive and affective, can be achieved in the shortest possible time".[86]

The findings of the Swedish research project will certainly be of great interest. In the meantime, however, there is an apparently well founded opinion, based on world wide experience, that the younger the child when first faced with a foreign language, the better will his learning develop. As a Swedish school inspector declared upon returning from a visit to a nursery school in France which had adopted the direct, natural method of learning foreign languages, "my research upon the teaching of foreign languages has always been based on the principle that language is not only a means of communication but that it is a form of behaviour".[87] In the nursery school, with their flexible and developing brain structure, young children are prepared to learn a foreign language similar to their own if they are involved in a real life situation in which they are forced to convey the needs that they desire to satisfy to other children or adults in that foreign language. "Indirect" learning comes later and it will never be so fruitful as the direct method. Personal, face-to-face relationships with children or teachers expressing themselves naturally in that foreign language seem to be the best method of acquiring that language at an early age. Language teaching by teachers who are not entirely masters of the other language, even if audio-visual aids are available, does not seem to be effective with young children, a belief that is borne out by French experience. For young children, learning a foreign language is something natural if it is part of the overall situation. They learn a new language not by reflective thought but through total experience in which their emotions, their social experience and their powers of expression are closely connected. The Swedish research project will shed new light on the issue, an issue of paramount importance in our time. It will help educators in the selection of the appropriate direct or indirect methods for the teaching of foreign languages.

Following much debate in Sweden up to that time, the Department of Foreign Language Pedagogic Institute of the University of Uppsala directed by Professor K. G. Ahlstrom, planned the project for the teaching of "English in the lower department of the comprehensive school, to extend from 1970-79".[88]

[86] *Ibid.*, p. 3.
[87] Mr. Tore Osterberg's words in a letter to Alice Delaunay, dated February, 1969, are quoted in her essay, "L'acquisition précoce des langues vivantes par la méthode naturelle", III, p. 1.
[88] School Research, 1969, 5, in which the project is described in detail.

Aims of Education

In Italy, too, where the 1962 law has introduced the study of one foreign language in the state junior high schools for 11 year olds in the first grade, experiments in the field of foreign language teaching are being carried out by many public and private primary schools, as well as by various centres. The "European Centre of Education" Multi-Media Division, directed by Professor R. Titone, who has done sterling work on the study of foreign languages, is concentrating upon research in the use of audio-visual methods in the teaching of foreign languages. At university level, the University of Florence Institute of Education, in conjunction with the English and Russian departments, has planned a research project on the study of foreign languages among children aged 4 to 8. In their preliminary linguistic and psycho-pedagogical approach to the problems involved, they have constructed the hypotheses to be tested, discussed methodological systems in a comparative framework and experimented upon educational devices such as puppet shows, drama work, video recording, etc., using younger children. The project is sponsored by the Italian National Research Council which has allocated a small sum for 1971.

There has been a growing concern for language education in the more advanced psychological and educational circles in the US and Europe over the past few years. There is, it is now increasingly believed, a need to advance the study of foreign languages to the lowest levels of school. This is now being done in most countries and research is now being conducted on the subject.

The study of foreign languages is, however, only one aspect of a wider issue extending beyond the didactic and scholastic field to the major problems of social and intellectual personality development. A solution is being attempted by

1) combining a respect for local culture, embodied in dialect, with the study and dissemination of the national language on the one hand and
2) pursuing a world culture and fostering internationalism in the population at large by encouraging children to take an interest in local, national and foreign languages.

Under these conditions, language education is important in many ways. It has the effect of improving the ability of children to express themselves, to think and to widen their social intercultural and international horizons.

The true benefits of language education will be felt only if it is closely related to linguistic research, a field in which great strides have been made over the past few decades, and to the study of child psychology. There must be a clearer assessment of the time at which children are ready for language learning, in the light of linguistic theory, if educational and didactic methods are to be improved in practice in the classroom.

2. INNOVATIONS IN THE STRUCTURES OF PRIMARY EDUCATION

BY

LAMBERTO BORGHI

In this chapter we shall attempt to outline the new structures of primary education which are already taking shape in educational and social theory and the strategies which are most likely to help achieve such structures.

Any discussion of the problem of structural change should be viewed in the light of the discussion in the following chapter about the aims of education in the context of what the future "should look like" in Europe and the world in the 21st century.

In the course of this chapter, we shall use the existing situation in various countries as a springboard for an attempt to forecast trends in the reform and change of school organisation. In this relatively short space, we shall try to condense the overwhelming mass of material derived from official and unofficial documents in European and extra-European countries[1] and to concentrate on certain major areas which

[1] I would merely like to mention a few documents: for West Germany, *Strukturplan für das Bildungswesen* issued by the Deutscher Bildungsrat in 1970; *Richtlinien und Lehrpläne für die Grundschule; Schulversuch in Nordrhein-Westfalen; Eine Schriftenreihe des Kultusministers* (1969); *Beiträge zur Reform der Grundschule; Arbeitskreis Grundschule e.V.* (2 vs., 1970); and *Grundschulkongress '69* (3 vs., 1970); valuable information is also provided by the magazine *Die Grundschule*, and by the bulletin, *Education in Germany*, published by Inter-Nationes. For France, *Institut Pédagogique National* publications, especially the *Recherches pédagogiques* collection, and the reports by the General Inspectorate of the Ministry of National Education. For Sweden, the *Läroplan för grundskolan* (1969), the bulletin published by The National Swedish Board of Education; the Reports published by the *Pedagogisk Centrum*, publications of the various Departments of Educational and Psychological Research of Schools of Education (especially those of Malmö and Stockholm). For the Soviet Union, the new primary schools syllabi; issues of the *Soviet Review of Education* published by the National Educational Academy of the Union of the Soviet Republics; *Planification de l'éducation en URSS*, a study by K. Nojko, E. Monoszon, V. Jamine, V. Severtsev, Paris, IIPE, UNESCO, 1967; and the article by A. Arsenyev and A. Markouchevich, "La réduction de la durée de l'enseignement en URSS", *Perspectives de l'éducation*, No. 1, 1969, UNESCO. For England, the main sources of information on the present situation of and the prospects for primary education are the Plowden Report, *Children and their Primary Schools*, London, HMSO, 1967; publications issued by the National Foundation for Educational Research in England and Wales and those of the Schools' Council; and the Times. Among the reviews of European comparative education, *Western European Education*, edited by Professor Ursula K. Springer, Brooklyn College, N.Y., is of special relevance.

we believe to be most relevant to the re-shaping of school structures and to the creation of new strategies to this end.

There are three major areas which are most open to discussion at the present time and which have the greatest educational bearing on the future. They are:
a. The general structure of primary education, especially in relation to the kindergarten and the nursery school at one end and to the middle school at the other;
b. the relationship between the school and the community;
c. the internal structure of primary education, particularly those organisational changes required for non-grading, team teaching and decision-making.

These three topics are closely linked and all are significant for the success of the educational process as a whole.

CHANGES IN SCHOOL ORGANISATION

Although there are still striking differences between European countries in the general structure of primary education, there are certain trends common to all nations which will probably gain momentum over the next few decades. Six is the starting age for elementary education in most countries in Europe. In Sweden and the Soviet Union, the statutory age for the commencement of primary education is seven. In England, the 1944 Education Act, institutionalising established tradition, decreed that every child has the right to education from the term after his fifth birthday and the Plowden Report recommended that "the statutory time by which children must go to school should be defined as the September term following their fifth birthday". The situation is, however, very fluid. There is a general trend to making the compulsory schooling age earlier and toward establishing close links between the elementary and the nursery school.

1. *The Soviet Union*

In the Soviet Union, according to the education plan for the decade 1970-1980, the statutory age for beginning primary school will be lowered to five by 1976. In the meantime, efforts are being made to persuade families to send their children to nursery school at least by the age of six. Achievement of this ideal, however, is being hampered by resistance from families, especially in rural districts, and by the lack of buildings and teachers. At present, about 50% of children attend the final year of nursery school, although there are wide differences between large cities and small towns. In Moscow, for instance, about 85% of six year olds attend nursery schools. The facilities are adequate to meet the demands of every family. The situation is very different in the newly developing industrial towns, where the supply of school places cannot cope with the demand, especially among peasant communities. One of the Soviet government's major educational tasks is to offset these inequalities. Its motivation in so doing is twofold: economic and educational.

Industrial growth in the Soviet Union is now dependent upon the female labour force. Today, many women able to work are in fact unable to take a job because of the shortage of nursery schools. On the other hand, in many Eastern Republics of the USSR, there is a large proportion of families with a high birth rate who are unwilling to send their children to nursery school. The State itself, fully aware of the obstacles still impeding the extension of compulsory schooling to six year olds, encourages families to teach their children at home. Special books are written to help parents and there are radio and television programmes to prepare children for primary school.

Nevertheless, the problem is still unsolved. The work of teachers is being made far more difficult because they have to cope with primary school children not having previously attended a nursery school. To counteract this waste of the teachers' energy and to enhance the success of primary education, special classes are held twice a week within the primary schools for children aged six and seven who have not come up from nursery schools. The inadequacy of kindergarten-level training and the existence of a large percentage of children not attending school of any kind before the age of seven, particularly in the rural areas, are having an adverse effect upon primary education achievement in the Soviet Union. This is officially a "punctum dolens" in Russian education today.[2]

2. France

West Germany, France and Sweden all believe, in principle, that the statutory age for compulsory school attendance should be lowered to five. In France there is a wide gap between the types of education

[2] We would like to thank the Ministry of Public Education of the Soviet Union, particularly the "Directorate of Pre-school Education" and the "Directorate of the School Planning Office for the Next Decade" for information provided on these problems during our visit to Moscow in May 1970.

provided in the nursery school and in the elementary school and, according to the administrators and educators, this must be bridged if an "organic relationship" is to be achieved between the two types of schools. The success of the comprehensive *cycle élémentaire désenclavé*, now being tested under the guidance and supervision of the National Pedagogical Institute, has raised the question of whether compulsory education should be lowered to the age of five in even more urgent terms. The basic aim in organising this *cycle* is declared to be the "untrammelled development of each child and the progressive advancement of his physical, mental, intellectual, aesthetic (including his emotional and artistic) maturation, as well as his social and personality abilities". Upon the primary school is placed the onus of "organic continuity with the nursery school". The basic principles underlying these experiments are "individualisation of education, maximum adaptation to the standards and working rate of each pupil, breaking up of class barriers and group mobility so that pupils can be moved from one subgroup to another at any given time".[3]

3. Sweden

In Sweden, the new syllabus for the *grundskola* (nine year compulsory comprehensive school) contains no mention of its relationships with the nursery school. However, it is the opinion of educational experts that as it develops the school will try to bridge the gap between these two types of school. The problem here, as in the Soviet Union, has its economic and educational implications. The issue, it is believed, is mainly political. New taxation legislation makes it imperative for women to work and, in turn, this means that the statutory age for starting school should be lowered from seven to five. This change is to be introduced within the next five years, but the problem is complicated by the relative shortage of nursery education today. Pre-primary schools meet the needs of only 30% of the population; from the educational point of view, it is considered important that the two schools be integrated to ensure not only the optimum intellectual development of every child but also his full emotional and social maturity.[4]

[3] Institut Pédagogique National, Département de la Recherche Pédagogique, *Expérimentation d'un cycle élémentaire "désenclavé"*, *Note explicative complémentaire au plan de la recherche*; and also (from the same Institute) *Programme de recherches* 1969/70, p. 71, *Expérimentation d'un cycle élémentaire "désenclavé"*.

[4] May we express our gratitude to Professor M. G. Ahlstrom, Director of the Institute of Education, University of Uppsala for furnishing us with this information during our visit in May 1970.

4. West Germany

The Structural Plan for Education approved in 1970 by the Education Commission set up by the German Council for Education recommended "the introduction of an initiation phase" (*Eingangstufe*) lasting one or two years for the five or the five and six year olds at elementary school and "the expansion of nursery school facilities to the three and four year olds".[5] As in the Soviet Union and France, the motivation for this reform was both social and educational. The "Structure Plan" pointed out that, in our contemporary society, children mature earlier and develop their learning abilities at a younger age. On the other hand, the family – particularly in lower social groups – has become less of a stimulating force. By advancing compulsory school attendance to the age of five, society would be able to provide remedial education for socially deprived children. The Commission report made it clear, however, that the aim of the structural reform was not merely compensatory. The principal goal was to "contribute towards improving the learning and decision-making abilities of all children". The new nursery schools should provide every child with the type of educational facilities that good kindergartens have provided a few privileged children in the past. "The learning process will be more closely integrated to develop children's learning capacities, effective social life, autonomy and satisfaction in personal activity".[6]

This plan is already being implemented in some of the German *Länder*. The largest *Land*, Nordrhein-Westfalen, has already approved a plan for an experiment to be completed by 1975 "with 50 pre-school classes, the long-term aim being to make it possible for all five year olds to attend school".[7]

5. Italy

No official provision has yet been made to bridge the gap between the nursery and the primary school. It was not until very recently that Parliament set up a State nursery school system by enacting the law

---

[5] "Federal Republic of Germany: Recommendations for the Reform of Elementary Education" (*Education in Germany*, n. 9, 1970; and *Newsletter/Faits Nouveaux*, Council of Europe 5, 1970, p. 14.)

[6] *Strukturplan für das Bildungswesen*, Deutscher Bildungsrat. *Empfehlungen der Bildungskommission*, 1970, pp. 301, 40 48.

[7] *Education in Germany*, n. 7/1970, p. 28. The Times Educational Supplement in its issue dated 11.9.1970 (p. 17) published the news that Schleswig-Holstein will be the first state in the Federal Republic "to make a pre-school year from five to six years of age compulsory, with effect from next year" (from a letter from West Germany written by Charles Whiting).

dated 18th March, 1968, although as yet only the first few steps have been taken to implement this law. The general syllabi (*Orientamenti*) for the school were approved by the government in September, 1969. The fact that approximately half of children aged between three and five already attend nursery school, most of them run by private and religious bodies, is no guarantee of their educational quality. There is, however, a growing concern with the organisation of local authority nursery schools and widespread recognition of the importance of nursery education in providing facilities for personal development and equality of educational opportunity for all. Educators of widely different persuasions all support the lowering of the compulsory school age from seven to five on economic, social and educational grounds very similar to those considered valid in Germany. The idea is gaining ground that a two year course for children from five to seven should be established and the issue is still being debated. Any such change would, however, make no substantial contribution to education if the teaching situation in the primary school continues to be at as low a level as at present, with poorly trained and paid teachers, no on-the-job training, little experimentation on new educational techniques and with powerful Catholic pressure to ensure the continuation of the denominational nature of primary education in State schools, violating the terms of the Constitution which guarantees non-sectarian teaching as well as freedom of religion.

Psychologists and educators in Italy have emphasised the need for a new two year pre-primary school for five to seven year olds, on the same lines as the infant school in England and the Montessori *Case dei bambini*, as a prerequisite for reorganisation of the whole structure of the basic school in Italy.[8] The striking differences that persist between children from differing social backgrounds in their learning ability and scholastic achievement are to a large extent due to the school's inability to help children overcome inequalities in the cultural and educational stimulation they receive in their home environment. The nursery school has a vital role in helping children to enrich and add to their range of experience and to broaden their social horizons, thus expanding upon and integrating the educational foundation laid by their parents. The nursery school serves the needs of all children, irrespective of social background, but it has a truly significant part to

[8] *Per la ricostruzione della scuola di base*, Bologna Municipal Authority, June 1969 (Recommendations made by two round table conferences organised by the Municipality of Bologna Education Department).

Innovations in the Structures of Primary Education

play in the case of children suffering from the effects of industrialisation and emigration by their families from country to town, and in the case of children from lower income groups in both country and town, in that it can help "to compensate for the frequent lack of cultural stimulation in the milieu from which the children originate".[9]

The outstanding number of failures in the primary and junior secondary schools among children from deprived homes has been attributed to the difficulties of social adjustment and communication in a new environment encountered by families emigrating to cities in the North from Southern Italy and to the common use of dialect in the home. Emphasis has been placed upon the close relationship between language and thought as the main factor in these failures. The nursery and infant schools can provide invaluable support by helping children to master their own national tongue, while at the same time it should be stressed that language learning "should originate from a deep and authentic motivation towards communication and form a living use of the native language".[10]

Two important projects now being advocated in the current debate in Italy on the structural reorganisation of primary education are a State nursery school, adopting methods evolved on the basis of advanced psychological and educational thought, and the creation of a new two-year pre-primary school along the lines of the English infant school.

6. *The English Influence*

The restructuring of pre-primary and primary education in Europe and the relationship between these two levels have been considerably influenced by experience in Britain. The Plowden Report recommended that the three stages of education, from infancy to adolescence, should be closely linked in the overall structure of primary education. The Report recommended "part-time nursery school experience for those whose parents wish it" as an "inseparable" aspect of the reorganisation of primary education into two stages, the former being a "first school" lasting three years, beginning at the "median age of five years six months" followed by a new "four year course in a middle school with

---

[9] Orientamenti dell'attività educativa nelle scuole materne statali, approved by the President of the Italian Republic on 10th September, 1969 (*Scuola e Città*, October 1969, p. 540). Similar attitudes had been expressed by A. Bassi in the article, Insuccesso e ritardo, *Scuola e Città*, April-May 1966, p. 147.
[10] *Per la ricostruzione della scuola di base*, Comune di Bologna, June 1969.

a median range from eight years six months to twelve years six months".[11]

The expansion of nursery school facilities has now become one of the most crucial problems in English education. The vital impact of nursery school education upon the general development of personality, both in infancy and during later periods, is generally recognised. In 1965, only 215,297 children between the ages of two and four experienced any form of pre-school education, either in nursery schools or in infant and junior schools. In January 1965, the total number of children aged two to four was estimated to be 2,100,000.[12] According to Plowden Report estimates, "in 1965 about 7% of all children in England were receiving some form of education in a school or nursery class... Three-quarters of nursery places are in classes in infant schools". The Report stated that in England, "nursery education on a large scale remains an unfulfilled promise".[13] The Plowden Report took a very close look at the educational case for and against this type of education. The conclusion was that such education is desirable not only on educational but also on social and economic grounds. It was not considered that the research findings supported "nursery education for all", but the Report relies "on the overwhelming evidence of experienced educators" as well as on the situations in other countries and upon the opinions of foreign educators. Special emphasis was laid upon the special need for the provision of nursery education to children "from deprived or inadequate home backgrounds", and serious consideration was given to available research findings "on the extent to which nursery education can compensate for social deprivation", with particular reference to the "consequences of social deprivation on the development of language and thought in children".[14]

THE IMPACT OF EDUCATIONAL DEMOCRATISATION ON CHANGING SCHOOL STRUCTURES

The structural reforms of primary education already introduced in certain countries and the reforms planned in others are closely linked to the process of educational democratisation which has gained momentum over the past decade. This movement has also been influenced

---

[11] *Children and their Primary Schools*, Vol. 1, p. 146.
[12] *Ibid.*, p. 109.
[13] *Ibid.*, p. 116.
[14] *Ibid.*, p. 119.

by the progress in research on cognitive knowledge, which in turn has been affected by the explosive accumulation of scientific knowledge in the recent past. Although the two trends are in no way identical, they have to a certain extent combined to reinforce the demand for earlier compulsory education and for the linking of primary and pre-primary education. However, there are certain substantial differences between the two trends and their implications. The movement to introduce greater democracy into the field of education has been particularly concerned with achieving the conditions that all children, irrespective of social background, need for their full personal growth – physical, emotional, social and intellectual. Educators are fully aware of the importance of the first few years of life in the process of development and they have stressed the urgency of establishing educational opportunities from infancy for all children, particularly, but by no means solely, for those from deprived or inadequate homes. Educators have also underlined the importance of involving the entire social setting within which children are brought up in this educational movement, thus extending the scope of educational reform and the demand for structural changes from the school to the community as a whole. In the case of this second trend, the main concern has been to speed up the children's rate of learning to help pave the way for successful technological advance. To accelerate and foster the educational process, limited mainly to children's learning abilities, has been the principal tenet of this movement. We have already suggested that the two trends are not always clear-cut or easily distinguishable. Their nature and implications are, however, very different: while the former relates more to the second model of society, a society dedicated to the personal development of all its members and to social and communal development – the latter refers more to the first model of society – based on the dominance of political and economic sub-systems controlled by private vested interests.

COMPENSATORY EDUCATION

The substantial efforts which governments are now making in the field of remedial education can be related to both trends. The reason why the stated goals have not been achieved, however, may be that they have no clear picture of the society of tomorrow. The main failings in the current remedial education movement are probably that it concentrates too much on speeding up the learning process and on helping children to master the technological instruments used to this end, without giving sufficient thought to their overall personal development, and that its efforts are confined to the environment of educational institutions, without altering the social situation responsible for depriving the child of his basic opportunities for growth and without involving the whole community in this process of change.

The Plowden Report singled out the compensatory education programme being evolved in the United States as one of the valid suggestions originating in other countries, believing "that educational stimulus for young children is of great importance, particularly for the deprived". The Report stated that "in the USA at the present time, Federal and other authorities and private foundations are providing large sums of money for programs of nursery education to counteract the effect of extreme deprivation".[15]

Compensatory education programmes have been conducted in the USA at three levels – pre-school, elementary and secondary school. The greatest impetus, however, has been in the provision of education for the pre-primary and primary school levels. These programmes have supported the conviction that work to ensure the success of education must start in the first few years of life and that nursery schools, kindergarten and elementary schools must be regarded as interdependent units. The development of unstructured, semi-unstructured and structured nursery school programmes has been mainly due to efforts to provide compensatory education for deprived children. As the authors of a report on current educational changes in Canada have noted, "some of the impetus for research into structured kindergarten and nursery school programmes has come from the attempt of the United States Government to do something about massive poverty problems. Before the Poverty Program began, pressure for early cognitive emphasis had come mainly from middle class parents who wanted their children to learn more and learn it faster. Now, however, the pressure is coming from lower class parents or rather, from their government representatives". The Toronto Report quoted Jerome Bruner's words to the effect that children from deprived backgrounds can benefit greatly from "structured, systematic pre-school enrichment and retraining programs which would compensate or attempt to compensate for the difference in the slum environment". The Report also quotes the "radical departures" from traditional kindergarten practices offered by the kindergarten programme recommended by Professor Orville

[15] *Ibid.*, p. 120.

Johnson of Syracuse University, a programme that is "planned in small developmental steps", i.e. direct and to the point, employing the techniques peculiar to programmed learning. "Professor Carl Bereiter and Siegfried Engelmann", the Report continues, "are developing a programme to help culturally disadvantaged children to catch up in a hurry... The programme emphasises direct teaching consisting of deliberately planned lessons involving demonstration, drill, exercises, problems and the like".[16]

Readers of the series of publications issued by the Education Office of the US Department of Health, Education and Welfare, describing pre-school and elementary programmes in compensatory education[17] are impressed by the wealth and variety of projects that are being developed to help children from coloured and poverty-stricken groups to "increase their potential for early success in school". The age of the children involved ranges from 15 months upwards to include children in pre-kindergarten, kindergarten, elementary school and even secondary school. The results achieved with the pupils are usually considered to be satisfactory. The cost of the programmes varies but it is on the high side, in many cases amounting to over $1,000 per pupil per year. A good deal of valuable experience has been gathered from these projects. There has been increased insight into the effects of early deprivation upon the individual and cognitive growth of children, and the knowledge acquired on cognitive and developmental processes has been skilfully applied in the conduct of the projects. The problems faced by the government and local boards of education has been so huge, however, that a wide scale solution could hardly be envisaged. The aetiology of the children's difficulties were so firmly rooted in the texture of American society that any attempt to cope with them within the social system as it now stands, while school continues to be organised upon the present lines, has been a task too great even for these

---

[16] *SEF Report E 1: Educational Specifications and User Requirements for Elementary (K-6) Schools.* Toronto, Ryerson Press, for the Metropolitan Toronto School Board Study of Educational Facilities, Copyright 1968, The Metropolitan Toronto School Board, pp. 105-106. J. S. Bruner's words are quoted from "The Cognitive Consequences of Early Sensory Deprivation", *Sensory Deprivation,* ed. P. Solomon (Cambridge: Harvard University Press, 1961) p. 203; the quotation from Bereiter and Engelmann is from their book *Teaching Disadvantaged Children in the Pre-school,* Prentice Hall I, 1966, pp. 48-49, and 63.

[17] Thirty-one booklets published by the Office of Education, US Department of Health, Education and Welfare, Washington, DC, describe the same number of projects in compensatory education as the pre-school, elementary and secondary school level. Information on all 31 projects has been provided by the Office of Education in the booklet: *It Works Series: Summaries of Selected Compensatory Education Projects,* US Government Print-Office, Washington, DC, 1970.

wholehearted efforts. The overall impact of these efforts was evaluated by President Nixon in his 1970 message on education, in which he stated that "the best available evidence indicates that most of the compensatory education programs have not measurably helped poor children to catch up".

THE DEBATE ON COMPENSATORY EDUCATION

The reasons for this setback are not solely the cost of the programmes and the magnitude of the task, but also the way in which the problems have been tackled and the programmes conceived. It is important that we consider and evaluate this criticism, as the movement for compensatory education is spilling over from the US to Europe and there is a world-wide need to offset educational and cultural deprivations of disadvantaged groups. Any discussion of the future of education will to a great degree depend on how we approach this problem.

The subject of compensatory education leads us to the issue of changes in the school structure, i.e. the relationship between school and community. Critics in the US and England on the concept of compensatory education and its impact on current projects consider this issue to be the most crucial one faced by educators today.

The main argument recently directed against compensatory education in both countries is that "it serves to direct attention away from the internal organisation and the educational context of school and focus our attention upon the families and children", thus devaluing the children's life experience outside school in their own eyes and leading to a loss of cultural identity and self-esteem as members of a family from which they come to think "something is missing". According to Professor Basil Bernstein, "a wedge is gradually being driven between the child as a member of a family and a community and the child as a member of a school". Instead of separating family and community life from the school, the well-known British educational sociologist remarks, "parents must be brought *within* the educational experience of the schoolchild by doing what they do and this with confidence". While the concept of compensatory education drives home the belief that the main origin of failure at school is to be attributed to "deficiences within the community, family and child", radical changes must be made in the school structure and curriculum. On the one hand, "the contents of learning in schools should be drawn far more from the child's experience in his family and community", and on the other, "larger questions" must be raised regarding "the organisational contexts we create for educational purposes" by examining "the social assumptions underlying the organisation, distribution and evaluation of knowledge", and the effects on education and educability of the fact that "the power relationships created outside the school penetrate the organisation, distribution and evaluation of knowledge through the social context of their transmission".[18]

The American counterpart of this criticism was recently voiced by a Ford Foundation Program Officer, the author of major works on urban education, Mario D. Fantini. He stated that most Federal programmes in compensatory education were based on the assumption that the present structure and management of the school should not be changed, but rather that something had to be done "to add-on" and strengthen existing programs". "The central problem concerns the learner and not the school". Attention is diverted from the school to "environmental and cultural deficits". This means that children are stimulated "to adjust to schools" rather than focusing attention on the need "to change the school". The main task is to shift attention and concern "from the learner to the institution". Fantini agrees with B. Bernstein's analysis of the situation and his evaluation of its needs, stating that "the classroom must be expanded to include the community". A major problem arising in America today is pinpointed by the statement that "public school systems... must strengthen the role of the community in school affairs... through the establishment of sub-systems which are community-based or community-oriented". The school as an institution must evolve by developing new structures in which the responsibility of the community is more widely felt than is the case today. The reaction of substantial groups of the coloured population in the United States against integration programmes over the past few years is based upon their refusal to assimilate the culture of a white dominant group, a culture transmitted to them through channels – school – in which they had no say. The movement towards separate school systems is inspired by the desire of minority groups for a cultural identity and for democratic participation in the control of public education. The current trend towards separation should be viewed in perspective as conductive to genuine integration based upon an "orchestration of diversities" (to borrow Horace M. Kallen's expression) by creating "partici-

---

[18] Basil Bernstein, "A Critique of the Concept of Compensatory Education", from *Education and Democracy*, D. Rubenstein and C. Stonemann, Ed., Penguin Books, London, 1970, pp. 111-121.

patory systems" which "maximise decision-making for all the parties which have an intrinsic interest in the quality of schooling".

This infusion of "new energies and resources... into the educational system", a process that is vital if true change is to be introduced, will create new public attitudes towards education and schools. Minority group awareness of isolation from society may gradually give way to a feeling of belonging. "If handled sensibly, the current demand for participation in control of public education can be a means of greater connection to society". However, it would be a mistake to overestimate the power of the school to solve the problems of society. "The school as a public institution does not have the capacity to deal with the diversity of its consumers. Public schools are asked to provide the solutions for many social ills: poverty, racism, alienation, powerlessness, while responding to the manpower needs of an advanced technological society. In short, public education has been given a mission for which it currently is not prepared. Faced with these growing demands, schoolmen have responded in the only way they could, with an add-on strategy, i.e., building layers into the standard educational structure. The basic charge for the 1970's, therefore, is institutional reform".[19]

This insight into the solution to the problem of inter-relationships between school and society sheds new light on the issue of structural reform of the school. The two authors quoted above, who to a certain extent voice the viewpoints of leading educationalists and sociologists in the United States and Great Britain, visualise the relationship of school and society as being reciprocal in their effects. The community must of course play a greater part in school affairs and "the contents of learning must be drawn much more from the child's experience in his family and community", but new public school sub-systems must also be created "which are community-oriented". It must be the school which expands towards the family and the community. Although it will benefit from their influence, it must in turn exercise its influence upon them. A model of a society which emphasises personal and communal values can come into being once social life comes to mean a wider fellowship of human beings, with reciprocal communication on a world wide basis, in which class distinctions, racialism and alienation have been abolished. The dominant aspects of such a society are cultural and educational throughout. It is true that no educational

---

[19] Mario D. Fantini, "Urban School Reform: Educational Agenda for Tomorrow's America", *Current History*, November 1970, pp. 267-330.

programme can compensate for social deprivation; the only solution is to abolish social deprivation.

School structures must, therefore, be transformed in line with changes in other social structures which must be considered as forming an integral part of the school.

THE TREND TOWARDS INTEGRATION

These general assumptions lead to certain suggestions as to changes in school organisation in its relation to society, in the content and process of learning and the organisation of teaching within the school.

Two structural changes in particular have special bearing on future-oriented education in Western Europe. These changes, however, are not limited to Europe. First of all, education should be seen as a unitary process and no internal division reflecting developmental stages in the growth of personality should be used to justify barriers between different levels and types of school. Professor B. Bernstein expressed this view very clearly when discussing relationship between the pre-school and the primary school, saying that "it would be foolhardy indeed to write off the post-seven years of age educational experience as having little influence" and that "minimally what is required *initially* is to consider the whole age period up to the conclusion of the primary stages as a unit", adding that "in order to accomplish this, the present social and educational division between infant and junior stages must be weakened".[20]

The Plowden Report and the law creating State nursery schools for children from 3 to 6 in Italy represent a move in this direction. Many compensatory education projects in the USA have also been organised along these lines.

Certain other countries in Europe, such as Sweden, the Soviet Union and most Communist countries have closely linked primary and secondary education without, however, extending their unitary concept of the school structure and of the educational process to the pre-school.

Many progressive educators in Italy have advocated the establishment of a unified school, incorporating the pre-school, the primary school and the junior secondary school, asserting that the *scuola di base* cannot be broken down piecemeal into "disconnected and often conflicting stages". Demanding the creation of a "truly unified school"

---

[20] B. Bernstein, *Ibid.*, pp. 113-114.

covering the ages 3 to 16, they have declared that "the same principle applies to the later stages of schooling". These educators affirm that if this new type of school "is to achieve its proper goal and to go even beyond the limit of its current goals, it must become a centre of permanent education, fulfilling its social function by initiating projects, debates, research and experiments in which the whole surrounding community cooperates. Such a school would demand that all its structures be entirely democratic".[21]

CONTINUITY BETWEEN PRIMARY AND SECONDARY EDUCATION

The lack of continuity between primary and secondary education in most European countries today is one of the major obstacles to scholastic success. All schoolchildren are affected by this division between school structures and curricula, although underprivileged children suffer more. The switch from class teaching to specialisation is a process that requires thorough preparation and careful consideration of each child's rate of development. Since there are no institutionalised links between the two school stages, it is impossible for teachers to meet these needs. Teachers, especially in the secondary school, strive to inculcate middle class values and this makes the gap between pupils of different social classes even wider. This is the reason for the continued existence of selective systems of admission to secondary schools and organisational differentiation at lower secondary school levels, following the same lines as the divisions of the social classes, a phenomenon still to be found in several European countries.

The trend towards the establishment of a unified middle school, which first took shape during the early and mid-sixties in France, West Germany and Italy, has led to major structural school reforms in these three countries. The Soviet Union has established a comprehensive eight year school, now being extended to ten years to include comprehensive secondary school education for all children from seven to seventeen. The concept is that this should be a unified structure, but it includes three distinct phases: primary, middle and secondary levels. In Sweden there is a nine year compulsory comprehensive school (*grundskola*) for all children from seven to sixteen. In that country subjects are taught by specialist teachers from the seventh grade, while all subjects are taken by the one teacher in the first six grades, forming

[21] Bologna Municipal Authority, Education Department, *Per la riconstruzione della scuola di base*, Bologna, 1969, pp. 13-14, 20.

the primary school, which is divided into a lower and a middle department.

In England, for various educational and social reasons the Plowden Report suggested that children should no longer be streamed at eleven or begin secondary education at that age. In considering the new structure of primary education, it recommended "a three year course in the first (at present the infant) school" for children from five to eight, to be followed by "a four year course at the middle (at present the junior) school" for children from nine to thirteen. Although the Plowden Report suggested "a median age of twelve years six months on admission to a secondary school", it agreed with the results of the Scottish Council for Research in Education to the effect that, as far as "the appropriate age of transfer" is concerned, "there is no one correct age... The transition from primary to secondary education should extend over the whole period from age ten to age thirteen".[22]

The Report did not, however, envisage a unified structure for primary and secondary education, but merely emphasised the need for regular professional contacts between primary and secondary teachers and for "increased opportunities for individual work in secondary schools" to "reduce the overlap in children's work before and after transfer".[23]

The important factor in current British reform is that the primary school will continue beyond infancy into adolescence, thus paving the way for more far-reaching transformation of the school structure, leading to a unified school system which will ensure "continuity and consistency between the stages of education",[24] while introducing those internal differences in teaching and the curriculum which are necessary to meet the developmental needs of children at different ages.

This concept of the achievement of continuity between primary and secondary education by means of structural coordination is no less important than the concept we have already discussed, continuity and rational structural coordination between pre-primary and primary education. Whether efforts to make the school system more democratic in Europe succeed will depend upon this two-fold transformation.

---

[22] *Children and Their Primary Schools* (Plowden Report), Vol. I, p. 146.
[23] *Ibid.*, pp. 164-165.
[24] This is the title of chapter 12 of the Plowden Report.

THE "SCUOLA-QUARTIERE" (SCHOOL AND NEIGHBOURHOOD) MOVEMENT

The structural change arising from this concept is the creation of a community school system which allows for the control and management of the school by "the newly emerging public – students, parents and the communities who are becoming increasingly aware that they should be involved in any decision on the programme options for schools in their localities" and for the educational process itself in close liaison with teachers.[25]

A political movement has recently been gaining momentum, under the impact of the student movement: this has been set up to counteract the centralised school organisation prevailing in most European countries – the principal exceptions being England and Switzerland – and against the "entrenched bureaucracies" which exercise a pervasive and paralysing control over schools. In Italy, over the past three years, the *Scuola e Quartiere* (School and Neighbourhood) movement has spread to several areas of the country. About one hundred groups attended the national meeting held in Florence in June, 1970. These groups of students and teachers have organised afternoon and evening courses for primary and junior secondary school children in working class urban districts. Their goal was to create a "counter-school" as an alternative to the existing school structures, accused of being agencies discriminating in favour of middle class children. The main points made by the groups starting the movement are the following: "The ever more serious crisis in existing school structures and organisation, especially in areas that have seen recent urban expansion, has forced families to set up a popular organisation to pursue their right to study, to control educational systems from below and to set up district post-schoolday courses".[26]

This movement has sprung up from small groups that have formed spontaneously, lacking a well-defined nature; it has declared its goals of change not to be "confined to the cultural and pedagogical sphere", as in the case of contemporary programmes organised and carried out in other European countries over the past few years,[27] but as essentially

---

[25] Mario Fantini, *Ibid.*, p. 270.
[26] *Scuola e Quartiere*, by "Doposcuola – scuole serale – comitati di genitori di Firenze e provincia", Tipografia La Stamperia, Firenze, 1969, p. 14.
[27] *Project Compensatory Program* – Utrecht University Department of Education, *Western European Education*, Summer/Fall 1969, Vol. I, n. 2-3 ("Compensatory and Pre-school Education"), p. 17.

political. The movement has attempted to create new channels of communication and new methods of joint action between intellectuals – students and teachers – and the working class. It is not yet possible to assess the achievement of the movement. The operating groups realised that if their campaign for a reform of school structure and educational contents were waged from outside the school, it could be successful only if coordinated and parallel action was carried out by teachers within the State school. At the Florence meeting in June 1970, an appeal was issued to teachers to reject "the role assigned to them by the establishment... to experiment within their own classes with new teaching methods which would originate from mutual work and be projected into social life"; the meeting also asked them to "associate themselves with those forces outside the school fighting for the creation of new instruments of counter-power that could tackle the problems of the school and the social struggle".[28]

It is considered vital that the teachers' outlook on the role and goals of the school be changed in order that new school structures may be created allowing close links between the school and the community in a joint effort towards mutual change.

One of the main difficulties faced in this period of transition, in which we are attempting to set up a new type of school and to rid society of present inequalities between social groups, is the middle class mentality of teachers.

This drawback is already generally recognised. In Cuba, for instance, the new revolutionary government has introduced a drastic measure whose aim was to create a new class of teachers drawn from the peasantry. These were to be trained in three special teacher-training institutes at the expense of the State, two in the mountains and one in the outskirts of Havana. It was believed that their social origin and training would fit them to teach in the small villages and towns throughout the island, as they would enable them to establish close links between the peasant culture and the culture of the cities.

In any reorganisation of the pre-primary and primary school and in the decentralisation of the overall educational structure, allowing greater autonomy for the schools which will be brought under community control through a "federation of semi-autonomous school districts" (Fantini), the aim must be far more than merely to raise the

---

[28] The resolutions approved by the National Meeting of "Scuola e Quartiere" are quoted from the article by B. Incatasciato, "Convegno nazionale di 'Scuola e Quartiere'", *Cooperazione educativa*, September 1970, pp. 7-8.

quality of teacher training. It is true that higher standards are certainly necessary in several European countries. In Italy, nursery and primary school teachers are still training in special secondary schools. They lack psychological and sociological understanding of the children they are to educate and of the cultural needs of the communities in which they will be called upon to serve. The length and quality of the training courses for teachers to work at all school levels must be made equal, if school structures are to be fully reformed.

A respect for and enhancement of cultural differences – an essential factor in the process of democratisation of school structures – are dependent upon the introduction of new subjects and new methods of teaching and learning into the schools.

A FRESH APPROACH TO THE EDUCATIONAL NEEDS OF CHILDREN FROM MINORITY GROUPS

Research conducted by Martin Deutsch and co-workers over the past few years on disadvantaged children and their social environment led him to the conclusion that more information on the cultural background of children "should make it possible to devise increasingly appropriate curricula". Deutsch goes on to say that "the curriculum must be reorganised to provide for establishing a solid base for the special learnings that are necessary" for underprivileged youngsters. When the middle class child enters school he comes into contact with an environment whose values differ little from those at home, especially as his teacher's outlook will be prevalently middle class. The working class child and the child from a minority group, on the other hand, feels himself stranded in an alien environment. It is the function of the school to make the child feel at home in his own sub-culture and to develop a self-image based upon that culture. Building upon this solid foundation, children from such groups should be helped to broaden their horizons and to appreciate the values of the predominating culture.[29]

Basil Bernstein's analysis of the differences between middle and working class children in the way in which they use language has emphasised that "the speech of the middle class child generates universalistic meanings, in the sense that the meanings are freed from the context and so understandable by all; whereas the speech of the work-

---

[29] *The Disadvantaged Child*, Selected Papers of Martin Deutsch et al., Basic Books, Inc., New York, London, 1967 (quotations are from chapters I, VI, VII, by Martin Deutsch).

ing class child generates particularistic meanings in the sense that the meanings are closely tied to the context and can only be fully understood by others if they have access to the context which originated the speech". Since it is the proper function of the school to help children to become more aware of and to develop universalistic orders of meaning, this can be achieved by the teacher and the school only if they recognise the validity of the culture of every child in their classroom, thus creating the psychological basis for the internalisation and use of universalistic meanings by children from working class backgrounds. Bernstein makes the issue clear when he states that "the introduction of the child to the universalistic meanings of public forms is not compensatory education; *it is education*". If it is agreed that this is the purpose of education, if the teacher's culture is to enter the consciousness of the child, then the child's culture must first penetrate the consciousness of the teacher. "This may mean", Bernstein argues, "that the teacher must be able to understand the child's dialect rather than deliberately attempting to change it".[30]

The establishment of a new two-way channel of communication between the school and the community is not an essential factor merely because of the close rapport between emotional and learning factors and the need to motivate working class children and local communities in their attempts to achieve a type of language and thought bearing universalistic meanings. As Goethe used to say, "*Gott ist im Detail*", the universal is in the particular. If the school rejects the many cultures brought there by children of different ethnic and cultural backgrounds, then it will never achieve its goal. For this reason, teachers must have both anthropological and sociological training to prepare them for the future-oriented school for which they are to be responsible.

Respect of children's sub-cultures, based upon understanding and knowledge, is a sine qua non for the success of the educational process. Each culture represents a specific method of "coming to terms with some of our deepest feelings about the world". In this sense, it has "a rational as well as an emotional component". Its rationality is born of "emotion recollected in tranquillity". The introduction of the emotional and imaginative elements of popular culture into the classroom by children from different ethnic and social groups will enrich the learning process. It is the right way of overcoming the conformity and the levelling-down of the traditional school. One of the main features

---

[30] Basil Bernstein, *Ibid.*, pp. 116-120.

of any school devoted to helping each child develop in his own way through individual teaching must be its understanding and appreciation of all that is characteristic of each pupil's culture. Recent research on dialect has postulated a return to dialect as, in the words of an Italian critic, "a sign of individual escape from the dangers of mass culture, for the use of a standard language by the mass consumer and advertising media is one of the most dangerous vehicles of that culture".

To appreciate the imaginative and emotional aspects of popular culture does not mean that we should underestimate its intellectual elements or undervalue the importance of its thought processes in education. Culture is a living organism which closely links emotion and the intellect in a single social whole. The need for what has recently been termed "education of the emotions" is particularly relevant when rethinking the school curriculum, not only "to meet the effective challenge of the mass media", but also to make the school more receptive to individual differences among children. By this means, their culture or sub-culture can become an innate source of their involvement and participation in the educational process.[31]

CURRICULUM CHANGES IN THE LIGHT OF STRUCTURAL CHANGES IN THE SCHOOL

a. Nongrading

The third aspect of the structural changes now being made in the school is closely related, although not restricted, to the problem of adapting the school curriculum to the needs of underprivileged children. For such children to experience success in the learning process is acknowledged to be a major incentive to their educational advancement. Failure at school can cause emotional disturbance, and that failure may be induced by organising the school around an over-rigid curriculum of structured subjects which pupils are expected to master. Neglect of the emotional factor in turn sets up a further barrier to the expansion of these children's learning capacity. If the elementary school is nongraded, each child can proceed at his own pace. If such a change to the school structure were introduced, it would be a major

---

[31] For some of the ideas which are developed here with regard to the education of the emotions, we are indebted to the book by G. H. Bantock, *Culture, Industrialisation and Education*, London, Routledge and Kegan Paul, 1968, although we do not agree with the author's views with regard to the need for a different education for the different social classes.

factor in overcoming the disturbing effect of not moving up from one class to another, provided that teachers are prepared and professionally trained to satisfy the needs and interests of individual pupils.

Evidence of these positive results has been gained from the introduction of a nongraded approach in certain compensatory education projects conducted over the past few years in the United States. The "early childhood project" for disadvantaged children, for instance, began in New York City in 1962 under the direction of Dr. Martin Deutsch and the Institute for Developmental Studies "in the form of an enrichment program for pre-schoolers". Later, it was extended to the third grade, incorporating seventeen classes in four State schools by 1967-68. The project report states that the programme placed "emphasis upon individual pacing, regardless of the grade in which a child finds himself".[32] The report also declared that significant gains were noted when the project adopted the "nongraded programmed approach".[33]

Nongrading is, however, an educational innovation that can benefit all children, for it promotes the subjective feeling of success in school and allows individualised teaching. In its planning and implementation it is not only a means of improving learning, but is conducive to a radical change in the educational process as a whole. While the experience of nongrading inevitably produces a new kind of interaction between pupils and teachers and among the pupils themselves, it also makes it necessary to take a fresh look at the problem of the relationship between school and society. The basic idea and purpose of nongrading is the recognition that children's personality growth is a continuous process, a process in which the satisfaction of their emotional and social needs is no less important than their intellectual development. The resources not merely of the school but of the community must be brought to bear so that this aim may be achieved to the greater benefit of every child. By grouping and re-grouping pupils according to their needs in different areas of learning and ability in different school activities, an individual and at the same time a flexible educational environment will be created. This continuous process of grouping and re-grouping, characteristic of the nongrading system, is based on the fact that, in Richard I. Miller's words, "at the point where an individual pupil no longer finds his needs identical with those of the

---

[32] *It Works: Early Childhood Project*, New York City, The Early Childhood Project of the Institute for Developmental Studies in New York City, US Office of Education, Washington DC, p. 4.
[33] *It Works Series: Summaries of Selected Compensatory Education Projects*, Washington, DC, 1970, pp. 3-4.

other members of the group, the philosophy and practice of nongrading or continuous progress enter the picture".[34] The "horizontal aspect" of school life, the necessary process of grouping, is an ingredient of the "vertical organisation" of the nongraded school.[35] The process of grouping is, I believe, necessary for it satisfies the need for socialisation, a need no less important than the need for individual attention. The full importance of grouping will become apparent, provided that we pay due attention to the social and emotional aspects of the learning situation. Bearing in mind that the underlying purpose of all current attempts to introduce innovations into education is to promote the development of the child's overall personality, we must be careful not to identify nongrading with indivualised education to the point of affirming that "ideally it might be best to instruct one pupil at a time".[36] Socialisation of the child is a primary educational task which is unlikely to be fulfilled by creating a rigid, uniform and enclosed classroom structure within the school. If we can enable children to create small and flexible groups and to experience a variety of group life in the various phases of their daily work at school, we shall provide them with a better socialising medium than the traditional classroom. To achieve a balance between individual and group activities within the school is an essential educational goal. Its realisation may come to be recognised as the great achievement of, but also the source of difficulties for, nongrading. Both aspects of education call for great care and skill on the part of the teacher, based on study and experimentation. In the nongrading system today, too much stress is laid upon unilateral individualisation. This may be one reason for the growing concern among American teachers at the rapid ("too rapid", according to some) expansion of nongrading in US schools. Swedish school authorities and educators are devoting more attention to the educational implications of outright and one-sided individualisation. In his report on innovations in Swedish education, Stuart Maclure has stated that this aspect is the most important and problematical issue in the education of that country. "Individualisation", he declares, "is one of the primary objectives of the system ("the work of the school will be focused on the individual pupil...") ... From the teacher's point of view the question which is likely to arise is whether there is

[34] Richard I. Miller (Ed.), *The Nongraded School*, Harper, New York, 1969, p. 91. The quotation is from a paper prepared by Fred C. Jaquette, Director of Instruction, Mesa County Valley School District No. 51, Grand Junction, Colorado.
[35] *Ibid.*, p. 90.
[36] *Ibid.*, p. 91.

any conflict between the cooperative goals of the school and the pedagogic necessity to individualise instruction". The author of the OECD Report concludes that "sooner or later the incompatibility between individual and corporate objectives will have to be faced".[37] It would properly be more correct not to speak of "incompatibility between individual and corporate objectives", but rather to stress the concern for the two-way relationship that exists between individual expansion and empathy and, on the other hand, between the experience of interpersonal situations in group activities and in community life and individual development. The problem is not so much theoretical educational goals, but rather the psycho-pedagogic training of teachers, organisation of educational activities and the need to structure the school in such a way that common cooperative goals may be pursued by children as part of their personal formation. Psycho-pedagogic theory also plays its part, shedding light upon the contribution of children's personal experience on the learning process and the formation of attitudes. Nongrading – regarded as the "major form of individualised instruction"[38] – will probably also be seen as the major educational agency for socialisation, by creating non-coercive methods of communication within the school.

b. Team Teaching

The nongrading system could not work without cooperation among its teachers, in other words without team teaching. The staff must work together to assess the needs of each pupil and to provide him with the best possible care that each individual teacher can offer in the various areas of learning and social experience. One of the most positive aspects of team teaching is the cross-fertilisation of each child's personality as he is exposed to the coordinated influence of various adults who are significant to him and whose patterns he can internalize. It would of course be possible for teachers in a graded school to collaborate in working out and implementing a plan of studies. Conversely, team teaching may not be introduced during the early phases of a nongraded school. In due course, however, these two aspects are bound to merge. As one author has expressed it, in a nongraded school "a

---

[37] OECD-Centre for Educational Research and Innovation, *Innovation in Education – Sweden* by Stuart Maclure, Paris, June 1971, p. 48.
[38] OECD-CERI, *Innovation in Education – United States*, by Leila Sussmann, Paris, June 1971, p. 21.

teacher's room no longer is hers alone nor is a specific room full of pupils. The staff works together as a team".[39]

To help children to solve their developmental problems is a task incumbent upon all the teachers in a school, not one isolated teacher. The staff must work together to pinpoint the specific needs and attitudes of each pupil and to provide diversified yet harmonised forms of assistance, once those needs and attitudes have been identified.

Although nongrading is one of the main factors in educational change, supporting the view that the child is the focal point of the school, team teaching is enormously relevant in accelerating that process of change. Through team teaching, the authoritarian character of traditional learning situations in the school, rooted in the hierarchical relationship between pupils and teacher in the self-enclosed classrooms of the graded school, will decline and slowly disappear. Teachers' self-sufficiency and their adoption of a "monological" type of communication were closely interrelated aspects of that school situation.

There is no doubt that these procedures started to decline nearly eighty years ago, with the birth of the progressive movement in education. In practice, there has been cooperation among teachers in a great number of schools over the past few decades, but the rigid organisation of the graded school made cooperation more difficult. Team teaching institutionalises and thus reinforces the willingness of teachers to collaborate and to share responsibility. It is a system in which authoritarian attitudes and behaviour patterns are unlikely to re-emerge.

The stress on the organisational structure of the school implicit in these remarks does not imply that team teaching reinforces the bureaucratic aspects of educational institutions, for if this were true it would be no innovation. We heed the warning that the opportunities provided by team teaching for altering rigid administrative procedures and fostering flexibility of grouping for the purposes of learning must not be regarded as ends in themselves. In the words of Judson T. Shaplin, "those who assume that team teaching, by providing greater opportunities for independent study, small group instruction, large group instruction and diversified groupings by ability, achievement and interest, automatically assures improved instruction are naive about the complexities involved. For organisation itself is unimportant and guarantees nothing. But the organisation, with its potential flexibility, may

---

[39] Fred C. Jacquette, *The Nongraded School* (Richard I. Miller, Ed.), p. 93.

offer a framework within which improved instruction may eventually develop. Team teaching thus focuses upon the responsibility of the team to take advantage of the opportunities offered to analyse the instructional needs of students, to provide optimum grouping for instruction and to adapt curricula and teaching methods to these new arrangements".[40]

This has led to a great variety in team teaching patterns and the conviction, as this author has stated, that "it is foolish to search for one particular ideal type of team organisation that can be applied in all situations".[41] The factor common to all types of team teaching is that teachers work together in establishing and implementing a teaching programme for a given group of students. The skills and talents of several teachers are pooled to meet the varying needs of pupils within a single group. By differentiating these efforts, teachers and pupils can increase their proficiency in various branches of learning without losing sight of the interrelations between subjects, both by coordination of different disciplines, no one of which is an independent and self-sufficient whole, and by shifting attention from the content to the process of learning. In this way, the curriculum can be unified while specialisation is introduced. The three main aspects of team teaching are that it makes allowances for individual differences between pupils and for any similarities between them in different areas, and uses these similarities in grouping the pupils; it takes into account any differences in the teachers' skills and interests, suggesting ways in which they can be used in different non-departmentalised areas and activities of learning; and it is concerned with the development of a comprehensive but flexible curriculum. The team teaching system can be horizontal, in that teachers can be assigned special responsibility either for helping a given group of children in different areas such as mathematics, science, reading, creative arts or social studies, or for taking different sub-groups of pupils for a single unit of learning. In the words of the American author of a recent OECD Report on innovation in education in the United States: "The teaching team decides on various time combinations for different units of instruction. A given level of social studies may meet in a large group once a week for an hour, in small discussion groups twice for 30 minutes; and then have an hour of scheduled independent study. The school may cycle its schedule every week or every three

---

[40] Judson T. Shaplin, "Description and Definition of Team Teaching", *Team Teaching*, edited by Judson T. Shaplin and Henry F. Olds, Jr., Harper, New York, 1964, p. 12.
[41] Judson T. Shaplin, "Toward a Theoretical Rationale for Team Teaching", *Ibid.*, p. 65.

days, or in any way that seems desirable. It is the computer that makes this flexibility possible".[42]

Horizontal specialisation in this two-fold form is often matched by vertical specialisation, characterised by what the same author has called "a hierarchy of authority and skill". For example: "a teaching team is made up of a Team Leader who is a master teacher and a trainer of teachers, a few Associate Teachers, a few teaching interns and several para-professionals who do secretarial work, help with discipline and housekeeping and possibly with some teaching and student counselling".[43]

The introduction of team teaching will be beneficial only if it is implemented with great care and attentive study, exploiting the findings of advanced educational technology. Nongrading is also advantageous to team teaching in that it requires careful organisation of the learning environment and assessment of both the pupils' needs and the teachers' skills. Those who defend the graded system do so on the grounds that teachers like to take full responsibility for the learning process of their own individual group of children, fostering pupil-teacher interacting and creating a stable environment for their pupils. These are basic needs and they can be met by a team only if the teachers have reached a high standard of training – didactic, methodological, cultural and social. They must have attained a high degree of emotional and personal security if they are to act as a team and in turn offer security to the pupils in whose care they are called upon to share. Only under these circumstances can a combination of team teaching and nongrading show its true worth. Henry F. Olds, Jr., has ably pointed out the alliance between these two forms of educational innovation: "At any level, the more rigid the concept of gradedness held by the school system, the more difficult it will be for the team to exert any influence in this area, and, among other things, the more difficult it will be for the team to provide an adequate educational environment for extremely talented or extremely retarded children".[44]

Like nongrading, team teaching cannot be regarded as an isolated feature in the present movement for the improvement of education. The Report of the Study of Educational Facilities sponsored by the Toronto Metropolitan School Board, published in 1968, made this point very clear. "The advantages apparently offered by team teach-

---

[42] OECD-CERI, *Innovation in Education – United States*, p. 22.
[43] *Ibid.*, p. 22.
[44] Henry F. Olds, "A Taxonomy for Team Teaching", *Team Teaching*, p. 106.

ing" it points out, "seem most likely to be obtained where team teaching takes its place as one of a set of innovations out of which a more satisfactory learning environment is constructed".[45] The prerequisite for the success of all attempts at innovation is undoubtedly a high level of teacher training. This will to a great extent determine whether team teaching develops into a "horizontal-collegial form" or into a "vertical-bureaucratic" form, thus reinforcing "the formal authority structure".[46]

THE EDUCATION OF TEACHERS

It would be misleading, however, to imply that educational innovation is limited to the improvement of teacher training, however important this may be in the above context.

To go to the roots of the problem, the far-reaching change in the school system, of which teacher training is an intrinsic feature, is only one aspect of the process of social transformation. The central function of cultural institutions will be fully recognised only if a new type of society is created, emphasising the pursuit of communal goals. As already pointed out in the first chapter of this report, in such a society culture will be regarded as the essential instrument for bringing out the creative powers of individuals and for implementing the process of innovation. New educational structures will be considered as the primary ingredients in this process of change, motivating teachers' awareness of their new role in a changing society.

We do not underestimate the role of teachers in the society of tomorrow. We can only warn against overestimating that role and suggest that consideration be given to the relationship between changes in society and the changing role of teachers in dialectical rather than in causal terms. A good way of outlining the function of the teacher in future society is to bear in mind the criticism constantly being levelled at schools in their role as agencies for the adaptation of individuals to existing institutions. The claim that society must be "de-schooled" is being voiced ever more widely. Teachers, too, are indicted in that they are regarded as the main instruments for the transmission of the dominating values of the profit- and power-seeking classes of society to the new generation, thus helping to perpetuate the existing order. Whilst claiming to provide children with an "objective" education,

---

[45] SEF Report E 1., *Educational Specifications and User Requirements for Elementary (K-6) Schools*, The Metropolitan Toronto School Board, 1968, p. 53.
[46] Dan C. Lortie, "The Teacher and Team Teaching", *Team Teaching*, p. 279.

detached from social and political issues, teachers in fact unknowingly transmit the prevailing sets of standards, beliefs and behaviour patterns. This accusation has been so widely made that many "counter-school" projects have been conducted over the past few years to create new links between the school and the community. The idea underlying these experiments is that the principal function of the school, and of the teacher who embodies the school, is to develop powers that enable individuals to become what John Dewey has called the "agents of re-organisation", rather than to transmit a cultural heritage. The main task of teachers must be to ensure that pupils cultivate and exercise creative imagination and reflective thought, in close and continuous contact with the more pressing problems of life and society today. Teachers can foster critical and creative attitudes in children by helping them to analyse and "decode" aspects and events within their environment, involving both themselves and all the other members of their community.

To fulfil the new teaching and educational tasks with which they will be faced in social and educational institutions, teachers will need better training than they have received up to now. If they are no longer to be at the passive end of research performed by other experts and researchers, teacher training for every school level must combine practical teaching and familiarity with those human sciences that help them to understand young people and society. The trend towards raising teacher training – especially for primary and pre-primary school teachers – to university level, thus abolishing the traditional distinction between teacher training colleges and other university departments, has been taking shape in several European countries such as England, Germany and Sweden, and is bound to gain momentum in the future. Worthy of note, in connection with this trend, is the recent announcement that in North Rhine-Westphalia, "students at the teachers' training college, Rhineland with departments in Cologne, Aachen, Bonn, Neuss and Wuppertal, training for teaching posts in elementary and primary schools, will also be able to take a doctorate". A similar item from Germany is that "student teachers at the newly-founded Trier-Kaiserslautern University will no longer be trained for specific types of schools but rather as "stage teachers for specific age groups (1-4 school year, 5-10 school year, 11-13 school year). As a rule the course of study for the first two groups is to last for eight semesters and for the last group ten semesters".[47] Something is at last stirring

[47] *Education in Germany*, No. 6/1971, p. 19.

in the otherwise stagnant position of teacher training in Germany, as in most countries. The 1971 OECD Report on Educational Innovation in Germany reviewed the "structural plan" issued by the Council for Education of the German Federal Republic. It pointed out that "there are also suggestions on how to improve... the desolate state of teacher training today". The teacher training programmes that now exist and the present low state of the profession, the OECD Report remarked, "threaten to nullify any new educational policy, however progressive it may be". This is why the Report described as "a key proposal... the provision of university-level training for all teachers". This new training "would basically involve the study of education, and the social sciences and pedagogics, with systematically integrated teaching practice".[48]

New research projects, such as the project on "New Functions and Structures of the School – The School and the Community", to be carried out by OECD in 1971-72, emphasise the need for any new study course for teachers to include sociology, anthropology and statistics, in addition to the psycho-pedagogical disciplines necessary to teachers dealing with children and adolescents.

Recognition of this need, which has emerged from our brief reference to the German proposal that university training be provided for all candidate teachers and to the OECD-CERI research programme, also emerges from a cursory analysis of the teacher training position in other European countries and certain study projects which appear to be related to this subject.[49]

In France, primary school teachers are trained in *écoles normales*, which provide general and professional education for student teachers. Each *département* has one such school for boys and one for girls. The *baccalauréat* testifies to the successful completion of a course of general education. Professional training is both theoretical and practical. Teaching practice, which is compulsory for all student teachers, includes training either in "laboratory schools" annexed to normal schools, or in "practice schools" or "classes". Contact with the social problems of education is provided through courses organised jointly by the Ministry of Education and the CEMEA teachers acting as leaders and monitors in the *colonies de vacance* or holiday camps.

---

[48] OECD-CERI, *Innovation in Education – Germany*, by Helga Thomas, Paris, June 1971, p. 17.
[49] OECD-CERI, *New Functions and Structures of the School Draft Description Paper*, by Susanne Mowat, *The School and the Community*: A Proposal (mimeographed).

A guiding principle of the CEMEA is that "all educational activity should rest upon a knowledge of the environment in which that activity is performed. Its aim is to diminish any inequality between individuals originating from different social and cultural milieux...".[50]

Seminars and discussion or study groups on various areas of learning such as new maths, language, etc., are organised by teachers' associations and by the Ministry of Education. This vast programme of in-service training and re-training of teachers is eagerly welcomed by the profession. One problem, however, as yet unsolved, is the continued separation of teacher training institutions (see *écoles normales*) from the university.

A recent report issued by the *Institut Pédagogique National* stated that "abolished during World War II, normal schools for primary teachers were restored after the liberation of France. But there has been constant debate over the past few years on the problems raised by these schools. The main issue has been the question of whether teachers of the future should receive two years' general, university-type education and whether the normal schools should be used for professional teacher education alone".

In England, as in many other countries including the United States, the process of raising teacher training to a higher educational level has been continuing for many years. Although some progress has been made in France and in Italy, pre-primary and primary teachers are not yet trained at the level of higher education. The situation in England has been summarised by Edmund J. King as follows: "In England it was only after the *Robbins Report on Higher Education* (1963) that the education of most teachers was even notionally termed 'higher education'. Even now a large part of it is dubiously admitted to that category, although the universities have shared in the guidance, examination and sometimes teaching of courses for teachers in colleges of education. Proposals in 1970, if fulfilled, bring more university-level work into colleges of education, and in wider variety".[51]

Edmund J. King's analysis of the position of the teaching profession in various countries is most illuminating, especially upon coming innovations. "There is a demand for higher quality and a better teacher-

[50] CEMEA, Coopération Internationale, Orléans, 1970, Bulletin No. 12, p. 7. See also CEMEA, *Quelques principes qui guident notre action* (Articles rédigés à partir des conférences prononcées par G. de Failly au Rassemblement des CEMEA à Caen en 1957), Extracts from Nos. 3, 4, 5 and 23 "Instructeurs", November 1965, pp. 2, 30, 31.
[51] Edmund J. King, *The Education of Teachers, A Comparative Analysis*, Holt, Rinehart and Winston, London, 1970, p. 15.

student ratio in *all* branches of education. On top of that, the structural changes we are considering demand not merely high quality during the initial preparation of teachers, but continuous in-service education and re-education. This new education for teachers can no longer be of a purely informative or pedagogical kind...; it also needs contemporary social and political pointing, with sensitive reference to contemporary world events and present 'crises of decision' ".[52]

A further crucial aspect of the training of teachers is the dual system still in existence in many countries, whose effect is that training is provided through special teacher training institutions and university departments.

The author informs us that there are two main methods: "The first to be mentioned is the most recent one, whereby most or all of the education of teachers takes place on the 'university' plane. The alternative method most commonly found is to employ university graduates (often untrained for teaching) in academic secondary schools, but to train and educate all other teachers in colleges at a lower-than-university level". Dr. King mentions the conclusions reached in Frank Bowles' study on *Access to Higher Education*: "(a) that university systems which included teacher education tended to be broader-based, both academically and socially, and therefore offered more growing points; and (b) that the university systems on the 'multiversity' pattern also had higher powers of student retention. Thus the latter developed more high-powered talent quantitatively than higher education systems constructed on an élitist assumption. They also produced better results qualitatively in the long run".[53]

To turn to England, the Robbins Report recommendation has been accepted that colleges of education should be "placed in the higher education category". On the other hand, the very important suggestion that these should be "grouped within schools of education forming an integral part of a university and transferred from any other kind of control" was not accepted. The reason for the non-adoption of this specific recommendation was, Doctor King explains, mainly backstage politics. "Local education authorities and independent foundations and religious bodies in control of the colleges of education opposed surrendering or diminishing their control".[54]

Teachers have less freedom to decide on matters of organisation and

---

[52] *Ibid.*, p. 72.
[53] *Ibid.*, p. 80.
[54] *Ibid.*, p. 81.

curriculum than they do on content and method of teaching. It is the "head teacher who decides how the school should be organised, what books and equipment should be used and on the relationships with parents. The head has wide areas of discretion". The information supplied by the 1971 OECD Report on Educational Innovation in England is supplemented by further information to the effect that "the head, in turn, is subject to a number of restraints". Furthermore, in curricular matters, where teachers "traditionally have been the source of authority, they increasingly find themselves as one among many with a view to contribute". It is in this field that innovation represents a specific threat to teachers.[55] Teachers might find it hard to share their authority with other administrative bodies and the community. But it is of paramount importance that teachers develop the capacity to interact with the public at large, especially in the light of recent calls for the establishment of close links between the school and the community. The creation of community schools, the devising and implementation of projects in the course of which teachers extend their educational role outside the school, following up children and adults in their own homes or in those places frequented by the children and their families, where they are most at ease, are important forerunners of coming innovations in the organisational structure of British education. Teachers' Centres, of which there are now 500 all over the country, created at the suggestion of the Schools Council and set up partly by local education authorities and partly by colleges of education or universities, have substantially contributed towards building up professional self-confidence among teachers, overcoming their feeling of isolation and demolishing the traditional barriers between schools, establishing inter-school liaison. Problems relating to the curriculum, method and content, the use of audio-visual material and continuity between primary and secondary schooling have been widely discussed. In this initial phase of their existence, the main attraction to teachers seems, however, to be the opportunity for meeting and exchanging views in these centres. Professional discussions on curricular matters, however important, take second place. The OECD 1971 Report already mentioned states: "At a recent Schools Council Conference it was discovered that at many centres the emphasis was almost entirely on open discussion and the exchange of views and not on devising

---

[55] OECD-CERI – *Innovation in Education – England*, by Anne Corbett, Paris, June 1971, p. 9.

specific contributions to teaching within certain subject areas".[56] The author of the Report comments that the Teachers Centres' "potential is obvious, their achievement less so". I am inclined to emphasise the positive aspect of the work of these Centres, in that they promote interaction between British teachers and provide them with a forum for the discussion of issues other than those relating to the curriculum. It is certainly remarkable that the Working Party Reports on Curriculum and Method, which formed part of the Project entitled "Middle Years of Schooling", issued in 1969 by the Schools Council, evolved five principal aims for the middle years of schooling: "to develop a spirit of enquiry; to cultivate values concerned with exploration; to satisfy the curiosity of the child as fully as possible; to stimulate curiosity; and to stimulate enquiry and investigating minds".[57]

All the teachers responsible for the 71 reports on the topics stressed the need for developing curiosity, the spirit of enquiry and investigation. They identified the main purpose of education as the fostering of independence of judgement, an ability to go beyond what has been imparted and is known, discovery, innovation. The spirit by which British teachers are guided may explain the far-reaching and profound changes which have taken place in British education, mostly at primary school level, over recent years. The task now facing British education is to channel that spirit of discovery and enquiry towards matters worthy of the effort. The attitude recently expressed by Jerome Bruner is of interest. "Education", Bruner declared in London in 1970, as Edmund King relates in his book on *The Education of Teachers*, "must no longer strike an exclusive posture of neutrality and objectivity. Mankind can no longer tolerate infant mortality, ignorance, racism, crimes in the street, pollution, war and aggression. 'Problem-solving' as an educational device must be given a chance to develop in the field of these and other problems such as marriage and the family, birth control and the real issued facing individuals and society".[58] It is an encouraging fact that "teachers of teachers" such as Jerome Bruner and Edmund King take such a wide and all-embracing attitude towards the problems of education which so greatly affect teacher training.

Social change is profoundly affecting what is going on in education

[56] *Ibid.*, p. 12.
[57] The Schools Council, *Middle Years of Schooling Project*. A Preliminary Digest of the Reports received from the Middle Years Working Parties established by the Project in 1969, Project Broadsheet Number One, p. 6 (mimeographed).
[58] E. King, *The Education of Teachers*, p. 111.

today. Most of the young people starting up their career as teachers feel closer to their pupils than to their parents, owing to the generation gap. A student teacher, Edmund King remarks, may readily feel this same estrangement towards "older teachers and the establishment". "Though this situation introduces its own problems, it is a hopeful sign if only because civilising discussion can really continue on the really critical points of the educational process".[59] Today, teachers must be open to the problems not only of their pupils but also of the social environment from which those pupils come. "Education", E. King adds, "cannot be something confined to school". Educators must be aware of the influence which environment exercises on the formation of their pupils, and they must draw upon the environment, using it as material for education. "In the long run education will be 'drunk in' daily as the Florentine child daily drinks in his city's history, works of art, music, passions and social problems". It is from their home and environment that children draw their *"attitudes and perceptions"* which influence learning "more than *what* is in the curriculum or what *techniques and programmes* the teachers use to teach it". This is what, according to Edmund King, forms "the ecology of learning, from the consideration of which we see the folly of separating thoughts about learning and the school from studies of an educative ecology in an educative society".[60]

In no other European country have we found such great concern on the part of teachers with the changes introduced by social transformation as we have in Britain and Sweden.

What teachers in England are learning from their experience at school in contact with their pupils and their pupils' families and within their Teachers' Centres, student teachers in Sweden are expected to learn during their college education. The Schools of Education Statute (1968: 318) makes it clear that "the task of schools of education is to train teachers in scientific principles", and also that "the aim of this training is to provide the students with such knowledge and ability that they can take an active part as teachers in realising the goals of the school for which they are trained". What is required of future teachers is, therefore, not only to acquire the groundwork of pedagogics, of methods of pedagogical research, of psychology, especially psychology of personality and development, but also to learn the ability to get to know pupils and to collaborate with them, with the other

---

[59] *Ibid.*, p. 114.
[60] *Ibid.*, p. 128.

teachers and with the environment outside the school. This in turn demands personal attitudes of open-mindedness, tolerance, "spirit of cooperativeness", "interest in people", as a basis for understanding "how pupils are affected by different conditions at home, at school and in society at large". These skills and personal qualities will be first developed in a few years of training, but it is also a continuous lifelong process. This is why student teachers are expected to acquire "through their training... an open and critical attitude to their own future profession and a readiness to renew their working methods" with the view that "teacher training should be a step in a continuous educational reform". To this effect teachers are obliged to participate in further training courses held on special study days... generally sponsored by the local education authority" and in other training courses organised by the further training departments of the schools of education, with voluntary attendance.[61]

The factor that distinguishes the Swedish scene from that of other countries, with the exception of the United States, is the amount of research being conducted into the effects of educational innovations upon the actual performance of teachers and, as an outcome, on the new demands which the ascertained results of innovation place upon teacher training. As a Swedish author has clearly expressed it, "any teacher training programme that takes no account of reasonable predictions of new teacher functions misses an essential point".[62] Empirical investigation into the results of such innovations as educational technology and individualised teaching, namely, "systematically developed and evaluated instruction" to adapt teaching to individual students' needs, abilities and interests, is of particular interest when predicting future teacher functions. A relevant discussion on this point is a study by Karl Gustav Stukat, from the Department of Educational Research, Gothenburg School of Education, reprinted from Research Bulletin No. 4, October 1970, *Teacher Role in Change*. Reviewing and comparing available studies "on highly individualised instructional systems", Stukat lists those expectations as to the teachers' role in such systems which are supported by empirical research, thus influencing the introduction of new procedures into teacher training. "Emphasis on continuous diagnosis and evaluation of individual students, providing the students

---

[61] The National Swedish Board of Education, *A Survey of Teacher Training in Sweden*, pp. 3, 15-22 (mimeographed).
[62] Stukat, Karl-Gustav, "Teacher Role in Change", Department of Educational Research, Gothenburg School of Education, *Research Bulletin*, No. 4, October 1970, p. 1-20.

with material for independent study, counselling and guiding him in his short and long-range plans, are examples of teacher functions that will become increasingly valid in the future, irrespective of whether advanced technology is utilised or not. Another reasonable prediction relatively independent of how far extreme individualisation will go is that the teacher will spend more of his time interacting with individual students and small groups. Likewise, team arrangement in some form or other for common planning and execution of instruction will probably become more widespread...". What available empirical knowledge does not prove is that teachers will be relieved from the routine tasks which devolve upon them in conventional education. "It is also uncertain whether most present systems for individualising teaching afford better opportunities for teacher-student interactions of the kinds that promote complex problem-solving skills, creative thinking, realistic goal-setting and social emotional development, to mention a few educational objectives that are expected to be more efficiently reached in individualised teaching".

The results of the comparative analysis of available empirical studies "strongly suggest", the author concludes, "that in the development and revision of individualised instruction systems, the teacher functions should be given as much attention as other aspects of the system". These results, based on experimental research into the essential role that the teacher will still be called upon to perform in a school situation characterised by advanced educational technology, are shared by other contemporary authors of articles, handbooks and institute reports, as Stukat indicates. He quotes E. R. Hilgard's article on "Teaching Machines and Creativity" (1964) which argues that, while teachers may benefit from the use of the teaching machines in the expository mode of teaching, "in the hypothetical mode of teaching-learning, meaning discovery, exploring possibilities and judging between alternatives, a human teacher is irreplaceable". Stukat adds that "when considering the convergent-divergent thinking dichotomy, Hilgard finds unique contributions for a live teacher essential".

A central issue in the education of teachers is whether, how and to what extent such basic innovations as individualisation and educational technology affect teachers as they are increasingly introduced into the school. Research on the effects of educational innovation proves to be an essential part of innovation itself. It should be added, however, that if research is to become a truly inseparable aspect of innovation in education, teachers themselves must develop positive attitudes toward experimentation and enquiry, acquiring adequate knowledge and skills to conduct research both during the teacher training period and the various periods of on-the-job training. The formation of attitudes, habits and skills in educational research is an essential part of the education of teachers, a point stressed by Torsten Husén in his paper on "The Role of Research in Teacher Education" read to the 5th General Conference of the Comparative Education Society in Europe, held in Stockholm in June, 1971.

Husén emphasised that "the potential for reshaping the school will greatly depend upon the extent to which teacher education can be reformed". If we wish to avoid teacher education becoming "a conservative element in the school system" and instead want a school that is able to tackle and work upon "radical new conditions emerging in a changing society", Professor Husén said, "the teacher training insititutions must be so designed as to foster the spirit of enquiry and investigation, as well as undogmatic criticism of the established order". He added that "this cause will be further fostered if the student teachers take part in the institute's research work, even if only to a modest extent". He emphasised that "research into problems that are thrust up by the continuing work of educational reform should be pursued *in close contact* with teacher education itself. For this purpose the contact must not be restricted to guiding student teachers and teacher trainers to the methods and results of research; instead, these groups should be actively involved in the research work". For this same purpose, "every teacher training institution ought to be equiped with a *laboratory school for experiments and demonstrations*".[63]

There are certain final comments which may be pertinent to the various teacher training issues that we have discussed.

Seen in perspective, a primary need in the reform of systems of teacher education is that teachers themselves must become the instruments of their own training. Continuous teacher training is essential for educators if they are not to be mere pawns, holders and transmitters of petrified routine, the tools used to preserve the established order. An essential part of this new kind of training is familiarity with research methods. Research is vital in changing the attitudes of teachers towards educational and social institutions. Open-mindedness towards investigation will enable teachers to become the effective agents of reconstruction. Teachers must, therefore, have a voice in determin-

---

[63] Husén, Torsten, "The Role of Research in Teacher Education", *Teacher Education, Proceedings of the Comparative Education in Europe*, Lund, 1972, pp. 124-125.

ing how the school shall be organised, the content of study and teaching methods.

Cooperation among teachers must be fostered by a profound change in the method of teacher training and teaching itself. Personal interaction among student teachers and between students and their college professors is an essential instrument that will help them to acquire emotional and social maturity and to achieve higher cognitive goals such as problem-solving and divergent and creative thinking. There should be increasing stress on independent and small-group study in the training period and these should occupy a substantial part of their curriculum. Student teachers themselves should be allowed a great measure of responsibility for the organisation of their syllabus and school life. Respect for the personality of the student teacher, his person-to-person interaction with his colleagues and teachers, his involvement in school and community life, must be regarded as essential ways of developing his capacity for discovery-based learning and self-motivated enquiry. This type of education demands close cooperation between colleges of education and the universities. University education is a necessity for all teachers from the nursery school through secondary and higher education level.

Team teaching is a result of this higher standard of teachers. It testifies their ability to cooperate, to reject authoritarianism in thought and behaviour, to their dedicated commitment towards helping each one of their pupils to attain his optimum level of development.

There is an intrinsic link between team teaching in its most mature "horizontal" form and non-grading, the best possible instrument for individualised teaching. If each pupil is allowed to learn and develop at his own pace, in the light of his own needs and abilities, he will be able to make his own unique contribution to group life. In the education of teachers, increasing attention must be paid to this interrelationship between individualised education and the development of social attitudes in children, one of the most crucial aspects and pressing problems in the education of teachers today. The topic calls for further research, both on its theoretical assumptions and on its methodological application.

As the teacher learns to recognise the needs of each pupil and to help him develop to his fullest capacity, he must acquire an intensive interest in the child's family and social background, familiarity with the community itself, an appreciation of the importance of adult education, the education of parents and continuous education.

Teachers must, therefore, not only be deeply involved in the living problems of present day society, with true empathy for the deprivations from which so many people in every country suffer, but they must also develop the ability to "decode" the conditions causing oppression, to "enter into communion" with the oppressed and to give them genuine help in freeing themselves. A social sense and sociological ability should be closely linked. In his report to the Stockholm Conference of the Comparative Education Society in Europe, June 1971, Professor Saul B. Robinsohn stressed the need for teachers to study sociology in order to become better acquainted with "the social conditions of education and educability, the school as a social system and the class as a social group, the effects of differentiation and selection, fundamentals of socialisation and identity formation". This wide horizon ought to be imparted to student teachers in their regular programme, not only to provide them with an adequate "understanding of specific institutions and processes", but also to help them to build "a basis for that new thinking on education which stresses its emancipatory role in society".[64] This more profound knowledge of the child and of society demanded of teachers, together with intimate involvement in the problems of the deprived young and adult members of society all over the world and the need to furnish educational and social help to all, can be acquired only through a life-long process of education. The continuous training of teachers is a necessity in our present society and it is one which will no doubt be increasingly felt over the next few decades.

During the past few years, there have been attempts to develop agencies, methods and programmes for continuous further training of teachers, not only in individual nations but also on a continental scale. The Council of Europe has done pioneer work in studying ways and means of achieving international coordination through projects that involve the teachers themselves in the continuous process of education. Contacts have already been established by conferences and meetings of experts. Although something has been done to cross the frontiers and to create channels of interchange, communication and coordinated action, there is still a long way to go in every country before the final goal can be achieved. The Report on *Further Training of Teachers* prepared by the Council for Cultural Cooperation of the Council of Europe for the Frascati Meeting of April 1971, clearly described the situation. "Reports from different countries almost consistently

[64] Saul B. Robinsohn, "Innovation in Education and the Curriculum for Teacher Training", *Teacher Education*, Lund, 1972, p. 48.

show", the Report declared, "the predominance of a centralised and bureaucratic form of organisation, vertically controlled by one or more ministries by delegation of authority... almost always through a bureaucratic machinery, centralising and bringing to a summit level all new ventures, even those originating at the bottom". The Report bluntly denounced the fact that "there is no evidence in any of the reports of any official system or efficient machinery for channelling to the responsible authorities such further training needs, interests and initiatives as emerge from discussion and experience in teachers' associations". An exception to this universal system, however, was the "teachers' centres" in England and Wales,[65] already mentioned in the preceding pages.

The concern for creating organisational centres, free from the bureaucratic control of centralised authorities over teacher training and re-training, has been expressed in the experts' meetings. The draft conclusions and recommendations produced by the English-speaking group at the Frascati meeting of experts in April, 1971, emphasised the role of the national centres planning for the further education and training of teachers which, it stated, should use "the services of the supplying institutions: universities, colleges of education and teachers' centres organised by local education authorities". This range of initiative was regarded as essential in order to face "the possibility of a political problem, the danger of a central organisation with a bureaucratic structure imposing a particular social or political ideology and stifling regional or local initiatives designed to meet local needs and aspirations". The document went on to say that "this danger was particularly apparent in countries where teachers were civil servants or officials". The organisational structure of centres coordinating the further teacher training programmes was considered to be an important aspect of the problem of offering incentives and the motivation for further training. There were two particularly significant suggestions as to ways of promoting teacher interest in further education:

a) "the creation of forward-looking attitudes should begin in school and be maintained during training. The involvement of students in simple research into curriculum development would encourage such attitudes. The quality of further training and education must be intellectually stimulating".

---

[65] Council of Europe, Council for Cultural Cooperation, Committee for General and Technical Education, *Further Training of Teachers*, by Professor G. Gozzer, Strasbourg, February 1971, pp. 6, 8.

b) "the function of teachers in developing social awareness was seen as both an important responsibility and a form of motivation".[66]

Even more striking suggestions as to ways of motivating innovative attitudes and behaviour in teachers were provided by the conference of the Comparative Education Society in Europe, held in Stockholm in June, 1971. The paper presented by Hartmut W. Frech, a member of the research group at the Institute for Educational Research in Berlin, on "Innovative Behaviour and Teacher Education" seems particularly relevant in this respect.

Analysing the existing teacher training programme in various countries today, Mr. Frech underlined the fact that "teacher training, with its great research activity and its readiness to try new programs is almost exclusively concentrated on the training of social behaviour in the classroom, on the acquisition of knowledge (using "innovative methods" for transmission) and on specific areas such as the education of culturally disadvantaged children". The study emphasised "the shortage of programme for the education of innovative teachers and research on contents, methods and organisational patterns most appropriate to prepare student teachers for innovative activities in the school system". The paper remarked that "only for some years past, since an alienated generation of students has begun to demand change within educational institutions and the surrounding society, a few cautious attempts to train teachers explicitly for innovative behaviour have been made, for instance at Teachers College of Columbia University (1968; Joyce, 1969) or at the Cooperative Educational Research Laboratory (CERLI, Goldman, 1969)".[67] Mr. Frech remarked that "in these programs the socio-political aims of innovative teacher behaviour are discussed and special courses for preparation for the role of change agents in the school are developed (see Allan and Krasno, 1968).[68] But these experiments also seem to be determined by a restricted definition of innovation". The missing factor in these projects was very clearly pointed out by the author. "The function of the school as a mere service sub-

[66] Meeting of Experts on "The Further Training of Teachers", Frascati, 2-6 April 1971: *Draft Conclusions and Recommendations*, Council for Cultural Cooperation of the Council of Europe (mimeographed).

[67] Bruce R. Joyce, *A Guide to Teacher-Innovator*: A Program to Prepare Teachers, American Association of Colleges for Teacher Education, Washington, DC, 1969, Office of Education; Samuel Goldman, "Futurists in Education". In-service Program for CERLI Staff, 1968-69. Final Report. Cooperative Educational Research Laboratory, Inc. Northfield, Ill., Office of Education, 1969 (quoted in Mr. Frech's paper).

[68] Dwight W. Allen and Richard M. Krasno, New Perspectives in Teacher Education. Department of Elementary School Principals, Washington, DC, 1968 (quoted in Mr. Frech's paper).

system of the specific economic production process has not been reflected or criticised. Thus research or change in the system contributes to the stabilisation of this system". In the opinion of the Berlin Research Group, any project concerned with developing innovative attitudes in students will be successful only if innovative ideas are carried by people characterised by innovative vigor. Of these two factors, however, ideas and people, "the persons, methods and rationale involved in the process of realising one initiative or a series of initiatives are of greater importance than the (primarily intended) idea of this initiative... It has been proved in the course of our argument that research on innovation without persons who translate this argument into adequate research projects or political decisions will reduce ambivalence in innovation in favor of a durable strategy appropriately adapted to system maintenance". An effective programme aimed at fostering innovative attitudes should shift the emphasis from "innovation" to "innovative behaviour" of teachers. The author suggests that "innovative behaviour of teachers would be an activity of promoting and selecting contents, materials and organisational devices with regard to the new need structure and corresponding cognitive and emotional patterns of pupils, with the goal of progressive change of social conditions". It is no small a venture to establish the conditions for innovation in schools and three important initial steps should probably be taken: "promotion of self-autonomy", "fostering a critical and political engagement" in the pupils; and "working with the other teachers for change in the structure of the school".[69]

The Berlin Research Group analysis is an important piece of work contributing to a better understanding of the problems involved in the education of teachers. It serves to define the aims of teacher education and the role of teachers in bringing about a new type of society.

---

[69] Hartmut-W. Frech, "Innovative Behaviour and Teacher Education", *Teacher Education*, Lund, 1972, pp. 63-72.

3. PROGRESS IN EDUCATIONAL PSYCHOLOGY

BY

FRANCESCO DE BARTOLOMEIS

INTRODUCTION

One of the main standards by which the value of a society can be judged is, according to Urie Bronfenbrenner, "the concern of one generation for the next".[1] When we survey the progress made by educational sciences and educational achievement, the striking factor is how greatly practice trails behind theory, due to the specific lack of social commitment towards education. The bulk of our scientific knowledge on teaching is still unexploited. There is an urgent need for more specific and effective planning of the educational means to reinforce the socially innovating force of the school. But what are our planning goals?

Today, mass education is no longer a problem encountered only at the primary level. The period of compulsory schooling is already 8 to 10 years and in certain countries there is a tendency for this period to be prolonged. A growing number of young people are continuing with their education to higher levels, including university. Technology, it may be believed, will play the leading part, imparting rationally selected subjects, immediately correcting the reply given by the pupil and allowing him to regulate his own rate of learning. But when we consider the three basic sectors of advanced psycho-pedagogic research – structure learning, creative production, inter-personal relationships – it is clear that technology by itself is one-sided and restrictive.

Now that the excitement over the miracle of technology is dying down, now that we realise the error of thinking that the future of education lies in a single direction, despite the expectations aroused by certain superficial novelties, a completely new line is being taken in both educational thought and in educational practice.

---

[1] U. Bronfenbrenner, *The Two Worlds of Childhood*, US and USSR, Russel Sage Foundation, New York, 1970, I.

The contribution of educational psychology is to determine the optimum conditions for non-unilateral development, how to form groups from among the mass, how to increase intercourse and cooperation between individuals and groups, how to mobilise creativity and to ensure the functional relevance of educational experience.

The type of communication with which we are concerned is no longer limited to the field of language and knowledge, but is extended to living in general, where reciprocal communication is never without its difficulties and sometimes cannot even be initiated.

The confused and conflicting growth in the number of stimuli, partly due to the predominance of technology in advanced industrial societies, makes adaptation even more difficult. Adaptation is an ambiguous term; we should, perhaps, use the expression, "constructive and appropriate responses", or imaginative projections into the future.

When discussing the future, a basic contradiction usually arises: we believe that the solutions we are putting forward are truly revolutionary, whereas in fact we merely reveal a sad lack of imagination in that these solutions are based on a limited outlook (for example, blind faith in technology).

EDUCATIONAL PSYCHOLOGY AND THE FUTURE OF EDUCATION

Is implementation lagging behind research or is there a crisis in the field of social sciences?

Before we launch out upon bold forecasts as to the future development of research, we should analyse the current situation so that we can measure the gap between research findings and educational achievement and can try to find the best way of narrowing that gap. This method of looking at the future has one not inconsiderable advantage: it is realistic, in other words it shows that the cultural instruments to promote some of the desirable changes to the school are already in existence. The only trouble is that, for many and varied reasons, these cannot be used to advantage in existing institutions.

Educational psychology is of course a young science and one that has made enormous progress in a short space of time, but it would be a rash man who would state that social science can produce ready-made theories and tested data that could bring about radical school reform, leading to the type of future with which we are now concerned.

We should not for this reason reject the wealth of new knowledge accumulated by psycho-pedagogic research in the light of the findings of child psychology, differential psychology, clinical psychology research on learning processes, on social and cultural conditioning, on group dynamics and inter-personal relationships, etc. But we must not believe in the existence of an overall body of knowledge that can be used as the basis for planning educational innovation, in other words for bringing about the school of the future.

Such a belief could be held only if all the findings pointed in the same direction, and this is far from proved. There is a crisis not only in the gap between scientific progress and practical realisation, but in the very validity of the scientific findings that do exist, at least those to which most frequent reference is made. There is a danger that the innovations which we think of as so radical will lead to a type of society which differs little in essentials from the society of today.

In recent educational psychology research, comprehensive and dynamic consideration of experience has gained more concrete significance; in other words, our attention has been concentrated on personal factors seen in a "field" of social relationships. As social relationships now stand, any reliance on independent and spontaneous process would be optimistic. In considering a specific problem of learning or adaptation or production, we must continually examine the problem in the light of our society, a society dominated by conflict, contradiction and disorder. We need a psycho-pedagogy which does not merely provide reassurance or artificial simplification, but furnishes new data. Education is such a complex process that its origins, methods of development and consequences cannot be verified by entirely didactic methods.

A variety of occupations, richness of stimuli, opportunity for creativeness, satisfaction of needs, freedom of movement throughout the school, extension of the school to the outside world: these are ideals that may never be realised unless there is a social perspective.

There is a need for planning and for checking on educational processes to throw as much light as possible on the subject with which we are truly concerned: the organisation of pupils' responses, not only intellectual but also social and emotional. Their power of response must be reinforced, their responses must become independent of immediate stimuli, experiences must be effectively structured, open-ended but coherent cultural frames must be set up so that any variation will merely add to the value of experience. All this is quite different from extrinsic, wasteful flexibility, where no account is taken of the results.

It is all too easy to be over-optimistic and to expect beneficial educational results merely from open-mindedness or flexibility.

The most significant new lines of development lie in an analysis of the social conditions which influence experience. In this analysis educational problems are enlightened by clinical psychology, a social science no longer limited to pathological anomalies but extending to the whole field of interpersonal relationships. Clinical psychology has helped to gain a deeper insight into the true significance of behavioural change, on the positive or negative effects of such change, on the relevance of change in terms of cultural gain, reinforcement of mental powers and the satisfaction of social and emotional needs.

The emphasis on the social aspect has another even more important effect: it can be used for a critical review of narrow research without a wide field of reference, of hypotheses divorced from reality and unfit for its change. A substantial contribution has been made both by structuralism (the principle of invariance is the first step on a long road towards freeing intellectual potential from artificial variants, induced by adverse experimental conditions) and by the reawakening of theory in response to the needs of a society, in which the division of labour is primarily responsible for serious detriment to human life, under-employing intellectual potential and creating class distinctions.

Educational psychology has made undisputed progress in the study of learning problems (review of learning content and methods, expectations as to the cultural levels that can be achieved, emphasis on conceptual structuring through problem solving, research in the form of organising and manipulating data, the discovery of general properties, the ability to generalise, to define and use laws) and of creative activity. Problems of inter-personal relationships have remained in the shade, even though socialisation is a predominating theme. There is a tendency to expect new solutions to emerge spontaneously through informal "liberalisation" and "democratisation", rather than planning for and implementing new solutions by specific research and action. While there is a widely felt need for a radical review of the psychological bases of education and for a study of its social implications, little genuine attention is paid to these bases and these implications, not merely in educational practice but even in the field of research.

Educational psychology, like every other social science, is in a state of flux: only through analysis, uninfluenced by assumed needs and rationalisation of what exists (relics of Hegel that have never been repressed), can we attempt to arrive at a more specific definition of its nature and its role as a social science. Use should be made of the criticism that structuralists have made of descriptive-inductive methods (a great step forward, which overcomes our inferiority complex when faced with a vast accumulation of accurate but irrelevant research) and of the principle of invariance, paradoxically, by the activation of deep-rooted structures (the universality of human nature against induced differences).

LEARNING AND CREATIVITY

The hypothesis that development is plastic undoubtedly occupies a pre-eminent position in psycho-pedagogy. Since psycho-pedagogic research has entered upon a new, more mature phase, even individual differences (used in the first decade of this century as weapons in the great battle against collective teaching which it was hoped would be replaced by individualisation) are now considered not to be inherent properties, but rather as products of an individual's interaction with his environment.

This has led to concern with the problems of learning in the light of the facilities and conditions that can be used to alter the course of learning, levels of achievement, the general influence of learning upon personality – the learning of sensory-motor abilities, of symbols, of concepts, of assessment criteria, methods of responding to stress exerted by the environment, social and emotional traits.

Are not the findings obtained when testing the hypothesis of plasticity now being called into question by structuralism? Although structuralism has been vulgarised, it is without doubt the most interesting innovation in the field of social sciences. The principle of invariance, the affirmation of the primacy of the intellect over the social, the return to the belief in the universality of human nature, the study of "profound models" of mental structure, grammar viewed not as a set of extrinsic, conventional rules but as a linguistic activity that follows the same rules as does thought (transformational grammar): all this is an implied criticism of the taxonomic and descriptive-inductive methods and experiments which, while technically correct, are irrelevant in that they explain nothing. Structuralism denies the significance of extrapolation but not the hypothesis of plasticity (variance), for it provides frameworks of reference which can be used in attempting to redefine plasticity by research. In consequence, individual differences can still legitimately be interpreted as products of complex response conditions.

In other words, plasticity and invariance are not in conflict. Structuralists emphasise the need to activate the basic structures and therefore to alter the current situation. It is understandable, therefore, that a structuralist such as Bruner considers the concept of predisposition to be ambiguous and affirms that predisposition can be *taught* – in other words, we can create the conditions that will foster the development of predisposition and do not need to sit back and wait until predisposition emerges.

The formal and logical powers of the mind, dear to the structuralist, are not forces which operate at full blast whatever the true situation. This has given rise to the search for points of structural production so that the processes of learning can be inserted at these points. Invariance is hidden, submerged, and it must be encouraged and brought to the surface.

Direct criticism has been made of the devalued significance of specialisation (a criticism that can also be levelled against the technical and social division of labour), of the type of specialisation which sets up barriers, crystallises, creates a hierarchy and rewards ability with privilege. Invariance and the identity of human nature are interpreted in progressive terms and are related to creativity. As Chomsky says, no discipline now takes pride in asserting its absolute independence from any other; we must free our scientific imagination from the fetters that have become such a familiar object in our cultural environment that we scarcely even notice them.

When defining the learning process there are two opposite approaches: the behavioural approach, which lays special stress upon stimuli; and the approach which accentuates the role of intention and of problem-solving. Both these contemporary explanations are productive. Learning by conditioning is of importance in problem-solving and vice versa. It is essential that psycho-pedagogy accept a variety of forms, so that drastic gaps are not left in the operating field.

At the beginning, experimentalists concentrated solely upon the processes of conditioning, using the stimulus-response formula, which may seem a rough and ready method if we overlook the difficulties of launching an experiment (Thorndike: connectionism and trial and error; Pavlov: conditioned reflexes; Guthrie, Hull, Watson, Skinner: behaviourism).

Other experts have emphasised the purposive element of learning – for example, Dewey's reflective thinking and Tolman's purposive behaviour. The five states of thinking described by Dewey in *How we*

Think (1910) are well known, as well as the three main intermediate variables identified by Tolman (the system of needs; the values-beliefs matrix; behaviour space, a concept similar to that of life space evolved by Lewin).

The contribution of *Gestalttheorie* is universally considered to be of fundamental importance as it is a precursor to structuralism. Its concept, that learning takes place, not by accumulating individual items that are subsequently static, but by the reorganisation and restructuring of wholes and forms (so that parts of a whole can be understood as parts of a structure), is a discovery which was used as a springboard for all subsequent theories.

According to Wertheimer "the whole process is often a kind of drama with powerful dramatic forces – with tension and dramatic structural changes, in the transition from not having understood structurally, from being troubled, to really grasping and realising the requirements".[2]

The theory of form, adds Wertheimer, does not underestimate the role of past experience but "tries to differentiate between accumulated aggregates on the one hand and *Gestalten*, structures, on the other, both in sub-wholes and in the total field, and to develop appropriate scientific tools to investigate the latter".[3] Certainly, when past experience is made up of fragmentary aggregates, of knowledge not understood, of mechanical reactions, it does not predispose one to tackle problems. Past experience is useful, therefore, only when it ensures a "structural transfer... in changed situations".[4]

These concepts are taken up in the theory of structured learning, whose most active exponent is Jerome S. Bruner. This theory, which lays emphasis on the differences in structures at the various levels of development, has been invaluable in promoting methodological innovation and in revising the content of learning, suggesting bold measures for anticipating and speeding up the process of learning, sharply diverging from the traditional "intellectual chronology" put forward by Piaget.

This change of direction would not have been possible had not structuralism made such strides over the past few years in the field of social sciences. Lévi-Strauss, in his brief essay, *Critères scientifiques dans les disci-*

---

[2] Max Wertheimer, *Productive Thinking*, edited by Michael Wertheimer, Tavistock, London, 1959 (1945), 57.
[3] *Op. cit.*, p. 65.
[4] *Op. cit.*, p. 66.

plines sociales et humaines (1964), did not exaggerate when he stated that only with the advent of structuralist research did social studies start to emerge from pre-history, discarding taxonomic and descriptive-inductive methods.

The basic assumptions and research techniques used by Bruner in his psycho-pedagogic research owes much to the structural anthropology of Lévi-Strauss and to Chomsky's structural linguistics.

Bruner's structuralism applies to the primary school, in that it defines the process of cognitive structuring from the active phase to the iconic and symbolic phase. Using methods of intrinsic conceptual organisation of the various disciplines as the point of departure, the symbolic form must be translated into an iconic or active form to obey the laws of learning that apply at the various age levels. This means that the "anticipation hypothesis" (i.e. any subject can be learnt effectively by any pupil at any phase of development) is realistic if it is combined with the principle of *translation*, according to which the learning of a given subject can and should be appropriate to a specific phase of development. But even at the lowest levels, there can be learning if stimuli organisation is produced by an appropriate response (the immediate stimuli being gradually withdrawn) by generalisation, by classification, by understanding of connections and relationships. All this becomes possible in the symbolic phase when the child has an effective command of his language.

Language, says Bruner, is the tool that enables us to travel in the realms of the possible, of the conditional, of assumptions that contradict factual reality. Words and sentences do not need to be immediately connected with experience. By the structural route, we progress from rules that refer to local similarities, sometimes related to irrelevant perceptive data, towards a subordinate type of grouping: the child understands rules of equivalence that connect a series of objects or phenomena by means of a "superimposed rule". As he becomes increasingly able to dissociate his responses from his immediate environment, he tends to use more sophisticated organisational principles than in the descriptive-inductive phase.

This is the point at which Bruner's thought converges with structuralism. For example, he affirms that we should not be content with analysing the diversity of languages, but we must determine the ways in which language as such, whatever the nature of language, influences cognitive processes. As we acquire greater understanding of the powers of the mind, we come to recognise the importance of symbolism in the cognitive process, and it is here that learning psychology and language psychology tend to merge.

Let us consider the symbol, in other words the means by which we dissociate response from the immediate data, by which we progress beyond the information furnished by stimuli. The realm of symbols can be explored by the child, provided that descriptive theories are replaced by a prescriptive theory which shows the most effective rules to help him acquire knowledge and skills. If, in the practical field, education is capable of exploiting the child's structural potential by teaching him how to use the instrument of symbolism, he will be able to launch out into the field of generalisation. Bruner states that eight year olds can understand the principle of conservation of energy (comprehension of an invariance) and the concept of second degree power (generalisation in the sense of understanding the nature of the relationship between a number of sets and the number of components within each set). Therefore, if descriptive research points out that, for instance, most six year olds have not grasped the concept of reversibility, prescriptive research must attempt to determine ways in which the child can be helped to acquire this concept.

Any subject is no more than the sum of its own methods, the set of strategies which it generates to define and solve problems. The quality needed is inventiveness, consideration of the possible and the probable. With this process of projection towards the future, the transfer of principles and attitudes is far more important than specific transfer, as it leads to maximum flexibility.

Structural learning involves purposive aspects (the desire to find a solution) and systematic aspects (use of a rational method to find that solution), but it also involves intuition and inventiveness.

Guilford reports that a growing concern with creativity occurred in about 1950 when the traditional intelligence tests were first criticised. The type of thought measured by such tests is not thought in itself, but only a method of using one's intellectual capacity for a given purpose (in other words, to find the correct answer). There is another type of thought, which has been given different names by the many authors who have been concerned with it; open (Bartlett), divergent (Guilford), fluid, flexible and original (Torrance), pregnant (Kneller), independent (Cruchfield), emergent (Taylor), tolerant to ambiguity and open to conflicting information (Rogers), and effective (Bruner).[5]

---

[5] For a first sketch see the article: F. De Bartolomeis, "Una svolta verso un effettiva innovazione: la struttura a laboratori", *La Ricerca*, Torino, 16 November 1969.

Creativity is a characteristic of the deep-rooted structures of thought, if proper incentives are provided, it is manifested in the processes of learning, production and language, in graphic, figurative and plastic depiction, in generalisation and in inter-personal relationships. According to the structuralists, creativity uses the subconscious as a basic symbolic function.

Creativity co-habits with what may seem to be its opposite (lack of productivity) but which in fact is a process of incubation whose duration cannot be predicted because it depends upon many variables: not only one's own working rate but also the substance and the relevance of the problem being tackled. Primary school programmes and methods can make use of the findings of the psychology of creativity only through organisational models, such as a "laboratory structure", which establishes no rigid timetable for learning and production and which does not segment activities.

The types of behaviour with which we are now familiar, the aptitudes that come to the surface, are not due to personal talents (and this shows how wrong we are to make uncritical dinstinctions between people of higher or lower ability) but to interaction with the environment, an environment that includes the school, which usually offers little stimulation. All research points to the same conclusion: the pupil structures the effects of adverse influences and is underemployed, in that he is given little or no problematical or creative work to do.

There is a growing belief that aptitudes depend on general experience and can be brought out by specific training. Through psychological analysis, without neglecting the importance of adverse societal influences and artificial impediments, light is cast upon *functional incapacity* which, being functional, can to a great extent be modified.

Examples of functional incapacity are a low level of aspiration, lack of initiative, failure to adopt systematic methods of research, substitution of creativity by flat and conformist thinking, failure to organise significant knowledge, failure to employ explanatory generalisation, non-comprehension and the resulting state of cognitive disorganisation.

Functional breakdowns (in other words, blockage, deviation, regression, non-employment of deep-rooted structures, etc.) affect not only cultural achievement but also – and this is far more serious – emotional maladjustment.

Creativity, formerly restricted mainly to graphic, figurative and plastic activities (which are still attempting to conquer a central position in education), has recently been viewed as significant of a new interpretation of intellectual powers and the methods of using those powers. Syllabi, timetables, the relationships between subjects, the organisation and employment of educational space, the type of work demanded of the teacher: all this is being revolutionised.

Although the creative processes are obviously important in expressive activities, we would do well to consider guidelines for further research on this field. In our opinion, the problem should be more closely linked with a sector which at first sight may appear to have nothing to do with school goals, especially the elementary school – the body of theories and findings of contemporary art which may exercise a decisive influence on the future organisation of productive aesthetic education.[6]

Educational psychology is opening up new horizons in the field of creativity by examining the significance and scope of the current revolution in the arts, including anti-art (a concept which made its first appearance in 1916 with the Dada Group in Zurich) and the use of new materials and techniques in an attempt to render our concept of painting, drawing and sculpture obsolete.

Lines, colour, space, matter (indeed, a vast diversity of materials) can be used, not for *sensitive* manipulation, but in the light of their formal and abstract values, in other words for *conceptual art*. Research on the psychology of representation, associated with analysis of the artistic manifestations of our time (a good start having been made by Arnheim), is no less important than research on the expressive ability of the child, for all these widen our framework of reference. This research can also be of benefit to what is considered "manual" work, when the shape of the product is an important feature (a field in which industrial design is of great importance).

We must mention the general acclaim that has been given to *brainstorming*, a method developed by A. F. Osborn to increase the production of ideas. This method, which was developed to meet the needs of industry, should be viewed with some caution, for it contains the seeds of dangerous manipulation of creative individuals: in other words it deprives them of the control of the whole process, preventing them setting out the problem in their own way in an attempt to arrive at a solution and from viewing the solution with critical eyes.

---

[6] A stimulating work, though at times confused, *Education through Art*, (1943) by Herbert Read; a more thorough work is by Rudolph Arnheim, *Art and Visual Perception*, (1954). See also F. De Bartolomeis, *Il bambino dai tre ai sei anni e la nuova scuola infantile*, La Nuova Italia, Firenze, 1968.

EDUCATIONAL PSYCHOLOGY AND CLINICAL PSYCHOLOGY

One of the most significant developments of psycho-pedagogy has been brought about by its encounter with clinical psychology. It is hard to understand why this encounter took so long, since:
a) Freud worked out his revolutionary doctrines more than sixty years ago;
b) from the very beginning of the Copernican revolution in education, stress has been laid upon motivation and the dynamic concept of education, as well as on the power of social and cultural factors to modify behaviour.

But to say that there is general acceptance of the link between clinical and educational psychology would not be the truth. Almost every teacher rejects it, while the general trend among specialist psychologists is to consider that it applies only in cases of deviation from the norm, it being taken for granted that such cases are the province of the psychologist alone.

Once it is recognised that there is no such thing as normality in the sense of a condition without difficulties, conflicts or disturbances and that the educator must therefore deal with behaviour patterns incorporating such problems, clinical psychology can no longer be viewed as a specialised practice employed only in exceptional cases. It must, indeed, be included in the training of the future educator.

We are indebted to K. Lewin and H. S. Sullivan – and it is by no means an accident that we mention a social psychologist and psychiatrist in the same breath – for their study of individuals in their interpersonal relationships, for their dynamic concept of behavioural problems, a concept that is not optimistic but that is aware of the complications ensuing from the position of the individual within society. Their thought has certainly brought about a new understanding of child psychology. Children do not develop by passing from one set stage to the next in an inevitable and linear progress.

Psycho-pedagogists have recently focussed attention upon the problems of interpersonal relationships. These highlight social and emotional variables not considered of paramount importance either in Dewey-inspired activism or in the theory of structured learning. In the most progressive field of educational psychology today, constant reference is made not only to psycho-analysis but also to new trends in clinical psychology, whose developments have a direct practical relevance to the organisation of education and to the vital contribution that can be made by the school psychologist and the social worker. As a result, the functions of all the experts involved in the educational process have been redefined.

The emphasis upon social aspects may pave the way for new developments, provided that the encounter between the educational psychologist and the clinical psychologist:

a) provides the tools for understanding and handling problems of adaptation, as clinical psychology has formerly always been concerned with difficulties and disorders, while the educational psychologist has always restricted his practice to what are considered to be less serious forms of maladjustment;

b) transforms psycho-pedagogic training, whose goals should be not only to impart a knowledge of the other person, the person at the receiving end of education, but also to provide the tools for such action. The teacher must gain insight into himself and – to borrow Freud's words – realise the existence of the subconscious and control the ways in which he represses his subconscious (withdrawal, diverting the repression into other channels which may reappear as disorder). In the future, psycho-pedagogic research will probably use the findings obtained by the merger between social and clinical psychology to promote a radical change of the basic professional training both of the school psychologist and of the teacher.

The study of educational psychology, like that of more specifically didactic subjects, in the training of teachers is an essential way of acquiring knowledge and psychological skill which can be used in educational practice. The ways in which the findings of psycho-pedagogic research are employed raises problems of no less import than problems relating to the scientific scope of this kind of research.

The introduction to educational psychology of future educators and school psychologists is the work of a specialist. The student will be expected to master the following two types of skill:

a) the ability to observe behaviour in a systematic way and to assess that behaviour. He must be able to compile data which will be used as a basis for action; this data will refer to the relative value of the subjects studied and to the child's interpersonal relationships and social and emotional traits (aggression, negative attitudes, lack of security, shyness, tendency to isolate himself, interference and disturbance, anxiety, inability to collaborate, exhibitionism, euphoria in the form of superficiality and irresponsibility, apathy, depression, over-gregariousness, the desire "to get his own back", etc.). The factors that lend themselves to direct observation are merely symptoms. If these symptoms are viewed in the light of the overall personality of the child within his life space, in other words in his social contacts, an explanation can be arrived at (causal interpretation) and effective action taken.

b) an ability to handle problems of interpersonal relationships. "The teaching of personal relationships" is too pedantic a term to apply to the skill that is in fact needed, which must be highly flexible and alert to every detail.

The teacher must observe not only the personal relationships of his pupils in the laboratory, on the playing field, in project work and during extra-curricular activities, but also his relationships in the whole field of his experience. The latter include: the pupil in his relationship with one other individual, with other pupils within his group (group psycho-dynamics), with the educator (or psychologist). The final objective is to improve the social and emotional balance of the children, increasing their output when faced with the stimulus of problems and the need for research.

The need to go beyond the bounds of a limited didactic definition of the "group" and to consider whether the group is truly justified from the social standpoint, in the light of the forces governing the individuals within that group, mean that we must turn our attention from educational and social considerations to specific research on group psycho-dynamics. This demonstrates the progress that we have made since Freud. Research conducted by E. J. Anthony, R. Battegay, W. R. Bion, S. H. Foulkes, H. Heziel and S. R. Slavson provide us with a new approach to the problems of socialisation and emotional adaptation to school.[7]

Since one of the teacher's functions is to act as the leader in a small group, it is essential that he should understand the dynamics of groups, the impact of conscious and subconscious motivations upon a group and the significance of the phenomena that rise to the surface.

The problem of small groups is of special relevance now that it is generally accepted that school should not be based upon the class unit but that pupils should be mobile within the overall educational space,

---

[7] For the pedagogical use of Bion's methodology see the work by E. Richardson, *Group study for teachers*, (Routledge and Kegan Paul, London, 1967). The distinction is made between the therapy group and the study group. While the latter has therapeutic aims, it is used to give the members of the group an understanding of the dynamics of interpersonal relationships, and so aims at training teachers to acquire the necessary ability to deal with such relationships within the school.

which should contain "points of activity" (true laboratories or laboratory situations or flexible specialised areas).

The group may be defined either by its size (number of members) or by its structure (the type of communication between members in the course of activities). The combination of size and structure will determine the dynamic physiognomy which the group will acquire. The dimension of the group is not measured merely by number, whether it consists of 4, 5, 6 or more members. The important factor is that the group should be able to solve cultural, social and emotional problems. Group dimension will depend on optimum communication (which can be ascertained by the quality of behaviour). Communication will not be achieved as soon as the group is formed but is a goal at which the group should strive through its learning and production activities.

Optimum communication has two meanings:
a) a set of uninhibited shared experiences which prepares the group to tackle and solve problems;
b) true cooperation between the group members without any control that may suppress conflict or social and emotional disturbance.

The group is a place which combines learning, production and socialisation. Only at an advanced operational stage will communication within the group become cooperation. At the beginning, the purpose of communication is to uncover latent conflict. We should not attempt to achieve cooperation without resolving inhibitions that would leave many major personal problems untouched.

The group must be of an appropriate size to foster cooperation and also to allow social and emotional problems to rise to the surface. It should be commensurate with the potential for communication. If a group is too large, some of its members will be excluded, intercourse between the members will be made more difficult and it will be impossible to attempt to solve conflicts. A conflict must be communicated before it can be solved, and it would be harmful to train children to suppress conflict which will only break out in other symptomatic forms.

It might be believed that by applying a structural concept to the group, individual potential would be reduced, in that the individual would only be a cog and would have to conform and adapt to the group structure. On the contrary, individual centres of activity would be reinforced, promoting socialisation and making use of intellectual instruments in response to the stimulus of problems, employing research methods.

In a group structure, each member can discover his own true nature by gradually discarding those factors which keep the group's level of achievement down by working against communication (inhibition, guilt, repression, destructive conflict, tension that makes it impossible to act). In a group structure, behaviour "melts" in that it finds new outlets and devises new forms of relationship, building up into a sense of belonging. The individual can progress from a situation of imbalance, in which many of his exits are blocked and he has to divert and waste his energy or create defence mechanisms in the form of inhibitions, to a situation in which channels of communication are created that provide an incentive for self-expression and self-realisation. This means that there are two "life spaces", two differing social situations, not one social situation as an alternative to an individual situation. Outside the group, the individual encounters an unbalanced social situation which affects his experience. The purpose of the group, therefore, is to give the individual a status in a network of interpersonal relationships. This purpose will be fulfilled more effectively if, through group experience, conflicts, defence mechanisms and distractions rise to the surface so that they can be channelled towards appropriate responses.

At school, a peer group is affected by interpersonal relationships outside the school. The field is even further broadened by research on the psycho-dynamics of family groupings (for example, studies by N. W. Ackerman) and on social and cultural conditioning in general.

Once clinical psychology is no longer restricted to the narrow field of pathologies, it is of even greater value, both in dealing with minor maladjustment (which may well become major) and in preventing disturbances. It is by no means fanciful to speak of school in terms of a "therapeutic community" (L. Hay 1965). A major problem in the school is that of social climate and the position of the individual in a network of personal relationships. This is a concept that has arisen out of research initiated, with different instruments and objectives, by K. Lewin (for example, the experimental creation of social climates) and by J. L. Moreno (sociometric tests studying the individual as the subject and object of choices related to various activities).

Now that social inequalities have been recognised, we can analyse their causes and plan for action which will, to the extent possible, promote equality of educational opportunity. Of special relevance is the problem of the disadvantaged child, the child who suffers from cultural deprivation. This affects his intellectual output, the processes of identification and identity, his self-image, stability, power of expression and his understanding of language, and all his personality traits in general.[8] Nonetheless, although the problems of the disadvantaged child and of cultural deprivation have entered into the province of psychopedagogic research, strongly influenced by sociology, we are still far from embodying its findings in concrete reforms. In the United States, the reasons for this failure are complicated by racial conflict and segregation.

The number of disadvantaged people is very high in every country. We must of course enact social measures; but is it best to tackle the problems by streaming or by reorganising the school so that it can devote more attention to the individual and so that a variety of groupings can be formed within the school, without comparing individual rates of work and achievements with an artificial standard applicable to all? This is a problem that we shall be discussing later.

"LABORATORY MODEL"

No great expense will be involved in discarding the class unit or in using specialist teachers; all that we are doing is to redeploy the school environment and the teachers. If we believe that the ideal pupil-teacher ratio is 25 to 1 in a traditional setting, this ratio is sufficient to allow of radical change in the organisational module.

Teachers' specialist training should include not only educational psychology and teaching methods but complete mastery of one or more subjects in the curriculum, to ensure the highest standard of teaching and to enable each pupil to pass from one level and rate of learning to another in different areas.

If teachers specialise in given subjects, even in the primary school, children will come into contact with several teachers, not just their own class teacher, and non-grading will be possible. A non-graded school is a school without classes, in which pupils can move up or down freely in the light of individual differences.[9]

"The non-graded school", explains Richard I. Miller, "is one without grade failure and/or retention, in the conventional sense; it has individualised instruction with the purpose of permitting youngsters

---

[8] For a review of recent research in this field see: *Education for the Disadvantaged*, edited by H. L. Miller, (The Free Press, New York, 1967). Also A. Davis, *Social class influence upon learning*, Harvard University Press, Cambridge, Mass., 1948: K. Eels, *Cultural differences*, University of Chicago Press, Chicago, 1951.

[9] Quite rightly a distinction is made between the ungraded school (that is, the traditional pluri-class) and the nongraded school.

to progress as they – individually – show competence to do so; and it permits sufficient flexibility in the curriculum to make teaching adjustments both in terms of intrapersonal variability (differences within an individual) and in terms of interpersonal variability (differences among individuals)".[10]

If the situation is to be coordinated and properly ordered, specialisation requires team teaching (in which teachers are at the same time at the disposal of individual pupils and of groups). Team teaching affects the decision as to the subjects taught, teaching methods, the purpose and assessment of education, as well as effective educational practice.

When team teaching and non-grading are combined, the ideal conditions are created to promote optimum individualisation and socialisation.

Reorganisation of the primary school is not merely a question of teaching. The important factor is the improvement in personal relationships, the creation of an atmosphere in which the new processes of learning and production will flourish. We believe that the "laboratory model" school allows of a type of teacher cooperation and pupil mobility in which experiments in team teaching and non-grading can develop beyond purely didactic goals.

We are surely justified in believing that the school of tomorrow will provide a setting that will foster not only efficiency, in that children will be able to attain higher levels of achievement formerly considered beyond their capacity, but also in which they will be able to attain a higher level of social and emotional adaptation in the absence of frustrations in their personal relationships, greater incentive for creative skills being provided as well as greater satisfaction of their need for security, acceptance and participation.

We must make maximum use of the flexible nature of children's development and cater for their potential for conceptual structuring, generalisation, research, acceptance of responsibility and participation in the decision-making process.

Today, children are encountering more and more stimuli in their everyday experience (the mass media and the changing conditions of life characterised by an increasing number of technological instruments). By focusing our attention exclusively on the type of stimulus (by debating, for example, whether the word or the image is more effective) we are diverted from considering the mode of response, the

---

[10] R. I. Miller, *The Non-graded School*, Harper and Row, New York, 1967, p. 131.

very factor which structures knowledge and skill. The problem of stimulation must be the subject of research, paying due attention to intuition and creation. If research is too systematically planned, it may become over-rationalised and promote conformist thinking so that all that is new, unexpected, invented and personal will be lost.

If we investigate the time pupils take or the rates at which they work during the various stages of the primary school, we can discover the optimum conditions for learning and production. Periods of *tâtonnement* or "feeling the way", in other words a continuous, open-ended attempt to solve a problem and a period of incubation (when the attempt is suspended on the conscious level but continued in the subconscious) are beneficial.

Tâtonnement and incubation, combined with freedom of movement within the school environment, non-formal interpersonal relationships, facilities for the investigation and circumscription of knowledge and the absence of an artificial breakdown of work imposed by set time-tables, are all factors in favour not only of the non-graded school (which may differ little from the traditional school except in the mobility of classes), but also of a more radical development, a "laboratory structure" primary school. It would, of course, be impossible to implement this new model immediately on a wide scale. Two points should be borne in mind, however:
a) the model must be perfected and tested through experiments, and to do this the laboratory system could be introduced into a few schools under the sponsorship of research bodies (university institutes);
b) this study relates to educational changes over the next thirty years, and if we are really determined to make a decisive change, time is on our side.

If we are to emphasise the importance of "learning by research" and the creative process in education, we must first determine what institutional and organisational measures are necessary to provide the setting for these activities. The traditional "all purpose" classrooms will be replaced by laboratory situations (specialist areas). In addition to the programming centre, directed by specialist teachers responsible for student groups, there must be social areas in which pupils – even though they are free to move from one laboratory to another – can satisfy their need to "belong". Laboratories must be centres of activity in an educational space in which all types of relationship can flourish.

In experiments on the use of fluid educational space, as in the British open plan schools, provision is always made for a "home base" that maintains the link between a given teacher and a given group of pupils in a specific place, especially at the beginning and end of the day or at intervals during the course of the day. This teacher has an overall picture of everything that the child is doing and can help and guide him in his work. The child is not submerged and lost in a social morass, but his individual personality is recognised and accepted.

The sense of belonging is certainly not promoted by the traditional class, dominated as it is by collective teaching which discourages the formation of groups, cultural initiative and flexibility.

Just as cultural skills have to be learned, social life must be learned through freedom of movement, meetings, rapports, initiative. The assimilation of new ideas within an educational space requires continuous adaptation, although the reasons for and the goals of that process of adaptation are understood. An optimum dimension must be established, in terms of number of pupils, teachers and other staff, and of the space available, to promote social mobility, full use of every area, integration of experience of the home group with that of other groups, sequence of activities, relationships with the other teachers and people within the educational space, the sense of belonging to a group.

An open plan school has no laboratories or specialised teachers, although there are specialist areas. These areas are, however, informally organised in that they are not clearly defined and they are not of a sufficiently high technical standard to make any positive contribution. To use the special skills of each teacher is not the same as team teaching. The results would be more successful if individual skills were extended beyond the sphere of personal interests and tastes to the level of subject specialisation, although not to such a point as to prevent cooperation between teachers. It is undoubtedly a promising factor that great attention is being paid to the interests of the teachers as well as of the pupils.

The open plan school is still in the early stage of experimentation. One of its advantages is that it encourages inventiveness, naturalness and freedom of movement; in other words, it creates an atmosphere that excludes those features which cause school to be considered as something unpleasant, artificial, dead and out of tune with the biophysical development and true interests of its pupils. There is every reason to hope that future developments will lead to greater flexibility, the abolition of classes, a variety of groupings and a more rational curriculum raising the level of school activities (paving the way to technological production) and using more appropriate means of evaluating the results of the educational process.

It is vital that laboratories, or at least laboratory situations, be available if learning is to be based upon research and if room is to be given to productive activities.

A laboratory is quite different from a classroom which is a no man's land where teaching activity predominates. A laboratory is space organised and equiped to promote research activity by the pupils, in which the teacher's role is to act as a guide and as a supervisor. A laboratory structure is necessary for the installation of equipment and for student mobility. The child goes to whichever laboratory meets his needs, where he will find the equipment he requires and the help of a specialist. The teacher is a research worker helping the pupils in their own research projects.

The laboratory structure might lead to confusion and segmentation if there were no programming centre to which the pupils can refer. This means that they have freedom of choice within the limits of what the school can offer. Teachers, for their part, must be able to keep a continuous check on what the children are doing and review the progress made by each in different fields.

With this organisational module and with the supervision and guidance of the teachers, providing far more personal and frequent contact than in the school of today, waste of time and effort is avoided. Another factor making for integration is the existence of groups and the pooling of the results of their work.

The result is a flexible organisation, open to adaptation, capable of satisfying the pupils' need to known the result of their work and to find out how to proceed with that work. If there were no planning and monitoring centre, if there were no specialist teacher, the laboratory structure would generate a degree of confusion that would make us long to return to the traditional timetable and classes.

The laboratory structure has been evolved in response to the need to align learning and production with research methods, taking into account the role of research in creativity. In the school as it exists, research and creativity are impossible. It is wrong to lay down a specific timetable and to create a classroom to be used for all activities in that it has an adverse affect on all the processes for which creative effort and socialisation are essential. Many of these processes require incubation and clarification, testing and re-testing, and would be impossible if they were interrupted by a set timetable.

The child must be given the opportunity to work through his problem without fixed time limits and work should not be suspended for arbitrary reasons. The traditional school timetable makes it difficult to concentrate, for it makes the child stop work just as he is beginning to achieve results. It makes sense to change once a task has been completed or when a pause may be beneficial, but to crowd a host of different subjects into a single day simply causes fragmentation and alienation from the problem. For example, half an hour's concentrated work on mathematics may be sufficient, but it would be absurd to prevent a child from spending more time on a specific problem if he needs it. When a problem is set, one must concentrate, conduct research, feel free not to have to face other problems making equal claims. In short, the laboratory structure makes it feasible to adopt a problem-solving and creative approach, the sole approach that will enable the child to build up structures, the nucleus around which all subsequent knowledge and work will be centered.

There are obviously other considerations besides the timetable. The time variable should be viewed in the light of the other variables: equipment and the type of guidance available (specialist teachers). There is a fourth parameter in the laboratory situation: the content of learning. This is a factor that requires radical rethinking, for laboratories could accomplish nothing if we continued to pursue the same old objectives.

The laboratory system introduces many changes compared with the traditional system, making use of many innovations: structured learning, research and discovery methods, attention to individual differences, the psycho-dynamic and clinical approach, the open plan school, non-grading and team teaching. In brief, these are the changes:

a) the laboratory system or model respects the nature of the process of learning and production which is given full rein in research. It allows concentration on the problem, planning, incubation and continuity of effort.

b) it includes a programming centre, and pupils can consult teachers who have an overall picture of their work and the progress they are making.

c) there is sufficient material and technical equipment to promote individual and group research and productive activities. This equipment brings the pupil into contact with modern culture, in other words he can, through his own personal work, acquire insight into the findings of various branches of learning, learning how to handle

Progress in Educational Psychology

the same instruments so that he can better organise and rationalise his research work.
d) it provides skilled assistance and guidance from an expert in the subject (who has been trained in teaching techniques and educational psychology) in each laboratory or laboratory situation (specialist area without specific material confines). This will have a beneficial effect on the quality of individual and group work. Specialist teaching is combined with team teaching, in which all teachers co-operate closely and are present full time.
e) with the incentive provided by the laboratory situation, through social contacts and intercourse, the pupil can work at his own rate, not to artificial, mechanical patterns that are alien to research and the conceptual structuring of knowledge. This means that the pupil, either alone or in a group, can work on a project without being restricted by time. The time he takes will be determined by his motivation, capacity and the objective requirements of the project itself. In this way, every child will attain the level within his scope, unhampered by lack of incentive and by negative conditioning. The laboratory model is a classless school and promotes vertical mobility.
f) the pupil learns to trust his own judgement; he accepts responsibility, he works towards objectives whose meaning he understands. The laboratory model creates a setting in which he can build up structures, gradually broaden his knowledge and improve the products of that knowledge.
g) the laboratory system provides for interdisciplinary research, the purpose being more the intrinsic nature of research, not the extrinsic relations between different subjects.
h) the personal relationships and groupings involved in the pupil's activities are enhanced by a general climate of acceptance and self-expression.
i) all pupils work in every basic laboratory, although they may choose one or more laboratories for the projects that they themselves prefer. This makes for rational and planned variety, very different from the breakdowns imposed by a set timetable, one of whose advantages is that it promotes physical and mental health.

TECHNOLOGY AND THE FUTURE OF EDUCATION

The reaction to programmed learning is almost always one of two extremes: optimists dream of the lucky beneficiaries of technology, teachers no longer carrying out the sole function of teaching and assessment, while pessimists are concerned and shocked, believing that programmed learning marks the end of any true form of education and a headlong lemming flight towards a mechanical age in which all individuality will be lost.

This concern is far from new: it arises every time some new technical development appears which is to revolutionise our living habits and behaviour. We still make the mistake of considering the effects of novelty from one viewpoint alone: the effects of the machine on the individual. We forget that the individual can respond by broadening his field of experience.

The problem should be considered from neither an over-optimistic nor an over-pessimistic standpoint. We must try to discover whether the new instrument is beneficial or harmful in itself and what will happen if that instrument tends to monopolise education rather than being only one aspect of the process. In our opinion, there is great potential in programmed learning but it is an educational aid that will not unsettle traditional methods. It may be a paradox, but its effects on individualisation are very similar to those of collective teaching if it is used to the exclusion of any other method.

When we attempt to predict the future, we must not allow ourselves to be blinkered by confining our terms of reference to technological development. Based on an analysis of present trends, we believe that other needs will make themselves increasingly felt, and these will by no means oblige the individual to make preponderant use of images and logical sequences in the processes of learning. There is already widespread awareness of the need to provide critical ability, the capacity to work out problems for oneself, the need for intuition and creativity to help us cope with the increasing number of stimuli and the tendency to form logical patterns. Many people have warned that methods that may be valuable as an instrument must not become the tools of instrumentalisation. Not for nothing is "structure", as conceived by the structuralists, formed by and rooted in the symbolic function of the subconscious.

Advanced experiments in fluid educational space, such as the open plan school, deliberately avoid concentrating upon the technological aspect. This may be somewhat too drastic an attitude, for we cannot counteract a danger by refusing to face it. It must not be overlooked that in certain cases technology may promote the processes of invention and production.

That mythical activity known as manual craftsmanship cannot by itself promote such inventiveness or productiveness; a more realistic attitude would be to consider that craftsmanship and technology might combine to improve the education of the future. We would be wrong, therefore, to reject technology out of hand or to welcome it uncritically, but we must broaden our framework of reference and carry out more advanced research to ensure that we grasp all the opportunities offered by progress in general, not merely by technology in particular.

A pupil who is taught through the channel of television, not by a mediocre teacher, but by a true specialist who gives the benefit of his experience to a vast number of students at the same time, is still a traditional pupil. A lesson which is assimilated by programmed learning alone may appear to be an innovation but it is in fact a step backward. It overlooks the importance of learning through personal initiative and research, as if the only differences between individuals lay in their intellectual capacities and their rates of learning, not in their whole personality. To consider the personality as a whole – and in this field the contributions made by dynamic psychology, social psychology and clinical psychology are invaluable – requires a standard of research and, in consequence, a standard of practical implementation which would be adversely affected by an over-narrow technological attitude, to the detriment of the individual and of the community.

The school which incorporates a laboratory structure makes optimum use of technological facilities but at the same time develops individual resources to the maximum as well as fostering socialisation and creativity in a healthy environment. Technology, if used alone, is repressive, authoritarian and indoctrinating; it provides no alternative to the traditional school but only makes its defects more glaring.

"In the school of tomorrow, the television camera will be the king, served by the computer, large screens and small screens, tape recorders and a terrifying number of teaching machines. The school of tomorrow will be the realm of electronics, audio-visual aids, magnetic tapes, invisible pulses and the punched card... Shall we pay a visit to this school of the future, starting with the elementary school?... As we go into a classroom with 20 or 30 pupils we see, instead of the traditional desks, a series of little wood and steel tables. There is no exercise book in front of the child, but a keyboard with four buttons. The teacher does not say a word but on his desk is a machine like a large tape-recorder, on its panel four automatic indicators and the same number of lights as there are children. If he needs to make a roll call, the children are merely asked to press a button".[11]

This is taken from an account by an Italian journalist visiting the New York World Fair in 1964-65 to see a display of the school of the future. It all seems a mere figment of the imagination, but since such a school is still based on seeing, listening and replying, these "electronic" pupils are no more than traditional pupils.

We have quoted from this account because it refers to something that was seen by 70 million visitors to the World Fair, and introduced to hundreds of millions through the press and television, and as it was considered to be the nec plus ultra of efficiency.

Programmed learning helps to:
– renew the content of education;
– structure the subject in logical form;
– make learning more individual;
– evolve a new concept of the evaluation of learning.

But is programmed learning really more efficient than the traditional methods? It is difficult to compare the two directly. To view the function of programmed learning in the school of the future in perspective, we must consider it not in isolation but in the light of research methods, the incentive it provides to creativity, expressive ability and socialisation. While the traditional methods apply to the whole of schooling, programmed learning is only one of the features of the new school. We must compare the two types of education in their entirety, not the old regime (a whole) with programmed learning (which is only a part).

Not every subject has a logical structure that lends itself to programming. The learning psychology on which the programme is based does not cover every possible form of learning. Education does not, moreover, consist merely of learning but also of production through use of intuitive and divergent thought. Divergence – in other words, creativity – is one factor that is not covered by programmed learning.

The principle that the student must learn one fact before he can go on to the next, proof of such learning being given by his reply, does not always apply. It may be valid when facts must be marshalled in logical order, when they follow one another in succession, but not in the case of cognitive organisation of another kind; creative work, for instance, needs varying periods of incubation, rough approximation, tentative excursions in different directions. On the other hand, pro-

---

[11] Livio Pesce, "Sono an dato a scuola del Duemila", *Epoca*, 3 Maggio 1969.

grammed logic is not the same as the logic inherent in the generating and transforming medium, language and behaviour. It is merely a logic evolved by the programmer to assist in certain aspects of structural learning.

All this means that programmed learning by itself is not synonymous with the school of the future, for it cannot cater adequately for the whole breadth of intellectual activity. Its aim is to make effective use of convergent thought (in other words, thinking that is directed towards assimilating the correct information supplied by the programme), using individual techniques. Learning is acquired through logical and structural understanding of the subject, which is broken down into component parts and arranged in an order which will enable the student gradually to build up his knowledge until he has become master of a cognitive whole. We would repeat, however, that the cognitive structures involved in programmed learning are by no means the same as the deep-rooted structures, the structures that correspond to the productive laws of the mind with which the structuralists are concerned.

Programmed learning fails to reach two important areas: research, which makes use of divergent thought, intuition and creation; and socialisation, a process that is hard to rationalise or circumscribe because it involves the subconscious and a complex set of motivational factors.

DIFFERENTIAL CLASSES AND DIFFERENTIAL TREATMENT

Research on the various ways of grouping pupils to provide the best possible educational setting began about 60 years ago. The main focus of attention was the needs of the less gifted and those who had a low achievement rate in traditional classes.

The people who investigated differences between individuals and tried to discover methods of providing individual education had great faith in streaming, especially for those of below average ability. To reduce the range of ability in a class, which was considered an obstacle to providing help to individual pupils, aggravating initial handicaps and failing to provide sufficient incentive for those of higher ability, seemed to be one of the most outstanding and unquestioned successes in the application of psychology to education. However, as psychological research advanced and tended to look at the personality as a dynamic whole in its life space, faith in the criterion of homogeneity started to crumble. Doubts arose as to whether the intellectual factor alone was responsible for differences or whether that intellectual ability, or lack of it, was due to personal disposition; social and cultural influences, it came to be believed, played a large part.

Today, stimulated by social and political concern with education and by experimental research, there is a growing trend in favour of the abolition of streaming. This may not, however, be a clear step towards progress: it may simply deny the existence of pupils with special difficulties and suggest optimistic solutions which, by leaving things as they are, evade the basic problems faced by the school and make poor use of psychology. This is the case when it is sustained that ordinary classes, organised as they are at present, can absorb pupils of different levels of ability as they represent a negative displacement from the norm. Critical abolitionism, on the other hand, a theory which supports de-streaming on the grounds that the mechanisms of the mind are adversely affected by external causes, is quite another matter.

The structuralistic concept of invariance provides another approach to the problem; negative differences are superstructures and if the basic structures can be activated, these differences will to a great extent be smoothed over.

If true progress is to be achieved, the advocates of de-streaming should support the idea that the whole school should be "individualised", that is, it should be made radically different from the existing school in which the performance and behaviour of pupils are reinforced by an educational régime which, instead of catering for their legitimate needs, uphold the mechanisms of social discrimination.

An additional point is that pupils may frequently be placed in lower streams not because they are of low ability but because their talents lie in different directions from those traditionally approved by the school. A lively child who refuses to conform to school routine and is capable of arriving at divergent solutions is very likely to be regarded as a trouble maker and will be punished or even placed in a lower stream than his ability warrants. Finally, streaming is a drastic substitute for differential treatment. A child must be considered as an individual, not by segregating him but by using educational measures that can penetrate those basic structures that have been neutralised or deviated by adverse social and cultural conditions. Differences should not be institutionalised; instead, there should be fluid individualisation in educational space which expands social experience and encourages the mobilisation of critical and creative powers in order to compensate for original disadvantages.

We have described the concept of "differential residue, i.e., the differences that remain after the removal of the effects of unfavourable social and cultural condition. This helped us to emphasise the need to turn the problem on its head: granted (a mistaken interpretation of individual differences, which are used as the foundation for methods of individualisation and differential teaching techniques without scientific justification and which are, in practice, ineffective), the following problems must be tackled:
- are the differences really negative or are they merely divergent?
- what kind of experience has led to the negative differences?
- what abilities have not been stimulated?
- what is the relationship between behaviour at school and the social and emotional factors?
- how can the obstacle be removed and how can we provide a favourable setting (achievement of structural invariance)?
- to what adverse extra-scholastic influences are the negative differences due?

This analysis shows that it would be arbitrary to speak of the "less gifted" (in terms of innate, natural gifts) or to differentiate between levels of ability as if these were not associated with experience.

Is the school capable of carrying out its educational role or do its programmes, methods and objectives reinforce the adverse effect of conditioning? This is the basic problem. It is not sufficient, however, to send pupils to an educational psychologist for a summary assessment, for it is the responsibility of the school to make a general critical examination of the problem. The aim of this critical review should be to find out whether:
- the teachers are professionally qualified in their own subjects and educational psychology;
- there is an opportunity for true individualisation and a wide range of activities, including the availability of laboratory situations and equipment;
- an adequate psychological, sociological, medical and educational counselling service is provided;
- the school is not making irrational demands so that performance is equated above all with the ability to conform;
- learning and output are motivated by a feeling for the problem and by research methods, encouraging cultural initiative, creativity and the acceptance of responsibility;

– topical problems play a central part, with the greatest possible stress being placed on culture;
– the academically retarded are not relegated to a back position and the maladjusted are helped to solve their problems of personal relationships, in other words, whether the prime concern is socialisation;
– the whole educational environment is conducive to mental health;
– cooperation from the family can be sought.

If the school is in default, streaming serves only to reinforce and aggravate the effects of social discrimination.

We have described this hypothesis to give some idea of the extent of the area of maladjustment which can be reduced or even eliminated. There is a vital need to overcome pseudo-differences or induced differences, to counteract the effects of conditioning, to distinguish between functional inability and personal limitations. The only form of differentiation which can be justified, we would repeat, is that form which affects the whole of the school, radically transforming it from the foundations up.

It is one thing to recognise differences, another to institutionalise them. Instead, we must deploy new methods and new organisational modules affecting the school as a whole (for example by "activity points", laboratory situations and specialist areas to facilitate the channelling of productive energy, individualisation and social intercourse). The whole problem of streaming or non-streaming, differentiation or non-differentiation, of separating the low ability children or even the highly intelligent, is one that has been untouched by the programmes, methods and systems of the traditional school structure.

A critical review of streaming is of value when planning for the future only if it is based on a school model of which there are as yet few examples. Team teaching, the open plan school, nongrading, laboratory structures and, to a lesser degree, the dual progress plan (Stoddard) are all developments which will help to eliminate not only streaming but the very division of the school into classes for what are considered to be normal children. This is a far more radical innovation than can be brought about by educational technology alone.

WORK AS AN INTRODUCTION TO TECHNOLOGY AND THE MANAGEMENT OF SOCIAL SERVICES

It is one thing to enjoy the fruits of technological progress – and, in that enjoyment, we usually stress the fact that we live in a world that is dominated by technology – and quite another to receive a technologically orientated cultural and functional education. A technological education helps to combat the alienation of technical conditioning. Manual work, a form of technology, must be a major feature of the school of tomorrow for many reasons – cultural, social and emotional adaptation.

If the school of tomorrow is to produce "electronic and computerised pupils" linked not with one another but with mechanisms that can transmit information and check replies with astonishing speed, there will be no place in that school for manual work which, in the primary school, is very close to craftsmanship, and which is very far removed from the industrialisation of educational processes.

The expression "manual work" is not in fact the proper term, for it lays the emphasis upon the sensory-motor aspects of tasks which, while they are carried out with the hands and tools, are intellectualised, in other words they substantially modify basic education and, far from being one-sided, contribute to both cultural and social development.

Contemporary educational psychologists have pointed out the educational value of work, continuing on the same lines as the pioneers of the "active school".[12] Up to the present, however, nobody has gone so far as to say that work is a process of socialisation capable of bringing out the full potential of man and of providing equality of educational opportunity to all. In other words, the democratic system of education can put up no convincing argument against the technical and social division of labour, although the same could be said with equal truth of the educational system in countries which have eliminated capitalism but not the hierarchy of power.

We now need to go beyond the level of specialised research on the educational value of work, however scientifically accurate this may appear. In fact, decisive steps in a new direction have been made possible not by this kind of research but by bold hypotheses combined with critical examination of ideological and political concerns. Specialist research is still conducted in an atmosphere of prejudice and camouflage and does not tackle the basic social (and political) problems, with the result that it confirms differences totally unjustified by the intellectual potential of each individual (and this in turn leads to

---

[12] John Dewey, for example, uses the concept of educational work to indicate not only the activisation of the school but also the social importance of the school both within its own community constitution and in respect of its need to be linked with progressive social movements.

the underemployment of individual intelligence through the division of labour, which is the true reason for alienation).

The barriers created by the division of labour constitute one of the reasons why the democratic school is still a class school, inspired by the ideology of the "industrial state". The concern of this ideology with progress in the means of production serves only to cover up the problem – the only truly significant problem – of man's relationship with production.

If the school is to continue to be inspired by that ideology, it will be the equivalent of progress in technology and science, which it is believed will bring benefits to all but which in fact is a poor substitute for a radical transformation of society. The division of labour and the division of society into classes[13] may be historical facts, but they are not warranted by substantial differences in intellectual potential.

Educational practice always lags behind the findings of science, but it is particularly inadequate in its relations to work. Manual crafts in the primary school do contribute a little, but these are merely sops and there is no systematic planning or method in their teaching and they lead to no substantial change. Even science, in specific research projects, may be ideologically predetermined and unable to face the problem of the relationship between educational work in the school and work in society.

There is a tendency for work activities to be considered merely as exercises, justified by their general educational value, but whose effects are bound to be wasted, as are those of expressive activities. We would repeat that while the social irrelevance of work in educational practice is deplorable, still more serious is the fact that psycho-pedagogic and didactic research on the subject is inadequate.

Actual social experience of work can contribute towards abolishing privileges or disadvantages, to achievement of equality of status not in the fictitious community of the school but in society at large. True progress will have been made when work in the school paves the way both to a new culture and to new intellectual processes and to new behaviour patterns.

A job that makes few technical demands is humiliating only if the

---

[13] Recent criticism is particularly incisive on the connection between the division of labour and the division of classes. For Italian contributions see: Michele Salvati and Bianca Bettalli "Divisione del lavoro" *Quaderni Piacentini*, n. 40, 1970; Carlo Donolo, "Progresso tecnico-scientifico e lotta di classe", *Quaderni Piacentini*, n. 41, 1970; Francesco Ciafaloni, "Divisione del lavoro e lotte operaie", *Quaderni Piacentini*, n. 41, 1970.

category of people who do that job is labelled as such. If a job is not humiliating, everyone must be prepared to do it. This applies not only to the school but also to a non-hierarchical society. In a forward-looking (but not a Utopian) vision of the society of tomorrow, we can discern two processes:
– minimisation of the *division of labour* (which is always alienating) as the result of technical and scientific progress; and
– the distribution of jobs among the largest number of people, so that everybody can do work that benefits *society*, the specialised activities, and engage in *free activities*.

In the field of science, there has been great emphasis upon "conceptual frameworks" and on "systems of ideas", but these ensure no more than efficiency. It would be better to place more stress upon "social frameworks" and on "political systems".

Research is of course conditioned by the type of problem being solved or the phenomenon being explained. In consequence, once it is realised that the problem is being considered in too narrow a sense, that the researchers are insensitive to the problem of the technical and social division of labour, there will surely be pressure to undertake research on the type of education that will really help to counteract this division.

If work no longer plays a subservient role in the school and if the exercises through which work is introduced to children are enriched, it has a major contribution to make to the new form of basic education. The goals are these: not merely manual dexterity and sensory-motor control, but knowing through doing, development of the perceptive and logical mechanisms (familiarity with the laws that govern the way in which the components of a product are fitted together), a readiness to adapt to objects, experience in cooperation, critical understanding of the role of production in society, laying the ground work for job mobility to combat hierarchical distinctions.

The aims of conceptual structuring and inventiveness as well as the social relevance of work mean that it is no longer possible to sustain the desirability of distinguishing between men and women's work according to the traditional concept of their roles.

Work must be associated with expressive activities in the future so that the object produced is not merely functional and appropriate for the use envisaged, but also aesthetic. This design of an object for a given function may differ very widely. This is the reason for the link between technology and aesthetic education, for the product must satisfy our need to make our mark upon our environment through the creation of beautiful objects.

The affinity of the materials and working techniques with the properties and qualities of a product is a point of departure for research of enormous interest. Our personal contribution to a product is to respond in an inventive way to the limitations imposed by the materials and by the techniques that we must use.

To conduct technological research means to plan, to select materials, to ensure that we have the proper means, to use tools, equipment, special devices, to make measurements, to experiment, to keep within the permitted tolerances.

Although we cannot expect primary school children to make very complex products, in planning for the final object children will be introduced to technical design, a craft that they will need to solve the problem of making the product suitable for its function. The inventiveness they need for this work of technical design can be effectively developed only if many conditions are satisfied: children think about materials, instruments, working systems and cost (and in this latter case they will come to realise that work is connected with the social science of economy).

Technological research has its roots in science, in the sense that an object is constructed and functions in accordance with principles determined by science, so that technological research is a way of gaining concrete knowledge of those principles. We do not merely observe phenomena, we recreate them for ourselves, carrying out experiments on their characteristics, ascertaining how they develop. We must not be content with one set of facts but must use these facts to make generalisations. Nonetheless, technological research is not the easy and direct result of science. In this lies the originality of technology; it requires the exercise of mental powers which is invaluable, too, in general education. To neglect technology means to deprive the intellect of a fundamental stimulus.

The links between history and technology are manifest: there are always technological components in historic changes. The production and use of new materials and tools, the invention of new mechanisms and processes, the shift from artisan work to more advanced levels of industrial production: these are all things which have altered working conditions, earnings, human conditions, educational systems, family life, leisure and the production and use of the arts.

Even when the school includes work, it is probably the most misrepresented educational occupation because it is given no social meaning and does not involve the intellect. It is hard to shake off the idea that the true work of the child is to study, to be educated. He is not expected to produce, to contribute to preserving or transforming the community in which he lives or to provide for his own needs and those of his companions. Educational work tends to be non-productive and irrelevant from the social point of view. In the desire to prevent work from being contaminated by over-professionalism, it is rendered fictitious. In most cases, therefore, the work done in the school is of a low technological standard and has no social purpose. Even when work activities are included in the school, nobody questions the rights or wrongs of the technical and social division of labour; this is accepted as natural. Everything is ordered to confirm the idea that even if the children are made to do certain very ordinary, humble things, these are only done as exercises and at a later stage the privileged will no longer have to do them. In the same way, no objection is raised to the fact that many of those who are given a basic culture at the school will then be directed towards occupations which make no cultural demands upon them. Work can develop its educational potential if it can be seen in its social context, if, through work, children can be introduced to production, one of the pillars of society. It would be unreasonable to argue that it is not the task of the school to work for abolition of segregation between social classes. Since work in the school provides contact with cultural problems and behaviour and is untrammelled by any concept of hierarchy of jobs, it has an essential role in that it can help to end the conflict between technical and manual jobs on the one hand and intellectual occupations on the other, as now exists in today's technical and social division of labour. This division works against a democratic educational curriculum and a society in which we are trying to eliminate inequality due to exploitation.

When the school occupies a new place in society, work will gain its full social significance as the organised activity of services for which the pupils are made responsible. Social sciences will be confined to a small cognitive circle without any practical relevance unless they are linked with a type of social education that is not institutionalised and imposed upon the pupils but that is the outcome of their own attempts to solve the problem of optimum organisation.

In the field of research, it is no longer believed that freedom of movement and initiative cannot exist when there are organisational modules through which this freedom and initiative can be channelled in a constructive form. In the same way, research on socialisation in small groups is tending to be integrated with the study of wider social settings, from the school environment to all the other environments which to some degree affect individual development. The psychology of the primary school child will take on a truly new aspect when research arrives at a better definition of production and organisation, extending his intellectual and social experience. This is a point that we must stress: although fluidity of educational space, the provision of incentives for creativity, the raising of the level of programmes, are all trends that already exist in the more advanced school innovations, the same cannot be said of those activities inaccurately called "manual". We believe that development activities will be one of the features of future changes in education, as they increase the pupil's capacity to respond and broaden his area of experience.

CONCLUSION

There is, as we have seen, a state of crisis in the social sciences, a crisis which also affects educational psychology. It is only partially true that research has leaped so far ahead of practical achievement that scientific findings must be vigorously applied if research is to be translated into practice in the future.

It is our belief that one of the most vital factors in the future will be scientific imagination, which is very different from the methods used in "narrow" research. The technical accuracy of narrow-based research may mask ideological preconceptions and may be used to justify the status quo.

We should question how a new school model – such as has already been created in several places, – can co-exist in a social order which attempts to perpetuate grave inequalities between men, precisely those inequalities that no school of psycho-pedagogical thought concerned with the essential issues should tolerate. The fact is that the new models of the school are too easily inserted into the existing structure of society and are not providing a true alternative that will compete with the current scale of values.

4. PERSONALITY, FAMILY AND SOCIAL FACTORS OF ACHIEVEMENT

BY

ORNELLA ANDREANI DENTICI

This is a report on the preliminary results of research conducted by the Institute of Psychology of Pavia University (Faculty of Arts) and Milan University (Faculty of Medicine) for IARD Association, Milan, and the Van Leer Foundation, The Hague. We hope they will help to clarify some urgent issues of school policy and educational strategy.[1]

The general aim of the project is to study factors which influence school achievement and maladjustment and to try out ways of counteracting the effects of cultural deprivation in early years.

The following specific objectives have been established:
1. Study of environmental factors (family, status) which influence the formation of intellectual structures.
2. Study of environmental factors which influence the formation of personality traits and the socialisation processes connected with success at school.
3. Correlations between social class and linguistic ability, both with regard to comprehension and production.
4. Typical profiles of under-achievers, compared with over and normal-achievers.
5. Study of methods of preventing maladjustment and under-achievement, especially enrichment of the pupil's concrete and linguistic experience and the devising of appropriate exercises.
6. Trying out these methods in experimental classes.

To achieve these aims, we worked in sequential phases, beginning with statistical analysis. First of all we explored the relationships between the variables correlated with success at school in a large sample (Sample A, No. = 2565); then we checked the first hypothesis, by

---

[1] The full report with technical details will be published in a book edited by the IARD Association, sponsored by the Van Leer Foundation. Our report refers only to the conclusions having greater relevance to the problem of new trends in education.

clinical and experimental methods, on a smaller sample taken from the former (Sample B, No. = 72); finally, we returned to the former to examine other aspects which emerged from the first analysis.

After examining the averages for intelligence and achievement tests in groups of different social classes, for instance, we found that the greatest differences were in reading ability; as a result we decided to make a detailed examination of linguistic ability in the small sample. Since only a general outline was evolved of the relationships between the social family environment and school adjustment in the large sample, we decided to embark on more radical research on the small sample, studying the affective, motivational and dynamic factors influencing inter-personal relationships in the family and at school.

Then, taking the preliminary findings derived from research on Samples A and B and comparing them with a wide range of reports and discussions in the literature, the team of educational experts decided on the type of action needed to counteract the causes of failure at school from the very start, working not only with maladjusted children or those whose achievement was decidedly low, but also, from the first year of primary school, with those whose lack of ability and mode of behaviour could well lay the foundation for cumulative deficit. In this way, attention is being directed not merely to children who are maladjusted *now* but to all those whose achievement fails to match their ability at any level and who may become maladjusted in the future when faced with greater difficulties in their studies.

The sample for the educational experiment, which we call Sample C, consists of 7 experimental plus 7 control classes, paired in intelligence and differing in social class, chosen because of the frequency of underachievers among the class 1 subjects of Sample A.

This experiment directed by Dr. Cavallini, which exploits a variety of remedial and enrichment techniques to combat the effects of cultural deprivation, particularly in language ability, is still in progress and will not be discussed here. We shall merely review the results of the psychological part, although these have not yet been fully analysed.

PART ONE – SMALL SAMPLE: FINDINGS

Since the subjects in the small sample were examined individually and chosen according to a factorial pattern, it was possible to carry out additional research aimed at analysing the dynamic processes which underlie and sustain:

A. the mechanism of intellectual operations
B. linguistic mediations
C. interactions between children, family and school.

A. *Intellectual operations*

Dr. Barbieri and Dr. Vegetti applied experimental tests, graded according to difficulty, derived from Piaget, to find out how subjects use time and causality concepts. We first tested the children's comprehension of simple time sequences and comparisons of duration, then the concept of age related to birth order, and finally the concept of old age and youth related to the life span. Three sub-tests involved a concrete operation, an intermediate and a formal operation. Our basic aim was to examine the effect of independent variables (status and intelligence measured by the Gille and Cattell tests) on the acquisition of reversibility and on the development of hypothetic-deductive thinking.

The results confirm the succession of stages found by Piaget. The social class being constant, we found significant differences between levels of intelligence; when intelligence was constant we found consistent but not significant differences between social classes.

This shows, on the one hand, that the results of Piagetian tests of operational level and the Culture Fair tests are comparable and, on the other, that status differences in cognitive mechanisms are not yet relevant at this age, when concrete thinking still prevails, though it is beginning to move towards formal reasoning. This is only true of non-verbal tasks, however, where interpretation of experience does not yet require the ability to generalise at a high level of formalisation. Even when intelligence is equal, there are slight but consistent differences in favour of the higher classes, namely in the most difficult sub-tests demanding a greater capacity for abstract thought; we can predict, therefore, that these differences will become more serious as the child grows older, as language ability certainly plays an important role in the development of formal thinking.

Further research is needed to confirm this hypothesis by repeating our test at the age of 11-14 years, in an attempt to identify the role of verbal formalisation in the comprehension of principles and in the development of formal reasoning.

To study causality, we employed questions on natural phenomena (origin of night and movement of clouds) and experiments on floating and sinking objects of different volume and specific gravity.

Here too, we found the Piaget stages: logic and ontological egocentricism, with its typical insensitivity to contradiction; finalistic explanation; and finally, physical explanations. The first two sub-tests, which required verbal reasoning (though this is based on everyday experience), are definitely influenced by the child's status. Subjects belonging to higher social classes tend to use physical or intermediate models, while a third of the boys from lower social classes use the egocentric model. Contrary to the findings of the test on time concepts, the most mature physical explanations of causality correlate with over-achievement and appear, therefore, to be more influenced by school learning. This does not occur in the floating test, which requires the subject actively to manipulate objects, as well as demanding explanation and prediction. In this task, the differences between groups are closely correlated with intelligence but not with social class.

Since the questions about time were in the form of realistic drawings depicting differences in age and duration in a concrete form, we may infer that the differences in operational level are not linked with social class but with individual levels of maturity, while the influence of status is apparent as soon as the operations involve the use of cultural information and verbalisation. The floating sub-test, which required the child to infer a physical law, proved of special interest for educational purposes, because it showed how active teaching based on experiments conducted at school can be understood even by disadvantaged children, unlike formal, verbal teaching that assumes previous cultural experience. It is important, however, that concrete experience also be verbalised to lay the foundations of abstraction and generalisation.[2] In this field, our Institute is studying, at junior high school level, the effect of methods derived from Suchman's Inquiry Training, which seem particularly promising in stimulating the discovery of causal relations and the formalisation of physical laws.

B. *Linguistic mediations*

The role of linguistic factors as mediators of the structures of cognition was investigated in two more research projects, using the same sample of children. Dr. Baldi and Dr. Duse examined written and oral production, analysing three essays and the stories told to four TAT tables by means of 90 language variables. These were divided into three groups:

---

[2] With regard to the relationship between thinking and verbalisation, note the important experiments conducted by Russian workers such as Vygotsky, Luria and others.

1. *morpho-lexical variables* (of a simple type, such as the number of nouns, adjectives, verbs and so on, and of the ratio type, such as the type token).
2. *syntactic variables* (such as the number and the type of sentences, various indices of subordination such as those of Loban, Lawton and the T unit).
3. *variables indicative of doubts and mistakes* in the use of language, repetitions, uncertainty, incorrect use of verbs and pronouns.

We made an analysis of variance to find out the effects of intelligence, status and discrepancy, to verify Bernstein's hypotheses on the elaborated and restricted code.[3] Our results confirm Bernstein's theories (1958-1970) only in so far as written language is concerned, while in oral production the most important differences proved to be associated with intelligence rather than status.

In particular, our investigation showed that individual temperament, status and intelligence, have a different influence on the various dimensions of language behaviour and that some of these may be more greatly affected by education.

a) In oral language ability, *productivity*, chiefly manifested by the number of words and of nouns, adjectives, verbs, adverbs and pronouns, is correlated with individual traits (probably with the "fluidity" factor) and is a function of the stimulus situation, also affected by status.

b) *The variables that show richness of vocabulary and lexical ability* are correlated with status and school achievement, both in oral and in written language.

c) On the other hand, *syntactic variables* are more closely related to intelligence than to status, especially in oral production. Yet our investigation shows the inadequacy of the measures traditionally used for measuring syntactic complexity and points out the need for new research to study the deep-rooted structures of language ability in terms of transformational grammar.

d) The various *indices of grammatical uncertainty and correctness* are most closely correlated to status and school achievement, and they rise considerably in upper class children, especially in the written language.

The minor, or sometimes even non-existent, significance of differences between social classes that we found in oral production provides

---

[3] We prefer this distinction which is clearer than the one previously used by the author in the expression, "public and formal language".

food for thought. In an informal situation, dissociated from the school, in which the child gave full vent to his imagination, talking about his personal problems, free from the patterns imposed by the school (as he was when answering the TAT), productivity increased and the only differences that were noted related to individual traits (not even to intelligence). Nonetheless, such productivity was marked by poor language, with limited vocabulary, grammatically incorrect and syntactically poor, as in Bernstein's restricted code. The fact that the differences were exaggerated in written language and in the Reading Test scores (for Vocabulary, Speed and Comprehension) shows up the great inadequacy of school. It could be said that differences between social classes are greatest in the abilities acquired at school, where there should in principle be greatest equality. This is especially serious, as it leads to a series of negative consequences not confined to low marks in purely linguistic subjects (mother tongue, foreign languages and classical languages): it means that the child is ill-prepared for learning other subjects for which reading is instrumental, reducing his ability to understand, communicate and conduct interpersonal relationships, condemning him to a position of inferiority and isolation that will give rise to a negative attitude towards school and finally (the most serious aspect) limiting the development of mechanisms of cognition, stunting the processes of symbolisation and abstraction.[4] As these results so greatly affect education, they emphasise the need for developing language ability through a well-planned series of experiences bringing out the ability to communicate, to compare different standpoints, to establish reversible relations, to infer laws and deduce their consequences and to construct and try out predictions and hypotheses. We are against both the rhetorical exercise of writing and speaking without doing (including mystifying forms such as "Talk about the subject you like best"), and the practice of spontaneous manipulation of materials without verbalisation.

The latter stimulates action but not speech or writing, is instantly exhausted and is not stored in long-term memory unless it attains the level of symbolic representation. Our findings on operational mechanisms point to three conclusions:

1. In traditional schooling, too much weight is given to speaking and writing, penalising children with language difficulties, particularly those from the poorest social classes. This by no means devalues the

---

[4] This should be viewed in conjunction with the results of our experiments on causality.

Personality, Family and Social Factors of Achievement

importance of teaching linguistic ability, but the true function of language is to act as a means of interpersonal communication and the structural vehicle for thought.

2. The aim must not be to teach grammar or vocabulary, not to set academic exercises, but to make use of the opportunities afforded by experience and social life to stimulate verbalisation, the exchange of views and to generalisation and the summarising of conclusions drawn from actual experience.
3. Learning situations must be set up that stimulate the child's development of concrete, and then of formal, reasoning. These experiments should also accustom him to following manipulation with verbalisation, formulating principles and hypotheses, and finally to dominate experience (as described by Bruner) through mastery of different kinds of symbolic language: verbal, numerical, musical or graphic.
4. Interpersonal relationship situations must be created that encourage communication and a comparison of opinions, both to stimulate "decentralisation" and the formation of operational patterns, and to foster a climate of spontaneity and anti-authoritarianism in which creativity is stimulated and rewarded, in which the ego can shed anxiety and tension and regain its autonomy.

It might be assumed that over-achievers, whose success is higher than their potential at the cost of greater anxiety, will prove to be less creative than their school fellows, despite being more "intelligent", according to the traditional type of test. We intend to verify this hypothesis when we examine the written work of the Sample A groups.

C. *The interactions between children, family and school*

As this topic has been studied on the basis of analytical data derived both from the small and the large sample, we shall present the results in Part Two, paragraph 4.

PART TWO – LARGE SAMPLE: FINDINGS

A. *Intelligence and achievement tests*

The scores in the two Culture Fair Tests (Gille and Cattell) and in the two Achievement Tests (Mathematics and Reading) were standardised as T-scores to facilitate comparison between groups and to compute indices of over/under-achievement. The group was composed on the hypothesis that it is necessary to identify subjects whose achievement is above or below their intellectual potential. If it is inferior, we can adopt an educational policy that will compensate for cultural disadvantage and remove the causes of emotional disturbance; if it is superior, the subjects are usually apparently well integrated but may meet stress situations later, for they are working at a level that makes continual demands upon their abilities due to an excessive desire for achievement or to family pressure. In this case, too, it is possible to apply educational techniques that prevent maladjustment by encouraging socialisation and the formation of stable personality structures.

To measure the discrepancy between achievement and intelligence, we chose the difference between the standardised indices obtained from combining the culturally weighted scores in Achievement Tests and the scores in the Culture Fair Tests. We then graded the discrepancy as "average", "positive" or "negative" on the basis of distribution, considering the norm to be between $+9$ and -9; this category included 50 per cent of the subjects. The difference is probably due to minor fluctuations in performance, measurement errors and so on.

We shall analyse in turn:
1. Differences in average scores in groups classified according to the father's and mother's occupation, education, socio-economic level, size of family and birth order.
2. Distribution of over/under-achievement according to intelligence and socio-economic levels.
3. Personality traits in different groups of over/under-achievers.

1) Differences in intellectual ability between social classes

We examined the differences in single sub-tests, total scores and cumulative indices of intelligence and achievement.

In dividing the groups according to class, we used a socio-economic index suggested by R. Havighurst, giving a weighting of 3 to the occupation and a weighting of 2 to the father's educational standard. We classified fathers' occupations in 6 levels, taking earnings and social prestige into account. The mothers were grouped in only 4 levels, since a very high percentage (80-85 per cent of every age) did not have a job outside the home. We also examined the influence of the educational level of each parent, keeping it separate from occupations, since the "housewife" category included women with an average or high level of education, a factor that undoubtedly has a bearing on the child's education. On the other hand, many fathers between 35 and 45 years of age, in a flourishing commercial city such as Milan, have attained high economic levels despite a low standard of education. Since, in addition to group tests, we compiled questionnaires on family aspirations, educational goals and the kind of educational assistance provided at home, we considered it important to distinguish between economic and cultural factors, both of which contribute to the formation of attitudes towards study, career aspirations and incentives and offer the children the support of economic stability and a cultural background.

On the whole the findings confirm similar research carried out in other countries, but they provide some clarification on the influence of each parent.

a) The average scores in all tests rise with social class, although the Gille Test appears to be less dependent upon culture since the questions are presented in the form of drawings of concrete objects or everyday situations, while the Cattell Test, although not verbal, is symbolic in form.

The greatest differences in achievement were found in the Reading Test, particularly in Speed and Comprehension, rather than in the Vocabulary sub-test. This is very important, because the ability to read rapidly and understand a written text, understanding the implication of a passage, is of paramount importance in most school learning.[5] To take the cumulative indices of intelligence and achievement, we found a difference of 14 T-scores in intelligence (from 95 to 109) between the lowest[6] and the highest class[7], but the difference increases to 23 T-scores in achievement (from 89 to 112). These differences are influenced to an extent by the occupational status of the *father*, which in practice usually determines income, but more so by the level of education of the *mother*, who is in closer contact with the child.

Since the greatest differences are always between the lowest and the intermediate level, it is probable that once economic and cultural conditions are levelled up to the average, eliminating extreme differences, if not all class differences, under-achievement due to social and cultural factors will disappear.

---

[5] We have, therefore, conducted research on language ability discussed in the preceding paragraph.
[6] Lowest class: manual workers, unskilled workers with only primary education.
[7] Highest class: managers and professionals with university degrees.

b) Under-achievement largely prevails in the lowest class, while over-achievement is more frequent in the top brackets and is more influenced by the mother's level of education. In fact, achievement increases when the mother's education was at least at junior high school level.

Other important factors are family size and birth order. Only children score higher in achievement, while children from larger families do less well (from 102 to 88); intelligence also decreases, but to a lesser degree (from 98 to 93). Only children are in the first group in reading ability, but not in the intelligence test (average = 98 compared with 100 and 101 for first and second children. The fact that only children and the first-born are more likely to be in the high achievers and over-achievers groups, combined with the influence of the mother's educational level, emphasises the effects of environmental stimulation and family care, particularly in the development of linguistic abilities.

2) Distribution of over/under-achievement to social and intellectual level

We examined distribution according to social and economic level and intelligence, because the analysis of group average scores produced less significant results as the positive and negative scores tended to cancel each other out. Normal-achievers are evenly distributed over the three social classes (20, 52 and 28 per cent); over-achievers occur more frequently in the upper class (28 compared with 18 per cent), while under-achievers are infrequent (11 compared with 30 per cent).

In other words, if we remember that over and under-achievers represent approximately 25 per cent of the population as a whole, working class over-achievers are inferior to expectation by one-third and higher class under-achievers are two-thirds inferior.

This phenomenon is complicated by the relationship with intelligence, which is also unevenly distributed, with an excess of gifted children in the higher class (37 compared with 13 per cent from the working class) and an excess of dull children in the working class (42 compared with 10 per cent from the higher class).

Since our "discrepancy score" was calculated as a deviation from intelligence, and indicates a level of achievement *relative* to intellectual potential, the range of *absolute* school failure is much larger than the discrepancy scores show. Furthermore, positive discrepancies (over-achievement) are more common in subjects of average and low intelligence: only 10 per cent of over-achievers are highly intelligent children, while 48 per cent are average and 42 per cent are low. On the other hand, 28 per cent of under-achievers are bright, 64 per cent are average and 8 per cent are dull. In other words, under-achievement is characterised by two fairly definite patterns: the first consists of intelligent children from upper or middle classes, whose failure is probably due to emotional and motivational factors; the second pattern is formed by subjects from working, or sometimes middle-class, children of average intelligence. Though this second pattern is approximately twice as common, we were impressed by the extensiveness of the first group. There is in fact a large negative correlation between discrepancy and intelligence ($r = -.40$).

The school must rapidly tackle a two-fold problem that may well lead to pathogenetic consequences: on the one hand, there are normal children who accumulate scholastic deficiencies and frustrations caused by social disadvantage and are likely to drop out of school, while on the other there are gifted children who lose interest in lessons that they find boring and lacking challenge or whose performance is inhibited by over-anxiety or the need for achievement. This is an enormous waste of talent, especially as we could recover borderline low intelligence children by planning an extensive enrichment programme during early infancy and nursery school.

In Italy attention has been focussed on the problem of below average children (which is certainly fair from a humanitarian point of view), but we tend to overlook the fact that the school does not develop the full intellectual potential of normal and gifted children. Educational psychologists should direct all their efforts towards evolving more effective teaching methods, based on a scientific knowledge of the cognitive processes, which will bring out the full potential of all, rather than trying to level all pupils to the *aurea mediocritas* through an education that eliminates difficulty and loses all its elements of challenge for the gifted, while at the same time it is too difficult for the disadvantaged.

It is worth noting that our discussion is based on traditional intelligence tests, which measure the capacity for convergent thinking usually fostered by the school, and that the waste of talent would probably be found to be greater had we assessed divergent thinking, initiative and planning ability, to which less attention is usually paid in the school.

B. *Personality and socialisation*

We divided the large sample into three levels according to status, intelligence and discrepancy. We are now studying personality mechanisms in different sub-groups by means of projective techniques, trying to identify the most frequent patterns of over/under-achievement.

We recognise that there may be an infinite variety of individual cases, because they are the outcome of an intricate combination of intellectual, emotional and social factors which interact to varying degrees. In a large scale examination, however, we must direct attention to personality and educational action. The premise of our research implies criticism of the over-clinical approach in educational psychology, which aims at adapting the individual to the existing structures. We support the belief that *if structures produce actual or potential maladjustment in so many children, those structures and educational methods must be changed*. However, we do not advocate the indiscriminate demolition of the established order and feel that more research is needed on its effect upon individuals at early ages and on the modes of cultural transmission through the family and the school, some of whose positive aspects might be exploited. As we shall see later, when considering the family, for instance, many current opinions require re-examination.

3) *Personality mechanisms in various groups of over/under-achievers*

This part of the analysis is still in progress, due to the complexity of coding projective responses for computer processing. At this juncture, we will discuss only a few of the preliminary findings. These are interesting in that they confirm our hypothesis about over-achievement as a source of *potential* clinical or scholastic maladjustment. In the School Frustration Test constructed by Dr. Vegetti, aggressive responses predominate in male subjects in all areas (frustrating obstacles being represented by schoolmates, teachers and parents, in decreasing order).

Constructive responses are more frequent in girls, who usually show more mature and adaptive behaviour, consistent with their greater precocity and their tendency to conform – factors that have already been revealed by other studies.

Aggressive responses are more frequent in school than in the family area, the highest scores being attained when they are directed towards schoolmates, the lowest when they concern parents. It is noteworthy that normal and over-achievers, particularly when from a higher social class, show strong aggression towards schoolmates and anxiety towards their parents. In other words, aggressive impulses that cannot express themselves towards adults cause the introjection of guilt; in over-achievers aggression is redirected against teachers, in under-achievers against parents. Anxiety responses are directed towards adults having authoritative roles and reach the highest frequency in middle-class over-achievers who consider competitive achievement to be a means of improving status. They are at the minimum in high intelligence normal-achievers.

Constructive responses, which denote a mature and successful attempt to resolve conflict and overcome obstacles, were few, as was to be expected in view of the youth of the subjects (9-10 years), but were more closely correlated with intelligence than with positive achievement. This fact was unexpected and merits further analysis based on an individual approach.

On the whole, these results confirm our comments on intelligence and achievement tests, i.e. that over-achievers form a more homogeneous group, while there are at least two main patterns in under-achievement which originate from various factors. The distinctive feature of over-achievers is a higher frequency of anxiety responses towards adults (in general) and of aggressive responses towards teachers, perhaps because they are driven by a strong need for achievement to acquire status. Since this need provokes excessive tension, spurring the children to overwork and to exploiting their energies to the utmost, it may contain the seeds of neurotic maladjustment which could reveal itself in the future, in high school, when children, particularly those of average or low intelligence, face difficulties that prevent them obtaining the success to which they used to be accustomed and preserving a positive self-image corresponding to their own or their family's expectations.

On the other hand, there is a wider variety of cases of under-achievement, which seem to be determined by cultural disadvantages in working class children and by emotional factors in high and middle class intelligent children. In the first case, the original cultural handicap is later complicated by the emotional troubles to which failure gives rise, while in the second case cultural inferiority is the consequence of inhibition, anxiety or withdrawal.

4) Interactions within the family and with the school

Part of our analysis was concerned with the relationship between class, the cognitive mechanism and linguistic ability, and will be supplemented by more thorough examination of the ways in which family culture affects not only performance, but also motivations, attitudes to study and career aspirations. Another part concerns the family as an emotional support and agent of socialisation. We employed projective techniques constructed for the purpose of analysing interpersonal relationships with adults and with peers in various home and school situations. These techniques employed ambiguous verbal and graphic stimuli to study affective dynamics and evoked a very wide range of responses, which took a long time to score objectively. Since we still do not know whether the tests used refer to the same level of projection, or how these levels are modified by different kinds of stimuli, in the present paper we will merely comment separately on the findings emerging from each test. At a later stage we shall discuss and further analyse the findings in two ways:

a) comparison between the three tests and examination of the comparability of parts dealing with the same areas.

b) a review of the conclusions based on clinical interviews of the subjects in the small sample in the light of the trends identified in the large sample.

DRAWINGS OF THE FAMILY AND INTERVIEWS WITH CHILDREN AND PARENTS

The findings shed light on the child's view of his parents, the child as seen by his father and the influence of the family on socialisation. This last point concerns both the cognitive aspect of family attitudes (what the parents *think* and *say* about socialisation) and actual family behaviour (what the parents *do* to promote social relations in the children, frequency of contacts with relatives and friends, contacts with out-of-school groups and so on). As dependent variables, we examined various aspects of children's socialisation, such as the number of friends, popularity index in the school class, affective expansion index, positive and negative views by peers, parents and teachers.

Summarising the most interesting data found by Dr. Cabassi and Dr. Calegari:

a) The grade and type of socialisation in nine and ten year olds closely

reflect family attitudes, revealing the educational policy of the family rather than individual character aspects.
b) Children's adjustment to family life is largely positive and free from conflict. Parental figures are seen as models with which the children identify and as a source of security and satisfaction of needs.
c) Relationships with teachers seem to be less satisfactory, and at the same time more heterogeneous, than with parents. They are largely determined by status and achievement, with distinct and definite patterns in the sub-groups according to social class, intelligence and discrepancy.

1. Family attitudes and level of socialisation

We found no differences between children from different classes in the number of their friends, in choices by peers, in choices of peers or in general in any index relating to personal relationships. However, "high" families have more frequent contacts with relatives and friends and more often stimulate relationships with out-of-school groups, such as cultural and sports clubs. This attitude is easily explained by the availability of more money, since most clubs and associations require a fee, sometimes substantial (admittance to church-organised activities is free but is linked to religious factors that are not acceptable to all). This strongly underlines the need for organising group activities in school or district centres to provide a valid option to arts or sports clubs which tend to isolate higher class children, enriching school activities by the practice of social behaviour normally associated with the members of higher classes. Children of a higher social class are seen by their teachers in a more positive light than lower class children of equal ability, if their achievement is good. It is interesting to note that highly intelligent under-achievers obtain 70 per cent positive evaluations if they belong to higher classes, but only 30 per cent if they come from the lower end of the scale. Inversely, low intelligence under-achievers receive 75 per cent negative evaluations if they come from the lower classes, but the percentage decreases to 50 per cent if they belong to higher classes.

In other words, teachers' assessments are based on intelligence and achievement, but also emphasise positive or negative aspects in the light of social origin. Upper class under-achievers often receive neutral or cautious assessments because teachers try to differentiate between intellectual potential and actual performance in school subjects, while in evaluating low class under-achievers the negative assessment of achievement reflects on intelligence and on behaviour as a whole, the "halo effect" probably being produced by the existence of socially undesirable traits and manners. Finally, it is worth noting that children of a higher social class are viewed more positively by their parents than lower class children of equal intelligence and achievement, while there is no difference in the views of them held by schoolmates.

The disadvantaged child is heavily handicapped not only by the objective difficulties he meets in school performance due to all the above causes, but also by a dual series of negative evaluations by adults, which probably play a key role in determining his attitudes toward learning and his self-image. This confirms the sequential model developed by Martin Deutsch and co-workers, who relate social disadvantages first with cultural deprivation and linguistic handicaps, and then with school failure and a negative self-image, which in turn determine more failure and frustration whose cumulative effects will often force the child to leave school early.

2. *Personal adjustment in the family*

The analysis of 2,500 drawings of the family by 6, 9 and 10 year old children showed that the children were well adjusted in the family, with a greater frequency of smooth relationships among the girls, a greater inclination to competition and denigration of siblings in boys and, as is obvious, increasing autonomy and independence in 10 year olds.

Though these characteristics are common to all social classes, we found social status differences when examining the children's appreciation of parental figures. Both sexes emphasise the role of the same-sex parent as a model for identification, but while more middle- and upper-class boys depicted their fathers adequately, lower class boys represented a higher percentage of those giving both positive and negative assessments of the father figure. This was marked by showing the father as larger or smaller in the drawing, by his central or non-central position and by the addition or absence of clothing details, ornaments and status/power symbols.

This fact can be explained by two different mechanisms of reaction to frustration resulting from the low social standing of the father: compensation by imagination or compensation by aggression or depression. The phenomenon is certainly due to child's perception of the social role of the father, because it does not appear with regard to the figure of the mother who is usually a housewife and whose role is at least apparently free from social class. Though the data are less extensive and the phenomenon less marked, these results echo the findings of American research on negroes, showing the relationship between a low desire for achievement and the frequent absence of a successful male model. We obtained another indicator of the relevance of the adult figure from the results of test F, constructed by Dr. Vegetti to examine reactions to frustration in different situations connected with school experience (marks, scolding, classwork and homework).

Statistical analysis revealed that responses are significantly different depending on whether the sources of frustration are parents, teachers or schoolmates. In the first and second case many intrapunitive responses appear, while in the third extrapunitive responses predominate, with frequent very strong and immature forms of aggression. This is probably because reactions are more controlled when directed towards adults than towards peers, against whom the child can express his aggressive impulses more freely.

It is interesting that the relationship with parental figures show signs of super-ego introjection and is smoother than with teachers. However, since adult figures on the whole have a determining influence on the most mature responses, in the education field (at least at this age) this should make us take a fresh look at the role of adults. The latter could provide models of cognitive and social behaviour which, if looked upon as supportive rather than as authoritarian, might stimulate more positive behaviour than peer models.

We need long term experiments on the acquisition of adequate models showing appropriate responses to frustration, ways of solving difficult intellectual and social problems and so on. It is a curious fact that there is little organised research directed toward studying the moulding of children's behaviour on adult models and suggestions, while teachers have always recognised, empirically and intuitively, the importance of constructive reactions, which they usually emphasise in intellectual problem-solving, naming them "goodwill, care, zeal, perseverance" and so on.

Though psychological and educational experiments on this topic are difficult to conduct in a scientific way because they require experts and the dedicated cooperation of the teachers, we should consciously aim at organising children-adult relationships in the family and school to perform two essential functions: the *cognitive function*, by offering information, correction, verification in language and reasoning, and the *emotional-social function*, setting an example by, and stimulating the practice of, constructive behaviour. Relevant to this subject are the results of research carried out by Lutte, Mattioli, Proverbio and Sarti on the European adolescent, which clearly reveal that when parents and teachers are chosen as ideal models, they are selected because they offer examples of conscientiousness, love of family, sensitivity, responsibility, altruism and sociability, while their intellectual qualities and professional competence are rarely mentioned.

CONCLUSION

Although the current research project is not yet complete, we feel that our findings offer useful tentative guidelines for educational action. They basically concern two areas:
1. The relationship between social class and intellectual abilities (Culture Fair and Achievement Tests, development of intellectual operations, language ability in the form of reading comprehension, lexical and syntactic ability, fluency and creativity).
2. The relationship between social class and personality traits (reactions to frustration, socialisation patterns in the family and in school, relationship with peers and with adults, career aspirations and identification models).

These two groups of problems have offered data which explain the most common typology of over/under-achievers and enable us to appreciate the underlying factors. Since the under-achievers are characterised by actual maladjustment and the over-achievers by latent, or potential maladjustment, we must face the dilemma of whether it is better to focus attention on achievement or on the psychological security of individuals. If we emphasise the former, as is usually the case in school, we increase emotional disorder (this is the problem of over-achievers), but if we do not foster the acquisition and development of basic abilities and full realisation of intellectual potential, children may drop out or encounter difficulties when they move into higher school levels (this is the problem of under-achievers).

From this point of view, while underlining the potential pathology implied in excess achievement sustained by anxiety and competition, we feel that the emphasis in educational psychology should not be on the clinical approach, but on applying learning theory, fostering intellectual curiosity in children who suffer from cultural deprivation (also to be found in the middle or upper economic levels) and promoting relationships between language and thought.

Finally, we suggest that more work is called for on the problem of the adult model, which we outlined when analysing family drawings.

This line of research is promising not only in its implications concerning the structure of the family, but also for the great and urgent problem of the selection and training of teachers.

II

THE CURRICULUM IN THE PRIMARY SCHOOL

5. MATHEMATICS

BY

LYDIA TORNATORE

INTRODUCTION

Over the past few years, there has been a growing concern with the rethinking of the teaching of mathematics and science, a concern rooted in social and economic motivations. A technological society demands a type of education that differs from the type of training imparted by the school up to this time, as we are constantly being warned by cries of alarm from every quarter, particularly over the past decade.[1] Mathematicians have not waited for the technological explosion before turning their attention to mathematics teaching – the *Commission internationale pour l'enseignement des mathématiques* was formed as long ago as 1908. In 1950, following a meeting between mathematicians and psychologists working on similar problems, the *Commission internationale pour l'étude et l'amélioration de l'enseignement des mathématiques* was set up. Nevertheless, the question received wide scale attention only when its basic social and economic import was realised. The OEEC *Bureau Scientifique* sponsored conferences of renowned mathematicians in Royaumont in

---

[1] The social-economic motivation of the present reforms is recognised as preeminent. Two examples among many! M. Glaymann, in a report to the General Assembly of APMEP in 1967, stated that: "Today, the power of a country is measured by its scientific potential. If we wish to continue to be one of the leading nations, we must give more and more pupils a scientific education. *This is not the case at the present time*: we are living through a period of crisis, young people are deserting the domain of science and are turning towards literary fields. To halt this process, we must rethink our education entirely, its content and its methods. Otherwise, within ten years, *France will be an intellectually underdeveloped nation*. This was the argument I put forward to the Minister of National Education on 4th July last to persuade him to implement a true reform, a reform which will actually *reform*...". (*Bulletin de l'association des professeurs de mathématiques de l'enseignement publique*, n. 257, March-April 1967, p. 119). N. A. Menchinskaya, in the report to a meeting of experts held in Hamburg in 1966: "The problem of improving education in primary mathematics arose in our country, as in others, with the exceptionally rapid growth of science and technology, and the corresponding need to raise the general level of mathematics. Naturally, this should begin in the primary school, where the foundations of learning are laid". (*Mathematics Reform in the Primary School*, UNESCO Institute for Education, Hamburg, 1967, p. 11).

1958, in Dubrovnik in 1960 and in Athens in 1963, which produced concrete recommendations for the "modernisation of mathematics teaching in the secondary school".[2] This concern soon spread to the field of primary education, for two specific reasons:
a) if radical change is to be introduced into the mathematics curriculum at the secondary level, based on an integrated concept of mathematical knowledge, it is obvious that the teaching of mathematics in the primary school must also be fundamentally revised;
b) the findings of psychological research revealed serious shortcomings in the usual concept and teaching of mathematics in the early years.

The combination of mathematical and psychological pressures and methods was to lead to radical change at the primary level as well. Educational theories have contributed little until now, for on the whole educational thought in the early part of this century has not been geared to continuous research[3] or review of the methods of teaching mathematics.

Although the movement for reform of the teaching of mathematics did not originate in the field of educational theory, today it has far-reaching educational implications, especially as this movement is extending its sphere of influence and inspiring similar movements in other sectors. In the first place, there is a renewed interest in the content of teaching, based on several different considerations. The first consideration is the concern for efficiency, the need to train people to master those intellectual tools that they need in a technological civilisation. The second consideration is the reaction against the educational aims that governed the first half of our century. Education as a means of training the intellect is contrasted to education as a means of socialisation; the value of receptiveness is contrasted to the value of direct individual experience; emphasis on learning specific subjects and on the introduction to abstract thought is contrasted to emphasis on learning in total experience situations. The third consideration is the concern for continuity of the developments in education theories over the first few decades of this century. In other words, when we study the problem of education more deeply, defining education as the "bringing

---

[2] Following these meetings the OEEC published: *Mathématiques nouvelles*, Paris, 1961; *Un programme moderne de mathématique pour l'enseignement secondaire*, Paris, 1961; *Mathematics Today*, Paris, 1964.

[3] The only notable exception is Decroly: the educational method theories of the Brussels Ecole Decroly have provided important groundwork. These were developed under the leadership of Paul Libois (see *Journées Pédagogiques*, "Mathématiques", OEEC Programme, Ministry of National Education and Culture, Brussels, 1962.

out of experiences", we find we have to consider the specific content of those experiences, their internal structure and their integration. In this context, the problem of content is closely correlated with the problem of method.

Up to now, the third consideration has not been the main issue. Now, however, mathematicians attempting to revise the teaching of mathematics have been the first to acknowledge the need for a generic theory and to recognise the importance of *method*. Fortunately, we seem to have gone beyond the phase in which it was considered that all that was required was to replace the traditional subjects by "modern" subjects. There is more extensive concern with educational research now than in the past, although this may not necessarily continue. There are other factors that militate against a rethinking of the problem: for instance, the products of modern technology may be introduced into educational practice on a large scale without any true thought for the consequences. Once we have embarked on this process of ever-increasing consumption, with its ruthless internal logic, we are in danger of thinking less of the great educational potential afforded by modern mathematics and being dazzled by the miracles of the latest technological invention. We must not confuse methodological progress with technological progress. It is a danger that is not peculiar to mathematics and science, but it is particularly grave in this sector.

There is another aspect which we should consider when defining the bases of the movement for the introduction of change to the teaching of mathematics and when investigating the direction in which mathematics may develop. There is a general problem of the *efficiency* of teaching, in that the number of people achieving satisfactory standards must be increased. It is a well known fact that the teaching of mathematics is very deficient in this respect, and the reasons for the difficulties encountered in learning mathematics and the failure rate has been receiving attention for some time.

It is of course important that everybody should acquire a grounding in mathematics, but greater emphasis should be placed upon the *function* of mathematics education, not only on its *efficiency*. Perhaps through an in-depth investigation of the problem of providing mathematical education for *all*, we may find a solution to wider educational and social problems (the contribution of basic education to abstract thought, problems of converting an elitist culture into popular culture, etc.). But there is also a danger of seeking no more than efficiency, as if this were a valid goal in itself. Too much emphasis upon efficiency could well lead to a questioning of the value of educational developments, at first generally accepted, and to prevention of their continuance. Here again, the future depends on whether we avoid over-simplification of the problem, as this may adversely affect the development of education by placing undue stress upon certain theories, dogmatically rejecting others that could well be integrated into a general theory of education.

THE ROLE OF MATHEMATICS

As with any other scientific discipline, mathematics is in a continuous state of development, expansion and re-organisation, especially in this century. The mathematics curriculum, as in the case of other disciplines, is outdated. At one time there was a general outcry at the gulf between the mathematics that are taught at school and the mathematics used by the research worker and the technologist. This is not an isolated situation, however, a gulf that occurs only in the case of mathematics: there is comparable gap between science and the type of scientific education imparted in the school, between contemporary history and the history taught at school, between contemporary linguistics and the way in which languages are conveyed to children. This outcry had one beneficial effect: it led to research and intensive experimentation. One of the undisputed merits of the movement, which has spread rapidly throughout the world, is that the curriculum of mathematics education from the infant school is now viewed in an integrated context. The fundamental importance of children's introduction to mathematics has been recognised.

The problem was first viewed in terms that were quite inadequate educationally and severely restricting from the mathematical point of view. There has undoubtedly been much ingenuity and error in the vast amount of research that has been conducted over the past few years on the introduction of changes to mathematics education, mainly because the problem has been viewed in an artificial light. The inadequacy of mathematics teaching in the fifties was considered to be an exceptional problem, arising from the radical differences between "traditional mathematics" and the "new mathematics". Many researchers worked towards translating new mathematics into a form that could be taught to young children. The first steps were to find out which were the most appropriate fundamental mathematical "concepts" on which to make a start (sets, relationships, structured sets, functions, etc.), studying ways in which these concepts could be made accessible to children. The problem in fact is a far wider one and does not concern mathematics alone. The structure of scholastic disciplines is usually built up on a theoretical framework that is already, or will soon be, outdated. It is becoming more and more apparent that merely to change specific subjects and revise others is not a satisfactory remedy. Teaching is not confined to transfer of knowledge even if, in the course of that teaching, all the psychological rules are applied. The task is far more complex: it is to devise appropriate ways by which children can make *mathematics*, bearing in mind the latest developments in mathematical thought.

In this sphere, we must first define our methods. At the elementary school level, to "make mathematics" can be understood in different ways. The manipulation of symbols, the discovery of structures through games, the expression of concrete situations in mathematical form, may each be considered as having the central role. Some systems opt for one method rather than another. In the system evolved by Dienes, for instance, the child practises mathematics by building structures and *invents* his own set of symbols to describe the structure that he has evolved. Papy advocates the use of graphs and manipulation. In other approaches, a mathematical route is constructed by incorporating several different viewpoints, as with the Nuffield project and the French experimental programme.

Turning to the subjects of mathematics education, some systems continue to give arithmetic the leading role while others introduce algebraic symbols to facilitate the understanding of arithmetic (as in the new Soviet programme). Other systems introduce the child to algebra and topology (Dienes, French experimental programme). Basic mathematical options obviously underly these choices.

Over the past few decades, the concepts evolved by Bourbaki have dominated the mathematics scene and have undoubtedly influenced the structuring of elementary curricula, of which the French experimental curriculum is the most typical.[4] The basic feature of Dienes' system is the attempt to achieve a balance between formal knowledge and intuition.[5] On the other hand, the British Association of Teachers

[4] N. Bourbaki, *Eléments de mathématique*, Hermann, Paris.
[5] See, for example, the introduction to *Building Up Mathematics*, Hutchinson Educational, London, 1960: and also "Sulla percezione astratta", in *Rivista di filosofia*, vol. XLVIII, No. 2 (April 1957), pp. 173-195; "Sulla definizione dei gradi di rigore" in Rend. Seminario mat. Univ. e Politecn., Turin, vol. II, 1952, pp. 223-253. According to A. Heyting, Dienes' intuitionism is different from "intuitionism" as a mathematical theory (see A. Heyting, "Intuitionism in Mathematics", in *Philosophy in the Mid-Century*, edited by R. Klibanski, Publications de l'Institut International de Philosophie, La Nuova Italia, Florence, 1958, vol. I, pp. 101-115.

of Mathematics has developed an approach which encourages the use of concrete situations to arrive at the process of abstraction. Its system is concerned with the value of "application", as in a matrix for mathematical activity rather than simply the application of acquired mathematical knowledge.[6]

The basic options are not only mathematical in nature, but to a certain extent arise from what one implies by education and are related to a given scholastic system. Furthermore, mathematical options are often closely linked with concepts of a psychological nature. A certain type of mathematics, for instance, may be considered as having more affinity to research findings on mental development, as is the case with Piaget, who evolved the concept of the equivalence between Bourbaki mathematics and psychological findings.[7] With the Dienes system, it would be difficult to distinguish between the mathematical aspect and the psychological aspect: his declared intent is to highlight the "constructive" aspects of mathematical thought, and it is obvious from his view of the "construction of structures" that he makes no specific distinction between the two points of view.

In addition to the relationships between "mathematical structures" and "mental structures", there are the issues of the relationship between mental development and learning, the teacher's role in learning, the place of mathematical activities in class work, the relationship between the acquisition of knowledge and education for creativity. The debate upon mathematics education is gradually broadening to cover these spheres, and this wider debate is likely to lead to new and different lines of development over the next few decades.

Any forecast is no more than an hypothesis: although we have dwelt upon those current developments upon which forecasts may be based, we are well aware that other factors may slow down or counteract these developments. The general trend appears to be that discussions

---

[6] "Mathematics involves the process of abstraction, starting with concrete situations, recognising corresponding structures and using one structure to solve problems presented by the other". "The teaching of mathematics also needs to be better integrated with contemporary applications in industry and research; indeed, these applications should often be the vehicle by which the subject is taught. To regard them merely as ancillary illustrations, as a sauce to be added after the meal is cooked, is to misunderstand their role in teaching. But it is not the applicability of the material which is the main point, it is its power to evoke a mathematical response from the pupil". (T. J. Fletcher, ed., *Some Lessons in Mathematics, A Handbook on the Teaching of Modern Mathematics*, by Members of the Association of Teachers of Mathematics, Cambridge University Press, 1965, pp. 1 and 3).

[7] E. W. Beth and J. Piaget, *Epistémologie mathématique et psychologique*, "Essai sur les relations entre la logique formelle et la pensée réelle", Presses Universitaires de France, Paris, 1961.

Mathematics

on specific areas of learning, particularly mathematics, are tending to merge to produce a broader and more rational debate upon the organisation of the curriculum in the elementary school. If we are sidetracked by too much abstract consideration of the content of learning, and if research on specific problems in different areas reaches different stages of maturation, these factors may delay or prevent general consideration of the curriculum as a whole.

RESEARCH AND PLANNING

A. There have been two main lines of psychological and psycho-pedagogic research closely associated with the problem of the teaching of mathematics and science subjects: Piaget-orientated research on mental development, and research on the learning process in the Soviet Union, based upon the theory that learning can make a fundamental contribution towards mental development upon the importance of language and upon the leading role of didactic problems (especially since 1944, the year in which the Soviet Academy of Teaching Sciences was founded).[8]

In both these systems, there has been widespread research on the *formation of concepts*, investigating the level achieved in the growth of basic concepts at different ages or through given programmes of learning.[9] Research on conceptualisation can be used for a narrow approach to the connection between educational planning and research. In planning, the focus is on content, i.e. there is a tendency to include basic knowledge of mathematics and science in the syllabus. The purpose of psycho-pedagogic research, it is considered, is to evaluate a child's actual potential for learning certain subjects. This restricted view of the function of research arises when research is conducted on a single discipline and the basic general theory is inadequate.

B. Over the next few decades, educational research will become easier, both because the research institution will be better organised and be-

---

[8] The orientation of learning research in the Soviet Union has been delineated since the 1930's. It was greatly influenced by the theories of Vygotski, later radically reviewed and revised. (See D. N. Bogoiovlenski and N. A. Menchinskaya, "The Psychology of Learning, 1900-1960", Brian and Joan Simon, ed., *Educational Psychology in USSR*, Routledge and Kegan Paul, London, 1963, pp. 101-161).

[9] J. G. Wallace, "Concept Growth and the Education of the Child", *A Survey of Research on Conceptualisation*. National Foundation for Educational Research, Slough, 1965.

cause there will be more finance available for the gradual improvement of methodology.[10]

There are, however, inherent difficulties connected with the organisation of research for a specific purpose while at the same time linking it with other fields of research. Research on the teaching of mathematics and science, for instance, has been mainly linked with research on mental development. Use has been made of only some of Piaget' theories rather than of his whole body of theories. There is a risk of neglecting the basic innovation at the core of the Piaget system: the hypothesis that mental development represents the formation of overall structures rather than the gradual acquisition of isolated skills. Perhaps, however, the difficulties encountered in exploiting the whole body of Piaget's theories in research and in investigating their educational implications are at least partly due to the very nature of those theories.[11] Piaget emphasised the "genetic" nature of his structuralism, distinguishing it from other forms of structuralism. The conceptual instruments and research methods evolved by Piaget tend more towards study of "structures" than towards study of their genesis. In addition, it is one thing to discuss genesis, but another to discuss learning: according to Piaget, the primary factors at the source of the operational structures of intelligence are maturation and "spontaneous" experience, while "acquired" experience can only accelerate or delay the process. In practice, the learning of logic and mathematics is not a factor of mental development, its only function being to act as a guide to *knowledge* of operative structures and to provide a symbolic language by which those structures can be expressed.[12]

The relationships between learning and development are often seen today in terms of a conflict between Piaget's approach, i.e. that learning is subordinate to development, and Bruner's approach, that development is subject to learning.

---

[10] See W. D. Wall, "The Future of Educational Research", *Educational Research*, vol. X, no. 3 (June 1968), pp. 163-169.

[11] The case of Hans Aebli may be interesting. He made one of the few attempts to develop educational implications from the psychology of Piaget (*Didactique Psychologique*, Delachaux, Neuchâtel, 1951). Later, in *Uber die geistige Entwicklung des Kindes*, Ernst Klett Verlag, Stuttgart, 1963, a concept of intellectual development is presented that, although starting from Piaget, modifies it considerably. He contends that this different thought helps to surmount the difficulties in applying Piaget's methods.

[12] J. Piaget, *Psychologie et pédagogie*, Denoël, Paris, 1969, pp. 45 et seq. The problem would be even greater if considered in the light of Piaget's thought on the relationship between "elementary structures" established during the development years and "Bourbaki structures". (E. W. Beth and J. Piaget, *Epistémologie mathématique et psychologique*, "Essai sur les relations entre la logique formelle et la pensée réelle", Presses Universitaires de France, Paris, 1961, p. 200 et seq.

In fact, this comparison is an over-simplification, for the relationships between development and learning are intricate in the extreme and require far more detailed investigation.[13] It should also be borne in mind that current developments in the social sciences, including psychology, broaden the terms of reference which have formerly governed research on the learning of mathematics and science, so that two extremely complex areas of research are now being investigated:
a) the relationship between mental development and the acquisition of culture;
b) the role of the learning of logic and mathematics subjects in the process of constructing cognitive structures during the age of development.

C. Planning for new mathematics and science curricula should be viewed in the light of an overall plan for education, so that we can make satisfactory use of research findings when planning new syllabi for specific areas.

So long as the replanning of mathematics and science education is due mainly to urgent social and economic pressures, there can only be an inadequate link with research. If new curricula have to be devised and introduced in the space of a few years, the usual route is as follows:
- an experimental programme is worked out for application in a few schools, with continuous assistance from specialists, such as mathematicians and psychologists;
- based upon the experience gained through this limited application, improvements are made to the subjects studied or their comparative difficulty, methods adopted, etc.

In this context, the most pressing research problem is evaluation. The subject has now been discussed for many years, but an appropriate methodology has still not been developed. The main problems encountered are probably in setting out the problem, for it is a difficult task to determine the effectiveness of a curriculum.[14]

---

[13] For example, E. Fischbein, "Enseignement mathématique et développement intellectuel", *Educational Studies in Mathematics*, vol. II no. 2/3 (December 1969), pp. 290-306.

[14] See M. Young, *Innovations and Research in Education*, Routledge and Kegan Paul, London, 1965. The problem of curriculum assessment has been theorised mainly in the United States. Today the role of curriculum assessment compared with curriculum research is a matter of controversy (see I. A. Abramson, "Curriculum Research and Evaluation", *Review of Educational Research*, vol. XXXVI, No. 3 (June 1956), pp. 380-395; R. L. Baker, "Curriculum Evaluation", *Review of Educational Research*, vol. XXXIX, No. 4 (October 1969), pp. 429-491; R. E. Stake, ed., *Perspectives of Curriculum Evaluation*, Rand McNally, Chicago, 1967.

The correlation between research on and development of new curricula will certainly be far more extensive in the future, both because of the foreseeable progress in educational research in general and because research on mathematics learning is now redefining its major tasks.[15]

Survey findings are now becoming available so that we can compare different social and economic systems, different school systems, different methodologies.[16] This will make it possible to approach curriculum reform over the next few years in due awareness of the many factors that condition mathematics learning. The very variety of the approaches possible in the field of mathematics education and the differing degree to which these approaches are in fact transferred into educational practice provide fertile ground for wide-scale comparative research.[17]

Finally, we are now in a situation in which we do not have to work out new mathematics curricula once and for all but must keep the problem under constant review. As mathematical sciences evolve, as new social and economic needs emerge, as progress is made in the organisation of the school and in educational technology, mathematics curricula will need constant revision.

Research should be carried out at two levels:

a) research on mathematics teaching as it exists and on changes to be made to the curriculum in the near future;

b) research on discernible trends that may affect mathematics education in any way.

If research is carried out on the second subject, long term planning should be possible.

THE DEVELOPMENT OF NEW MATHEMATICS CURRICULA

France

The new mathematics curricula for the elementary school (2nd January 1970) should be viewed in the light of the overall movement for the reform of mathematics teaching, a substantial contribution having

---

[15] E. G. Begle, "The Role of Research in the Improvement of Mathematics Education", *Educational Studies in Mathematics*, vol. II, No. 2/3 (December 1969), pp. 232-244.

[16] T. Husén, ed., *International Study of Achievement in Mathematics*, vol. II, Stockholm, Almqvist and Wicksell, Wiley, New York, 1967; D. A. Pidgeon, *Achievement in Mathematics*, National Foundation for Educational Research, Slough, 1967.

[17] J. B. Biggs *Mathematics and the Conditions of Learning*, National Foundation for Educational Research, Slough, 1967.

been made by the *Institut Pédagogique National* and the *Association des professeurs de mathématique de l'enseignement publique*. In January 1967 a ministerial commission was set up under the chairmanship of Mr. J. Lichnérowicz to investigate the teaching of mathematics. This commission first tackled the problem at the secondary school level only. In the meantime, the APMEP "Research and Reform" commission was drawing up a draft curriculum for the nursery and primary schools, while the IPN *Département de la Recherche Pédagogique* was proceeding with experiments under the direction of Nicole Picard, which had begun in 1964 and by 1968 had covered the whole primary school cycle.[18]

By these means, a path was mapped out for the curricular reform: the change was to be introduced in two phases, the first, involving mild innovations, to come into effect immediately while a revolutionary new compulsory curriculum was to be introduced into the preparatory classes in the year 1973-74, and into all primary school classes by 1977-78.

As a result the curricula introduced on 2nd January 1970, represent a transitional and preparatory phase. Their text was published by APMEP as far back as 1969, (although it was slightly different from the final version), under the title *Première étape... vers une réforme de l'enseignement mathématique dans les classes élémentaires*.[19] This publication also set out the curriculum for the more advanced phase, (i.e., the curriculum being used as the basis of research by IPN) for the specific purpose of emphasising that the first phase curricula being implemented in 1970-71 were merely a beginning. The authors stated that everybody embarking upon the first phase should be aware of the prospects to which this phase would lead.

The IPN curriculum drawn up by the APMEP Research and Reform Commission includes the introduction to logic (connectives, quantifiers) through work on sets, a good deal of work on relationships, a close link between arithmetical work and sets and algebra, the study of concrete examples of structures constructed on finite sets. In geometry, the main stress is upon introduction to topology. The theory of measurements is closely connected with practical experience associated with other sectors of learning.[20]

---

[18] "Projet de programmes pour les écoles maternelles et primaires" in *Bulletin de l'Association des professeurs de mathématique*, no. 258 (May-September 1967), pp. 272 et seq., *Le Courrier de la Recherche Pédagogique*, no. 27 (March 1966): "La Mathématique au cycle élémentaire", *Recherches pédagogiques*, no. 40, Institut Pédagogique National, 1970.
[19] Supplement to Bulletin de l'APMEP, n. 269 (July-August 1969).
[20] La Mathématique au cycle élémentaire, *op. cit.*, pp. 9-10.

The theoretical approach introduced by the curriculum is fairly clear: sets and relations, an introduction to function as the basic concept of algebra, algebraic structures, topology. Bourbaki's approach is clearly dominant.[21]

In methodology, the stress is upon "active" methods, often rather generic. Dienes has had some influence: there is fairly frequent reference to Dienes in the belief in the value of play in introducing the child to mathematics, even though this principle is not applied as recommended by Dienes himself (play has a less central role, while manipulation has very little).

The commentary upon the first phase curriculum makes observations on work upon arithmetic subjects in the experimental programme.[22] A transitional curriculum is being introduced not only because of the desire to introduce certain immediate changes but also to create a good setting for a far broader teacher training programme. For many years APMEP has been fighting for "permanent training" of teachers, and this has been one of the goals in founding research institutes on the teaching of mathematics at French universities (IREM). The APMEP recommendations in this respect were in fact made by the Lichnérowicz commission.[23]

England

In countries like England, where there is no central educational authority to set up uniform nation-wide curricula, old and new syllabi can happily exist side by side in educational practice. New curricula are suggested to, rather than forced upon, the schools. The situation is, therefore, profoundly different from that in countries with a centralised educational system.[24]

---

[21] G. Walusinski, "Mathématique d'aujourd'hui pour hommes et femmes de demain", *Le Courier de la Recherche Pédagogique*, no. 27 (March 1966), pp. 5-11; N. Picard, "Une expérience d'enseignement de la mathématique au cours élémentaire", *ibid.*, pp. 12-76.

[22] Ministère de l'Education Nationale, Circulaire n. IV 70-e, 2 January 1970 (Pédagogie, Enseignements scolaires et Orientation: bureau ES 1).

[23] "Rapport préliminaire de la commission ministérielle" in Bulletin de l'APMEP, n. 258 (May-September 1967), p. 255 et seq. The fundamental tasks of IREM were the organisation of in-service training for teachers at every level and development of research in experimental classes. During the school year 1970-71, there were seven IREM's in operation and the development of three more was announced.

[24] A comparison between the two situations was one of the topics discussed at a meeting held in April 1969. Participants included several members from the Association des professeurs de mathématique and others from the Association of Teachers of Mathematics. See D. Wheeler, "An Anglo-French Meeting", *Mathematics Teaching*, n. 47 (Summer 1969), pp. 19-20.

Mathematics

As in other countries, in England those concerned with radical changes in the teaching of mathematics at first concentrated upon the secondary school and later turned to elementary education, organising various ventures in the primary school.

In 1964, the Nuffield Foundation, working with the Schools Council, initiated the Nuffield Project. Many features of the Nuffield Project are worthy of note. First of all, it is mainly intended as a guide for the teacher. This has two fundamental implications:

a) the emphasis is placed upon non-rigidly pre-determined pupil activity, on manipulative procedures, on the mathematical study of real life situations.

b) the teacher's training is considered to be of great importance since he is the one who will promote and coordinate the children's experiences.

The teachers' guides included in the project are grouped into three series, corresponding to three types of work: Computation and Structure; Graphs Leading to Algebra; Shape and Size. The mainstream of the theory in these guides incorporates material from many different sources, and the final text is not in all cases an integrated whole. The curriculum is not based on one specific selected theory, but on a series of experiments in the field of elementary mathematics and science. It includes much arithmetical work, but also a great deal of work on sets and on relationships. Wide use is made of the child's environment[25]: the second of the three approaches in particular suggests elementary ways of describing facts derived from the children's everyday experience in graphic form, the end goal is to instill an understanding of statistical concepts and methods.

Another noteworthy contribution is a book upon mathematics in the primary school, edited by a group from the Association of Teachers of Mathematics, similar to another publication directed towards secondary school teachers.[26] The book's declared aim is not so much as to offer a ready-made programme but to provide information that the teacher can use to help the children "make their own mathematics". The authors believe that the goal of mathematics teaching should be to stimulate free mathematical activity by children and they suggest mathematical activities of a creative type that can be carried out with-

---

[25] See *Nuffield Mathematics Project, I Do and I Understand*, Nuffield Foundation, W. and R. Chambers and John Murray, p. 16.

[26] *Notes on Mathematics in Primary Schools*, by Members of the Association of Teachers of Mathematics, Cambridge University Press, 1967; *Some Lessons in Mathematics, A Handbook on the Teaching of Modern Mathematics*, ed. by T. J. Fletcher, Cambridge University Press, 1965.

in the primary school. Some examples of these are: the discovery of patterns (number patterns, paper-folding games, the use of Cuisenaire-Gattegno materials, arrangements of pins on a pegboard, etc.); the attempt to discover a general rule consideration of specific cases; devising several different ways of representing numerical relations in graphic form. The book also discusses the mathematical aspects of certain popular games or expressive and constructive activities. The main interest of the suggestions provided in the book is that they resolutely discard the more ingenuous method used by traditional mathematics teaching, the direct transmission of what is thought to be basic mathematical knowledge, even when this is done through ingenious tricks. The book, on the other hand, considers that the basis of mathematics is the process of mathematical thought applied in specific contexts to act as a stimulus to the child. The emphasis is laid upon the *creative* aspects of mathematical activity.

Soviet Union

In December 1964, a commission presided by the mathematician Markuschevich, vice-president of the Academy of Teaching Sciences, started work on the development of new curricula for Soviet schools. One of its terms of reference was that the elementary course should be reduced from four to three years.

The outstanding feature of these new mathematics curricula is, in fact, the way in which they accelerate learning. This acceleration has been made possible by the findings of psychological research on learning since the thirties.[27] The new mathematics syllabus for classes 1-3 (seven to nine year olds) includes arithmetic, elementary geometry (plane figures, perimeter, area), and elementary algebra.

Algebra is introduced at this stage to help the children to understand arithmetic and to prepare them for subsequent mathematical study.[28] The children learn to use letter symbols: from the very start, "x" is used to represent the unknown factor in an open enunciation[29], while in the second class letter symbols are used to express arithmetical

[27] N. A. Menchinskaya, "Some Aspects of Primary School Mathematics Teaching in Russia", *Mathematics Reform in the Primary School*, UNESCO Institute for Education, Hamburg, 1967, p. 119.
[28] Ministerstvo Prosveščenie USSR, *Sbornik programm dlja srednej obščeobrazovatel'noj školy* (USSR Department of Education, *General Education School Programmes*) "Prosveščenie", Moscow 1968, pp. 98-100.
[29] M. I. Moro, M. A. Bantova, G. V. Bel'tiukova, *Matematika*, Textbook for the first class, "Prosveščenie", Moscow, 1969, p. 23.

properties in a general fashion[30], preparing the ground for the concept of variables and making extensive use of tables[31], and solving simple equations.[32]

The philosophy underlying the new mathematics curricula was described by G. G. Maslova to the first International Congress of Mathematics Education held in Lyons in August 1969 as follows: "The mathematics syllabus in the first to the third grades is an organic part of the secondary school mathematics course, the main framework of this course being arithmetic of natural numbers and fundamental magnitudes. At the same time, children are introduced to elementary geometry and algebra. The preliminary study of algebra is an organic part of the system of arithmetical knowledge, as it enables the child to assimilate the concept of number, arithmetical operations and mathematical relationships. One of the fundamental principles of education is to provide a close link with the outside world. While we realise the importance of developing the power of abstract thought in children, we are nonetheless very cautious when we consider modernising mathematics courses in the primary schools. We are convinced that the pupil should not consider mathematics to be a system of arbitrary conventions, that he should not see mathematics as being any different from natural sciences. In the syllabus, the child will acquire mathematical concepts by using concrete situations that he encounters in his daily life, so that he will realise the types of problem to which the knowledge and mechanisms that he is learning during his mathematics lessons apply. In this way, from the very beginning he will develop a proper understanding of the relationship between science and practice. Children must always understand the true origin of the systems that they are studying. This approach is systematically followed up in subsequent studies".[33]

The justification for "cautious modernisation" is the refusal to consider mathematics as formal play. "We believe that it is quite unjustified

---

[30] For example of the commutative property of addition see M. I. Moro and M. A. Bantova, *Matematika*, Textbook for the second class, "Prosveščenie", Moscow, 1969, pp. 10, 11, 13.

[31] *Ibid.*

[32] *Ibid.*, p. 112 $(40-25) + x = 33; b-76 = 90-76; (52-17) - a = 18$.

[33] G. G. Maslova, Le développement des idées et des concepts mathématiques fondamentaux dans l'enseignement des enfants de 7 à 15 ans, in *Educational Studies in Mathematics*, vol. II, no. 2/3 (December 1969) p. 202. The reference to concrete situations implied *problem-solving*, which the programme emphasises (especially on pp. 100 et seq., and pp. 108 et seq. of *Sbornik programm, op. cit.* The problems in applied arithmetic are assigned by the teacher but it is considered important to accustom the children to formulating their own problems, according to directions by the teacher (*Ibid.*, pp. 102-103).

to place practical and formal education in two separate categories. It is not the objective of the Soviet school to develop the mind rather than to impart real knowledge ('brain sharpening' as, according to Doctor Dienes, it is known by some writers). For this reason, we are quite unable to agree with the suggestion that games or exercises in formal logic, games with symbols, etc., should be introduced into the junior classes".[34]

The concept of "sets" is introduced in the fourth grade (when education is reorganised, the fourth grade will be the first year of the secondary course, at the age of ten, with specialist teachers for each subject). In subsequent years children will be introduced to geometric transformations.

Sweden

The Nordic Committee for the Modernisation of School Mathematics has been working on changes to mathematics curricula since 1960. The countries involved are Sweden, Denmark, Finland and Norway. Its work has been greatly influenced by American thought and texts published by the School Mathematics Study Group have been translated.[35] Research on mathematics teaching is now being conducted at Malmö College of Education. New curricula are being introduced this year into the *Grundskolan*. The mathematics programme is not broken down by class, but by section and subject, stating the classes which will learn each subject in each section. For example:

"I. *Naturliga Tal*
 I.I. *Mangd och antal* (I)
 I.15. *Divisionsalgoritmen* (4-7)
 I.16. *Positionsystem med andra baser an tio* (3-7)".[36]

In most sections, it is planned that the introduction to the subject will take place in the first to the fourth grades. For example, in the case of statistics and probabilities:

"8. Statistics and probabilities
 8.1 Introduction of Statistical material. Tables and diagrams (2-9)".[37]

Thus the programme for the entire course of study assumes a unitary

---

[34] N. A. Menchinskaya, *op. cit.*, p. 121.
[35] M. Hastad, "The Activity of the Nordic Committee for the Modernisation of School Mathematics in Primary School in Sweden", *Mathematics Reform in the Primary School*, UNESCO Institute for Education, Hamburg, 1967, pp. 99-105.
[36] *Läroplan för grundskolan, Matematik*, Stockholm, 1969, p. 4.
[37] *Ibid.*, p. 5.

Mathematics

aspect. Explicit attention is given to the basic operations in traditional arithmetic and the introduction of techniques is a slow, careful process. Problems of measurement, geometry (fundamental concepts, including a first approach to transformations[38] and Cartesian coordinates are also taken into consideration. It is interesting that the determination of perimeters, areas and volumes is included in the *Matningar* section and introduced only in the sixth grade. In the first grade, the children are introduced to open sentences and, from the fourth grade, to decimals, fractions and negative numbers. The curriculum is followed by a commentary with suggestions on the various subjects.

MATHEMATICS AND CREATIVITY

It is difficult to foresee how our attitude towards creativity will develop over the next few years. It is a subject of special relevance in our technological civilisation, while at the same time it is vital for the development of our civilisation and will help to find a corrective for some of its consequences.

The learning of mathematics may provide fertile ground for studying the problems and implications of creativity in education, for two main reasons:
- it is easier than in other sectors to refer to the nature of mathematical activity on the adult level. It is now generally accepted that the mathematics of the mathematician is in many ways creative (although it is not so easy to reach agreement on the nature of this creativity or on its role in mathematical thought);
- Creativity in school mathematics cannot be dissociated from mastery of mathematical concepts and the adoption of ready-made processes. In creative mathematics learning, divergent and convergent thought are closely linked and interdependent.

The element of creativity may be injected into mathematics education in several different ways.

Value of Play

The "play" approach in mathematics is no novelty. One point should, however, be made clear: play does not necessarily promote creativity. The word "play" can in fact have several different meanings, just as

---
[38] *Ibid.*, pp. 15-16.

the relationship between play and its mathematical content can be understood in various ways. For example, the competitive element could be considered as a basic feature of play.[39] This theory is usually based upon the extrinsic relationship between the game and its mathematical content. It is not difficult to invent competitive games that require the use of mathematical knowledge and which help to reinforce that knowledge, or to devise rules of a mathematical nature. In such cases, the game makes use of mathematics as a tool and, in turn, is governed by mathematics, but the mathematics and the game are still substantially unrelated.

This is not the way of making optimum use of creativity in mathematics learning. We do not mean that we should never use this type of game but only that we should realise that such games are no more than tricks.

When today we discuss play as part of the creative approach, we mean something quite different. First of all, we imply optimum use of the creative aspects of mathematical thought and we do not consider that the main feature of play is competitiveness. If, by the word "play" we mean freely chosen activity, in other words an activity that is self-motivating[40], one which helps us to move in a "separate world"[41], these properties can certainly be found in mathematics activity. Once again, we must be cautious. To say that mathematics is like a game is one thing, but nobody would sustain that mathematics is no more than a game. If we evolved a teaching curriculum centered upon "play", we might neglect other no less essential aspects of mathematics.

Certain games suggested by Dienes are in fact bewildering. Take, for instance, games that use mathematical structures, in particular

---

[39] This is the theory favoured by T. H. F. Brissenden who suggests several games for the learning of algebra in the first cycle of the secondary school (T. H. F. Brissenden, "Learning Games in Mathematics", *Mathematics Teaching*, Autumn 1964, No. 28, pp. 51-57. Many competitive games at the elementary school level are suggested by L. G. W. Sealey, *The Creative Use of Mathematics in the Junior School*, Basil Blackwell, Oxford, 1950.

[40] "...Play is in fact the only, or the principal human activity in which the activity itself and its motivation coincide. We can say that play is 'pure' activity, meaning that it is in a certain sense self-sufficient and autonomous and that it does not tend to negate itself in any satisfaction of another type". (Visalberghi, *Esperienza e Valutazione*, Taylor, Turin, 1958, p. 154).

[41] "Play is not 'ordinary' or 'real' life. It is a 'standing apart' from it in order to enter into a temporary sphere of activity with an end in itself. Not being 'ordinary life', there is no compulsion for immediate satisfaction of desires and needs. It interrupts that process. It is a provisional action that is complete in itself and is accomplished for satisfaction received rather than for the execution of the action itself". Huizinga, *Homo ludens*, Einaudi, Turin, 1967, pp. 27-28.

those referring to the structure of vector spaces.[42] This type of activity may be considered as a game by children and through such games children may arrive at some sort of idea of their common structure and work out appropriate symbols. The problem that arises is as follows: can it be of any value to a child to perceive the identity of a structure through such artificial imaginative games? In mathematics, particularly in the Bourbaki type of mathematics, "structures" play an important part because they can be used to unify mathematical knowledge and free it from references to content. The mathematician may "play" at constructing formal systems; he may well believe that the construction of formal systems is "playing", but he is already aware of any value that his constructions may have in mathematical thought, he sees the connections and implications, while the child is obviously in a completely different position.[43]

From this point of view, we can see the limitations of the "play" approach. It may be very useful in certain ways but it may also falsify the role of mathematics education.[44]

Discovery Method

A good example of the "discovery method" is the Madison Project, which played an important part in the movement for the reform of

---

[42] Z. P. Dienes, *The Power of Mathematics*, Hutchinson Educational, London, 1964, pp. 106-109. Dienes distinguishes between three forms of play: explorative-manipulative play, symbolic play and play based on rules (Z. P. Dienes, *Uno Studio sperimentale sull'apprendimento della matematica*, Feltrinelli, Milan, 1968, p. 9 et seq.; original: *An Experimental Study of Mathematics-Learning*, London, 1963).

[43] "A mathematician, like a painter or a poet, is a maker of patterns... The mathematician's patterns, like the painter's or the poet's, must be *beautiful*; the ideas, like the colours or the words, must fit together in a harmonious way. Beauty is the first test; there is no permanent place in the world for ugly mathematics... A chess problem is genuine mathematics, but it is in some way 'trivial' mathematics. However ingenious and intricate, however original and surprising the moves, there is something essential lacking. Chess problems are *unimportant*. The best mathematics is *serious* as well as beautiful... The 'seriousness' of a mathematical theorem lies not in its practical consequences, which are usually negligible, but in the *significance* of the mathematical ideas which it connects. We may say, roughly, that a mathematical idea is 'significant' if it can be connected, in a natural and illuminant way, with a large complex of other mathematical ideas". (G. Hardy, *A Mathematician's Apology*, Cambridge University Press, 1969, pp. 84-85-88-89).

[44] In relation to mathematical games, in the *Journal of Mathematics Teaching*, no. 49 (Winter 1969): the question is examined and strong reservations concerning Dienes' and other similar games, are made. In favour, however, is A. Revuz in "Les méthodes de Dienes débouchent-elles sur la vraie mathématique?", *Le courrier de la recherche pédagogique* no. 27 (March 1966, pp. 84-86), who definitely accepts mathematics games (p. 86). There is also a condensed critique of Dienes' games in E. Fischbein, "Enseignement mathématique et développement intellectuel", *Educational Studies in Mathematics*, vol. II, No. 2/3 (December 1969).

mathematical teaching in the United States and which has aroused a good deal of interest in England. In describing the programme to teachers, Robert Davis speaks of "creative learning experiences" which he believes should replace the traditional type of lesson.[45] Mathematical subjects are presented in the form of suggestions and questions which help the child work out for himself the fact that the teacher wishes him to learn. The suggestions and the questions are put in such a way as not to require a specific answer but to let the child give his own answer. The routes by which it is suggested that the child should learn are the construction of mathematical symbols and "play" using these symbols. The child is helped to start constructing his own symbols by referring to imaginary practical situations.

As with the very different Dienes' system, the end result is that children make mathematics by "playing". They engage in a self-motivated activity in a "separate world", an independent but coherent world. Here again, though, there is a risk of developing a theory of mathematics learning that focuses upon certain aspects of this science to the exclusion of others.

Open-ended problems and situations

Emphasis upon the creative aspects of mathematics learning is usually linked with systems that stress the "autonomous" nature of mathematics, the need to direct learning from the very beginning towards the ability of "abstraction", in the belief that practical experience or situations have little of value to offer and might unduly restrict the schoolchild's ability to master mathematics, giving a false idea of mathematics by limiting it to an instrumental role. It should be pointed out that the "creative" theory of mathematics can, nonetheless, be combined with the belief that contemporary mathematics should place greatest emphasis upon the vast increase in the range of applications and that one of the main tasks of mathematics teaching should be to identify the paths of learning made feasible by this recent expansion in applied mathematics.

A guideline for the future is given in "Notes on Mathematics in Primary Schools":

"Mathematics is now applied to a very wide range of situations and is not confined, as it once was, to the mechanics of the physical world.

---

[45] R. B. Davis, *Exploration in Mathematics, A Text for Teachers*, Addison-Wesley Publishing Company, Palo Alto, 1967, p. 3 et seq.

Mathematics

Completely new fields of mathematical operations have spring up, some only a few years old. Operational research and cybernetics, to choose just two examples, are applications of mathematics to problems which formerly would not have been thought susceptible to mathematical analysis. Much of this work may seem a long way from the classroom and particularly from the primary school classroom. But its significance for the teacher lies in its demonstration of the vast number of things that are worth thinking about in a mathematical way. Mathematics is not just about numbers and space; it can be said to happen whenever the mind classifies and creates structures. This increases tremendously the range of experiences which turn out to be mathematically relevant and it makes it easier for the teacher to create situations for his pupils to use mathematics and find situations which release mathematical thinking. One practical consequence of this is that in the classroom mathematics becomes more varied and therefore more enjoyable. Another is that the child can explore situations which are within his experience, which yield quite profound mathematics and yet which do not require the technical equipment of memorised relationships and algorithms that traditional number work so often does.

If mathematics is not seen as restricted to a few conventionally accepted areas of experience, or constrained to follow a simple linear development, the teacher can encourage his pupils to range far and wide in their mathematical activity. They can explore situations which are incredibly rich in their mathematical yield. There are situations, some of which we mention, which are direct enough to be grasped by all children and yet which provide such a wealth of possibilities that they are difficult to exhaust. Faced with the responses of children to such situations, confident judgements about the mathematics appropriate for a particular age, or the precedence of some piece of mathematics over another, have to be abandoned. It becomes obvious that learning of mathematics is a complex activity and that children can work happily within this complexity".[46]

This is a plan for a mathematics curriculum not based on a list of mathematical concepts to be learned in a given order, but on a variety of suggested "situations" which allows the child to "create" mathematics on his own level. A "situation" is not a stated "problem" with only one correct solution. "A situation has the potential to develop in different directions. One situation may lead to several different pieces

---

[46] *Notes on Mathematics in Primary Schools*, by Members of the Association of Teachers of Mathematics, Cambridge University Press, 1969, pp. 2-3.

of mathematics and conversely each piece of mathematics may be reapplied to several different situations. Teaching from situations has in it *some* chance elements and, in fact, the element of chance is a necessary ingredient".[47]

To stress the "creative" nature of the child's mathematical activity – the fact that such activity should not be artificially imposed from above in sequences that reflect the systematic abstract construction of adult mathematics but should consist of free exploration of certain situations – shows that mathematical learning is beginning to be integrated into the overall educational goal, mathematical values being considered as closely connected with specific methodologies. In the future of mathematics education, it is essential that the debate should be conducted in such a way as to throw light upon these and similar problems. In other words, mathematics research should always be conducted in the light of general educational research.

MATHEMATICS IN THE CURRICULUM

Research on the teaching of mathematics cannot proceed unless attention is paid to the role of mathematics in the curriculum. This involves both consideration of the methods of mathematics education and an attempt to define its goals.

When determining methods of teaching mathematics in the elementary school, the first problem is to determine the extent to which mathematics should be kept separate from other activities. In recent years, there has been a move to keep it separate to ensure that mathematics does not become merely a way of learning how to do calculations in practical situations. Nonetheless, to believe in the autonomous value of mathematics does not necessarily mean that the links between mathematics and experience, or between mathematics and other areas of learning, should be severed.

The comments on the current *French experimental* curriculum include the following words: "There are two objectives in introducing mathematics to the elementary school: to promote good mental structuring,

---

[47] D. Wheeler, "An Anglo-French Meeting", *Mathematics Teaching* no. 47 (Summer 1969), p. 20, cfr. R. C. Lyness, "Applied Mathematics in British Schools", *Educational Studies in Mathematics*, vol. I. No. 1/2 (May 1968): "The main difference between problems traditionally set at school and those in real life is that the school problem is one that is known to be soluble. It is usually given verbally with just sufficient data, all of it relevant for the solution. Real problems are not like this and so we should give pupils more open-ended questions to investigate. We should present them with some material, leave them to suggest their own problems and find their own solutions. And the greater variety we can provide the better".

to provide children with an intellectual tool that they can use in a wide range of situations that they will be encountering in the course of their existence... At every level children discover and employ several methods of representation to:
- describe situations;
- organise the information that they have derived from their school, family or social life (the materials can be found in the study of language and general education subjects)".[48]

It cannot be said that the use of mathematical conceptual instruments to "describe situations" or to "organise information" has produced any experience of value as yet. In France, the main current concern is the connection between mathematics and language. Other areas of learning, called *matières d'éveil* or general educational subjects, are receiving less attention.[49] In the theoretical field, mathematics activity, described as "mathematising", was the focus of the conference on "How to Teach so as to be Useful", held in Utrecht in August 1967. There was a surprising degree of agreement at this conference. H. Freudenthal opened a panel discussion by stating: "I have the impression that we all agree about fundamentals. We are all convinced, I suppose, that mathematics has to be taught in such a way that people can apply it. We are convinced that this goal cannot be reached by simply teaching applied mathematics, but that mathematics has to be related to its applications at a much earlier stage, in a closer and more fundamental way, and that the ability to apply mathematics can be acquired only by starting students on situations that have to be mathematised. Mathematising has been an important concept in our discussions and I think that we all believe it can be learned only by starting from real situations which have to be mathematised".[50]

H. O. Pollock affirmed that this was as true for "pure mathematics" as it was for "applied mathematics". "...A fourth popular misconception is that applied mathematics is very different from pure mathematics and, in particular, that entirely different kinds of teaching are essential. If this were true, I think it would mean that we were teaching pure mathematics very badly. The attitude of both pure and applied mathematics is, at its heart, 'Here is a situation: think about it'. In applied mathematics, the situation is from some other field of human

---

[48] In "La Mathématique au cycle élémentaire", *Recherches pédagogiques*, no. 40, Institut Pédagogique National, 1970, p. 8.
[49] See: Y. Gentilhomme, "Enseignement mathématique et linguistique", *Bulletin de l'APMEP*, No. 273, (March-April 1970) pp. 89-130.
[50] *Educational Studies in Mathematics*, vol. I, No. 1/2 (May 1968), p. 61.

endeavour, for which situation we are trying to find some mathematical understanding. Our job is to make a mathematical model of this situation that will shed some light on it, help us to understand it, and, if we are lucky, even give us predictive power. How does this picture change for pure mathematics? The only difference is that the situation we are trying to understand is one from mathematics itself. In other words, and I admit this is somewhat over-simplified, if you are doing a mathematical problem purely for its own sake or for the light that it may shed on some other branch of mathematics, then you are acting as a pure mathematician. If you are doing a problem in the hope of understanding a situation outside mathematics, then you are acting as an applied mathematician. All too often, our teaching has failed to present this open-ended and constructive nature of both pure and applied mathematics. We almost always say to the students, 'Here is a problem: solve it' or, 'Here is a theorem: prove it' and very rarely say 'Here is a situation: think about it. Find out what the problem *should* be, or what the theorem is that you ought to be trying to prove'. Such radical improvement in pedagogy and student involvement will help the teaching of mathematics from many angles, not just the problem of applications".[51]

The problem of applying mathematics to the study of physics, or rather of coordinating the teaching of mathematics and the teaching of physics, was undoubtedly one of the most obvious reasons for the work at Utrecht. In his opening speech, Freudenthal gave an account of the meeting held with the physics experts in Lausanne in January of that year. He said that it was "a milestone in the philosophy of mathematics education"[52] and outlined the resolutions based on the co-ordination of the two disciplines.[53]

The concept of mathematics learning as a "mathematising activity" arose from the dialogue between mathematicians and physicists. The mathematician alone cannot develop ways of teaching mathematics

[51] *Ibid.*, p. 25.
[52] *Ibid.*, p. 3.
[53] The following is the text of the first two resolutions: "1. The teaching of mathematics and physics should be closely coordinated. Curricula should be adjusted to accommodate such coordination. 2. The physical world becomes intelligible through the formation of concepts and their mathematic formulation. Therefore, it cannot be admitted that divergence between mathematics and physics teaching in the secondary school may be due to modern trends in mathematics teaching which aim at encouraging *logical thinking* in pupils and their abilities for mathematisation. It is necessary to develop both the aptitude of pupils for identifying mathematical structures presented in situations encountered in physics (transfer of knowledge) and their skill in the use of key mathematical tools, particularly algebraic calculation". (*Educational Studies in Mathematics, op. cit.*, p. 245).

based on "actual situations", or rather the mathematician could do it alone but often has to use not so much "actual situations" as artificial examples devised for the purpose of demonstrating certain mathematical developments.[54]

Only if another area of education is investigated in depth (for instance a science subject or social studies or visual education) can we discover convergences and find ways of coordinating mathematics learning processes and other learning processes. If this is not done, apart from incurring the risk of creating artificial situations, there is another, perhaps more serious, risk: that the whole debate upon making mathematics arise from "true situations" will in the long run only lead back to the idea that mathematics is merely a tool and has no value other than that of being "usable". This risk can be overcome by the debate on mathematics education, by trying to clarify what is meant by "applied mathematics", by "useful mathematics", or whether we should use the expression "mathematisation". We should emphasise that the traditional focus upon the practical application of mathematics restricted the true potential of mathematics education. We must consider problems of methodology at various levels of education.[55]

This risk cannot be overcome if we confine ourselves to the area of mathematics. If the relation between mathematics and other subjects in the curriculum is not to be based upon "instrumentalisation", then every other subject, as well as mathematics, should be considered. "Here is the situation: think about it" should be the valid approach in all areas if mathematics is to play its proper role in the curriculum.

---

[54] "Mathematics should – in my opinion – be applied above all in natural situations, in domains external to mathematics, where a true problem is faced whose solution requires either mathematical method or the use of a mathematical theory that has already been developed. We must not illude ourselves that these natural applications can be replaced by the solution of problems posed in mathematics lessons. It is by the coordination and integration of different subjects of school education that we can solve this educational problem in a satisfactory manner. If the mathematics teacher attempts to show his pupils examples of the ways in which differential calculus of the theory of probabilities can be applied to biological problems, but if, during these biology lessons, the pupils never encounter a similar problem, and if this is the same with every other subject in the school curriculum, the young people's critical mind will start to suspect that their teacher's affirmations as to the importance of mathematics in other fields of human activity are not sincere".

[55] See the report by A. Z. Krygovska, *op. cit.*, to the Conference of Utrecht and the Panel Discussion, *op. cit.* H. O. Pollack reviewed the topic at the International Congress for the Teaching of Mathematics in Lyons in August 1969 ("How can We Teach Applications of Mathematics?", *Educational Studies in Mathematics*, vol. II, no. 2/3 December 1969). See also F. Conway, "A New Approach to Applied Mathematics for Schools", *Mathematics Teaching*, No. 46, Spring 1969, pp. 14-15; E. H. Bates, "Mathematics from the Environment", *Mathematics Teaching*, No. 47, Summer 1969, pp. 12-14.

There are two tasks to be tackled, the first of which governs the second:
a) we must study the connection between mathematics and other subjects in the curriculum. In doing so, the point of departure should be to identify the areas of mathematical education that are most suitable for use as the common ground on which links can be forged with subjects such as logic and statistics.[56]
b) planning of comprehensive and organic curricula, in which all disciplines are integrated as a whole.

THE TEACHER'S ROLE

One of the most complex problems when attempting to revise the teaching of mathematics is the training of teachers. It is now widely recognised that the problem is not confined to the need to train teachers in "new mathematics". Apart from changes in the content of teaching, there are very great problems of method and a very close look must be taken at the teacher's role and the role of mathematics education in general.

The main alternatives lie in the content of in-service training and the way of organising and running such in-service training.

In France, the problems of teaching the teachers have been carefully studied by APMEP. The Research and Reform Commission issued the following warning in connection with the proposals for a new programme: "the text of a curriculum is usually over-restrictive and not sufficiently precise to provide adequate guidance to teachers. This text will, therefore, be followed by notes and documents that will help teachers to understand the changes in the choice and the management of pupils' activities involved in this preliminary phase of change in education. It is hoped that teachers who work at the same level in every local authority area will meet in teams to decide jointly upon the educational steps they will take. If, for example, such teams meet on Saturday afternoons, they will be given active support by the pres-

---

[56] As for logic, the problems are enormous. The introduction of logic from the early school years has been analysed mainly by Suppes and Dienes. Logic is one of the areas of study in the French experimental programme. As for statistics, the activities for the introduction of combination problems suggested in the *Notes on Mathematics in Primary Schools*, *op. cit.*, section 9, pp. 201-223, should be investigated. See the combination games provided in the French experimental programme (M. Dumont, "Quelques Jeux Combinatoires", in *Le courrier de la recherche pédagogique*, no. 33, 1968, pp. 57-63). See E. Fischbein, I. Pampu, I. Minzat, "Initiation aux probabilités à l'école élémentaire", *Educational Studies in Mathematics*, vol. II, no. 1 (July 1969), pp. 16-31.

ence of a promotor (an IREM official) and by the provision of information documents. Once they have established their own methods of teaching in this way, teachers will be fired with enthusiasm and enjoy the satisfaction of having kept abreast of their times. This climate of freedom should eliminate dogmatism and allow room for the full expansion of young minds".[57] Especially since the school year 1968-69, many groups have been set up in France by regional groupings of APMEP, teachers in the Ecole Normale, IREM and the National Pedagogical Institute. The main goal is to provide "permanent education" through team work, combining the provision of the latest information upon mathematics teaching and consideration of the subject of methodology, both specific and general.

The Nuffield Project in England stated the problem in the following terms. If mathematics is to be an active and creative process for children, a way of acquiring experience of mathematics using actual situations as a springboard, teachers must have had experience of this type of mathematics in person. The most rational place for teachers to refresh their knowledge of their subject is in a mathematical laboratory where they themselves can engage actively and creatively in mathematics and cooperate with each other in devising ways in which their pupils can engage in mathematical activities.[58]

The group who edited the book entitled "Notes on Mathematics in Primary Schools" took a similar stand:

"It can be argued that the teaching of mathematics has concentrated exclusively on the attempt to transmit known mathematics and that it has done this in an incredibly narrow way. Our view of mathematics makes us see the job of the teacher differently. We are concerned with the creative side of the child's learning and with minimising the teacher's interference with this. Every time a teacher insists on his way of doing a piece of mathematics, rejecting any responses which do not seem to fit, he nibbles away at his pupil's ability to act mathematically. We believe in the value of the child's mathematics; that he

---

[57] "We must not lose sight of the fact that mathematics are only part of what teachers should be teaching, and that this part should be integrated within a whole. No reform of mathematics education would be significant unless the whole of education were reformed. Mathematics is an excellent instrument for the reform of all educational subjects. Permanent education should therefore refer both to the content of education and to its methods. With this in mind, the active method recommended for children is the same as should be employed when training their teachers. Teachers should take an active part in the processes of updating their knowledge and acquiring new knowledge, since without their participation nothing solid can be built".

[58] See D. S. Fielker, "Notes from a Math Centre", *Mathematics Teaching*, no. 51, (Summer 1970), pp. 18-21.

should have freedom to make it and use it and talk about it. The child may sometimes make mathematics that to an adult is not valid. Provided that the teacher avoids ex-cathedra judgements and has sympathy with what the child is trying to do, it is then proper for the child's mathematics to be put to the social test. In this way, the sensitive teacher can balance his pupils' need to think their own thoughts with their need to share and communicate with other people. The preservation of some degree of equilibrium between the demands of mathematics to be socially acceptable and the freedom to invent mathematics which may have meaning only for the inventor is the chief pedagogical task. In this sense the teaching of mathematics is not unlike the teaching of English".[59]

This kind of teaching makes far more exacting demands upon the teacher than if he were merely transmitting ready-digested knowledge in a given sequence. It demands that the teacher combines a taste for mathematical exploration, inventiveness and organising ability and it also requires that he have a high level of mathematical education. Unless one really "knows" mathematics one cannot see the mathematical potential of situations or guide and coordinate pupil activity in a mathematically productive way.[60]

The problem that arises in teacher training is to reconcile education in mathematical inventiveness and the acquisition of a general outlook that enables the teacher to identify the opportunities for mathematising in non-stereotype situations and to assess the mathematical value of any approaches to work that may arise in the classroom. It should be realised, however, that a single teacher will never be able to tackle the task of teaching mathematics in full appreciation of creativity and application. Only through group effort, assisted by specialists, can teachers carry out their task. Educational technology may in the future provide teachers with more sophisticated instruments which will

---

[59] *Notes on Mathematics in Primary Schools*, by Members of the Association of Teachers of Mathematics, Cambridge University Press, 1969, pp. 4-5.

[60] At the Conference in Utrecht, August 1967, T. J. Fletcher said: "... The approach I advocate is the investigation of mathematically pregnant situations which demand as little as possible in the way of technical prerequisites. Since the students are comparative beginners, this approach may lead to a series of separate puzzles, which are trivial because they are detached and unrelated to any general theory. Avoiding this real danger is a matter for the teacher's judgement, and the general theories must be introduced at the right time, when the pupils feel a need for them. The only safeguard against trivial and unproductive examples is the teacher's knowledge of how the subject develops later on. The teacher must choose problems that appeal to his students, whatever their knowledge at the time, and he should know how to relate them to the theoretical patterns which he intends to follow as the course proceeds". *Educational Studies in Mathematics*, vol. I, no. 1/2 (May 1968), pp. 167-168.

make teaching more efficient but not necessarily easier. These instruments can extend the teacher's range but cannot be a substitute for him. The major contribution that technology can make to education will be to assist with the individualisation of learning. Nonetheless, when developing and employing these sophisticated instruments, we must see them in the overall context of mathematical education, its function and its conditions. If we do not do so, these instruments will be no progress but rather a threat.

This is one of the many problems that teachers must face in their training over the next few years.

NEW DIRECTIONS IN MATHEMATICS EDUCATION

1. Of the many areas of elementary education, mathematics and science are the most sensitive to social and economic pressures, a fact that will undoubtedly lead to more rapid progress in this sector than in others, in the form of more research and greater awareness of the need for regular updating of the curriculum.

At the same time, it may lead to a limited concept and to imbalance. The problem of mathematics and science education can be solved only if it is viewed as an integral part of a complex and continuous process of research into the state of education today, bearing economic and social changes in mind and evolving a general educational policy. The inadequacies which restrict the role of science in society and in education are today reflected in the school. Once we have gone beyond the ingenuous form of scientific progressivism dating from the 19th century, we are governed either by concepts which minimise the role of science in the education of man, or concepts which judge science solely by its role in technological progress.

In fact, unless the role of science in society is defined in its true light, it is very difficult to solve the educational problem. In this case, any reinforcement of mathematics and science education becomes subject to the needs of technological progress. It is hardly surprising, therefore, that planning and implementation of this education today is unilateral.

For these reasons, the future of mathematics and science education cannot be considered as an isolated problem, for this would be severely restricting and would allow undue pressure by the needs of economic development.

The basic factors which affect mathematics and science education are associated with the development of today's society and the education of man for this development. If we view the problem in this way, the emphasis is placed upon the general formative value of mathematics and science in education: acquisition of skill in abstract thought and the extension of the applications to different fields; familiarity with methodology and personal autonomy; mastery of knowledge through doing and enhancement of inventiveness.

Otherwise, on the one hand there will be technological mathematics and on the other an educational psychology which will attempt to find expedients to preserve the abstract needs of human development. To follow this course would be to give up the attempt to find any basic solution.

2. In the movement for the reform of mathematical education, there is a current trend to extend the horizons of mathematics, to make mathematics the focal point for new trends affecting other sectors or trends that spread out from individual sectors to the curriculum as a whole.[61]

This applies in the first place to use of the findings of psychological research. The development of new mathematics and science programmes has, in various ways and at different levels, been associated with research on mental development and upon learning. As we have already stated, these connections have as yet been inadequate; nonetheless, there has been widespread recognition of their importance. The need to use psychological research has been recognised in other sectors when working on new recommended curricula. There are two fairly clear-cut trends in the use of psychological findings. First of all, the findings of psychological research are used to construct highly structured curricula to introduce a given subject and to form skills. Curricula of this kind help to make teaching more efficient and as such are of undoubted value. Mathematics and science could well be used as the test bed for further developments in other sectors of education.

There is a risk, however, that this work may lead to an over-narrow approach. To evolve a curriculum for a given subject is a technical problem that must be tackled using tested procedures that are frequently highly complex. There is a danger that we equate the problem of constructing a curriculum with the problem of the technical processes necessary to construct it.

With the second approach, the curriculum is considered to be a

---

[61] Significantly, since January 1968, the *Bulletin of the International Study Group for Mathematics Learning* has been retitled *The Journal of Structural Learning*.

Mathematics

basic problem affecting the education of the individual in the sense of the inculturation process, involving all the dynamic forces encountered by the individual in a social group and all the implications arising from the versatility of cultures or the existence of sub-cultures. To learn one form of mathematics rather than another or to learn a given form of mathematics in one way rather than in another is of no little importance from this point of view.

The way in which scientific and technological research is organised today makes it easier to work in separate sectors. Furthermore, technology is developing in its own way and is tending to predominate over other trends and other levels of research. In the field of education, technological progress is being made, especially in the field of mathematics and science, and this progress will probably become even more important over the next few decades. Its future role will depend upon the balance between the different levels of problems and research. The present situation certainly does not give rise to optimism. The very prevelance of the mathematics and science sector compared with other sectors of education is a basic sign of the difficulties being encountered in reconciling technology with education for purposes other than purely achieving efficiency.

3. A factor of the utmost importance is that progress in mathematical education is now beginning to be made in joint international comparative research. It is now possible to compare the influence on the educational level of different lines of mathematical research and to highlight different approaches based upon decisions extending beyond the field of mathematics.[62] This promotes research upon high level problems,

---

[62] A comparison of the important differences in French and English theory was made at the Conference in Exeter (April 1969). "Trevor Fletcher put this contrast to the meeting at its first session by asking how far the differences between *Some Lessons in mathematics* and Lucienne Felix, *Exposé Moderne des mathématiques élémentaires*, which represented quite different educational concerns – one with mathematical activity and the other with mathematics as organised knowledge. When the two groups discussed their pictures with each other, it seemed that to British eyes the French teacher was erecting a monolithic structure resting on the twin pillars of algebra and topology (although it was not clear what the pillars rested on), and to the French the British teacher was the busy organiser of a series of 'happenings'. Oversimplified though this distinction is, and therefore false to a good deal in both situations, it did serve to make the British teachers question their own lack of concern with an overall grasp of the structure of elementary mathematics, and the French teachers their neglect of the inventive powers of children, including the fact that they might be capable of inventing something that had not been intended". (D. Wheeler, "An Anglo-French Meeting, *Mathematics Teaching*, n. 47 (Summer 1969), p. 19). The role of the fundamental determinants of Mathematics Education was delineated by the Soviet Union representative at the Conference in Lyons. Markushovic, in his report, reiterated that the problems of Mathematics Education today do not have only one solution, and that, "responses are influenced by the goal pursued by general education in the country in question, as well

so that the debate on mathematics and science education will not degenerate into a mere discussion of teaching techniques.

Another advantage of comparisons is that they show how different social and economic situations and different scholastic systems influence research, experimentation and changes to the curriculum.

International cooperation has been very limited up to this time; only in the past few years has it become of any importance, partly due to the initiative of teachers' associations. This is an important fact, for it shows that those having greatest concern are not merely the people responsible for the organisation of teaching; the involvement of teachers is a good guarantee for the lasting success of any experiments.

4. The movement for the reform of mathematics education has now entered upon a second phase, in which there is greater critical awareness and more international cooperation.

In this second phase, work should be conducted on two separate levels. One task is to publish and consolidate knowledge as it is acquired. Even when new curricula are far from radical, an enormous amount of work is required to train the teachers, to assess the results on the spot, to make continuing improvements. The second task is to work out systems and lines of further action which may be applied to the school of the future.

The experience acquired by countries whose school system is centralised, such as France and the Soviet Union, and which are now reforming the teaching of mathematics on a national scale, can constitute a testing ground for the first task and provide useful information for other situations.

The requirement for general long term planning has already been realised in the first phase of the movement.[63] Goals have been determined, although we are far from reaching those goals. Nonetheless, we should continuously rethink those goals and embark upon research to prove that they can in fact be attained.

---

as by the forms which this education takes. Without attempting to draw up a comprehensive list of the factors that may affect responses to the above questions, I will merely mention the choice of philosophical concept by which mathematical science is envisaged. We are all agreed that there is an essential difference between the viewpoint of the mathematician who firmly believes in the idea that mathematics have nothing to do with reality (for example, Browner according to Heyting: pure mathematics are a free creation of reason and are not linked to experience) and the concept of mathematics as a science of the most general quantitative relations (relations in the philosophical sense) in the actual world (Engels)".

[63] See "Goals for School Mathematics", *The Report of Cambridge Conference on School Mathematics*, Educational Services Incorporated, Houghton Mifflin Company, Boston, 1963.

6. SOCIAL STUDIES

BY

GASTONE TASSINARI

THE EDUCATIONAL IMPLICATIONS OF THE TERM "SOCIAL STUDIES"

Although the term "social studies" is usually taken to refer to a specific area of the curriculum that includes history, geography and civic education, it is sometimes difficult to define in practice especially when applied to primary schools in European countries. It is of interest, however, that outside Great Britain this term is seldom employed in educational and didactic literature; even more rarely is it used in official academic curricula, although it is not entirely unfamiliar. In the recent curricula for the *Grundschule* in Nordrhein-Westfalen, for example, the term *Soziale Studien* is used when referring to one of the components of the *Sachunterricht*. Similar terms are also found in other educational curricula, such as *Sozialkunde* in certain German Lander, *Samhallskungkap* in Sweden and *Obščestvovedenie* in the Soviet Union for the final year of the 10 year school, in other words after primary school. These terms are normally used for only some of the subjects which we would list under the heading of "social studies", the subjects whose aim is to impart civic and political education, somewhat similar – although there are obviously substantial differences in the specific content covered – to what in the United States is called Civics, Government and Political Science.

It is mainly in the United States that the term "social studies" is widely used in drawing up the curriculum. Its origin is attributed to the Conference on the Teaching of History, Government and Economics held in Madison, Ill., in 1892, but it was officially recognised when the Committee on Social Studies of the Commission on the Reorganisation of Secondary Education was set up by the New Education Association (1916). In the secondary school, the adoption of the new term was seen as a specific recognition of the fact that history and geography, the two basic components of the study of man and his environment, were no longer sufficient to cover the complexity of rapidly changing events and relationships and the broadening of horizons.

While the term "social studies" expressed the need to make education more topical by making it relevant to the problems of contemporary life and by the enrichment of contributions from the new fields of social research (the affinity between the two terms, social sciences and social studies, is obviously not without significance), it also went some way towards meeting the need for change from the traditional disciplines that had emerged. Once history was viewed in the light of social studies, education would cease to be inspired by a romantic, idealistic concept of history, glorifying the role of great men and nations in altering its course. The bounds of history would now be wider so that the links between the various aspects of social life and the factors which had a bearing in their evolution could be perceived.

Similarly, in the field of geography, purely descriptive teaching which merely considered isolated characteristics of the environment and classified them in rigid categories would be replaced by the study of the relationships between the physical environment and the economic, cultural, and social life developing within that environment.

Finally, the very term "moral education" had proved to be inadequate because of its manifest spiritual connotation. Once it was viewed as a component of social studies, it would no longer apply to the teaching of abstract precepts but become a concrete way of approaching social life and the topical problems of the community.

Once the traditional subjects were imbued with the spirit and concept of social sciences, even they would have to come into line with the more vital trends in contemporary culture and would make a valid contribution towards the educational process.

At the elementary school level, the term "social studies" was introduced almost contemporaneously with the initial phase of the progressive education movement and, at least in the first half of the twentieth century, it implied the second meaning rather than an enlargement of the curriculum to new disciplines. Only in very recent years has there been any realisation of the need to extend the range of social studies in the primary school to fields other than the traditional subjects of history, geography and moral and civic education.

Most innovations in this area of education, especially in Europe, have been due to experiments conducted within the framework of the traditional breakdown of disciplines. This is still causing delay in accepting not merely the term "social studies" in everyday school practice, but above all the forward-looking thinking that the term implies. The study of housing, for example, may take a very different form depending on whether it is seen as part of history or as part of the social studies lesson. In the former case, the main focus of interest will be housing as it has evolved over a period of time, and the social context may be merely a footnote. In the latter case, the main concern will be man's living conditions and the bearing of ecology, anthropology, sociology and town planning on housing. The historical aspect is part of the investigation, as it helps to clarify the rest by providing comparisons with standards of living in other periods of our history.

On the subject of the content and methods of social studies, let us consider the following five points:

1. We use the term "social studies" to identify a specific area of the curriculum which is devoted to the problems of group living. It is a terrain on which several different subjects meet and combine: the "coordinated approach" is typical of social studies. This does not mean that we should not recognise the features peculiar to each individual discipline, since each one represents a specific way of viewing the many aspects of association. The controversy between advocates of the coordinated approach and of the subject approach, a controversy that has been at the core of the debate upon the teaching of social studies in the United States over the past decade, shows that this problem – despite its importance on the educational level – has not yet been satisfactorily solved. The reasons underlying the controversy are obviously not merely pedagogical, methodological or didactic in nature but are connected with the more complex problem of the content of study and the methodologies used in social sciences and their interdisciplinary relationships.

2. Direct contact with society, constructive and expressive activities and the very processes of communications established inside the school and with the outside environment constitute an integral part of social studies, not only because they meet the child's need for a concrete foundation upon which to build up his knowledge, but also because they provide an appropriate and effective means of helping children to study man and society. Some of the best methods of achieving this aim are the introduction of graphic and representational activities, drama, interviewing or correspondence between schools into social

studies. Through such activities, the researcher – in this case, the pupil – learns how to tackle research, to be a participant, not merely an onlooker. By being forced to marshal the facts that he is investigating, the researcher has to break those facts down and truly understand them. One of the methods inherent in the social sciences thereby becomes a basic component of the process of learning social studies.

3. Another factor which brings the teaching of social studies closer to the social sciences is that the terms of reference are broader than is generally the case with the traditional compartmentalised disciplines, especially in the primary school. In advanced experiments on the teaching of social studies, most of which were conducted as part of the progressive education movement, an attempt was made to find an alternative to the teaching of nationalistic and patriotic history, not concentrating upon political and military events but attempting to guide the child towards an understanding of those aspects of man's life which reveal the most elementary and most authentic forms of association, eliminating the traditional ideological superstructures to the extent possible. The life of primitive man, how man has learned to satisfy his basic needs, the study of environments that are very close to the child's own experience: these were considered to be the most appropriate subjects, as they would help to counteract racial and jingoistic prejudice and would promote a cognitive attitude very similar to the attitude appropriate to natural sciences, so that the child would gradually acquire a rational comprehension of social phenomena.

In practice, when these theories have been implemented without a proper critical awareness they have often led to misunderstanding and their true innovatory significance has been lost. The life of primitive man has been presented as no more than a fable or legend, it has provided the opportunity for escapism rather than making a real contribution to knowledge of society by shedding light on the simplest forms of life. Man's fundamental needs have often been conceived in the most general of terms, with no reference to the specific social and cultural context. Knowledge of the environment closest to the child has often degenerated into pure description, concentrating upon the picturesque and the folksy, or has even served to promote the acceptance of traditional values and to reinforce ethnocentric attitudes. This is no criticism of the validity of the needs demonstrated by teachers and educators working towards reform of this area of the curriculum from the first few decades of our century, but it does show that these needs are not yet satisfied.

4. These considerations lead us to a more general theme: social studies and values. Since the specific purpose of this field of education is to impart a knowledge of associative life, it should not neglect the principles, beliefs and ideals which express and are sometimes the foundation of social life, inasmuch as they are the causes of association or differences between individuals and social groups.

Recent thought in the field of social studies has emphasised two aspects of special significance. The concept of "value" has been extended to include not only the more general concepts of man's destiny and his highest ideals of conduct but also his needs, aspirations and ways of feeling and acting which motivate and direct his everyday experience and which individuals and social groups consider to be relevant to their existence. With this in mind, in social studies special stress is now being laid upon those aspects of man's life that the traditional subjects tended to push to one side, considering them to be irrelevant to "true" knowledge of civilisation and the intrinsic nature of man. The other aspect is the connection that has been established between values and the social-cultural context. Values are not considered to be principles unrelated to the realities of life, nor are they conceived as absolute and unchanging, but rather as created by man, the result of common beliefs, feelings and actions related to the conditions of life in given epochs and in given groups and societies.

Viewed in their social and cultural context, values acquire specific connotations depending on whether they help to maintain the social status quo or whether they are an influence for change, whether they are used to impose acceptance of, and to consolidate, positions of privilege or whether they help to make people more equal, whether they reinforce prerogative or whether they accentuate everything that unites men and overcomes the barriers of culture, race and nationality. The essential task of social studies is to foster a critical approach to the world of values. In so doing, social studies provide a lay alternative to moral education in providing certain principles and guidelines for conduct.

5. Finally, there is another important aspect of social studies: they have a direct bearing on things as they are and pave the way for concrete action to alter those things. Social studies would have little educational significance if they were confined to the cognitive aspect and if no account were taken of their practical purpose. In learning about social life, the child learns to participate in that life, he becomes aware of the problems and can work out rational plans for their solution. A commit-

ment to social life – or at least the formation of attitudes and skills through social studies that will help to promote this commitment – should lead naturally to social action. We should also add that social action provides the means of testing the effectiveness of intellectual and theoretical social studies. We must realise, however, that other influences, apart from formal education, have a bearing and may be more effective in relating the individual to social reality, making the children aware of the true problems of their times and of the society in which they live, thus creating a lasting commitment towards the solving of those problems. What used to be generally acknowledged as the purpose of social studies, "good citizenship", based on confidence in the current system and the certainty that one lives in the best possible form of society, a society which can evolve smoothly and adapt to the changing needs of the times, has proved to be abstract and anachronistic, corrupted by a form of detachment from social reality, since society is profoundly instable, incoherent and uncertain of its future. Society needs new ideas and more active and extensive participation in starting up the process of radical change.

For this reason, the inclusion of active work in some of the more significant experiments in the field of social studies is still entirely valid, especially when we project our concept of education into the future.

One of the most important innovations in twentieth century education has undoubtedly been the identification of an area of the curriculum dealing specifically with social life. Nevertheless, when the subject has moved from the realms of theory and experiment to everyday educational practice there has been much limitation, compromise and misunderstanding, not solely due to intrinsic resistance on the part of the school towards innovation. It is obvious that cultural conditioning and the forces working against social change also exert a strong conservative influence on this area of education.

We believe that the concept of social studies which we have attempted to outline is still only in the "design" phase, despite the fact that educational theory and experiments on social studies date from the early years of our century, for the social, cultural and educational conditions required to translate theory into practice have not existed until now.

CURRENT PROBLEMS AND PROSPECTS FOR SOCIAL STUDIES

In European countries, there appears to be little educational research on social studies and even less reform of the social studies curriculum in the primary schools. This belief is confirmed both by a review of recent pedagogical literature and by direct contacts with schools and research institutes during visits that we have paid to the countries to which reference is made in this report.

The social studies research situation is highlighted by the following data. The three books published in 1969 by the Council of Europe (Documentation Centre for Education in Europe, Education Research, European Survey 1968), which provide an account of the work of 109 research institutes in 18 countries, reveal that no more than 15 surveys on the teaching of social studies or social education in the primary school had been completed or were being carried out during the two year period 1966-68. This fact is borne out by the documentary information supplied by 37 research institutes in 14 European countries at the time of the Seminar for the Directors of Educational Research Institutes and Professors of Education organised by the UNESCO Institute for Education, held in Hamburg in November 1969. According to this information, the total number of research projects on the teaching of social studies and social education in the primary school was 12. The ratio between the number of projects and the number of institutes represented was far higher in this case than in the Council of Europe publication, the probable reason being that the UNESCO Institute for Education draws more widely upon information from Socialist countries in East Europe, in which, in accordance with Marxist principles, social education is of greater importance even at the primary school level.

The main concern of European educational research today is the teaching of mathematics, science (although there is marked preference for the former) and linguistic subjects. In the near future, however, we may expect greater pedagogical concern with social studies.

This would meet certain widely felt needs:

1. The need to bring educational thought closer to current thinking in social sciences;
2. The need to make use of the influence exerted by the modern mass media over today's children, especially by extending and organising their interest in, and knowledge of, social life;
3. The need to take account of changing social and cultural conditions

in our continent and in individual countries due to technology, the growth of international relationships and trade, economic and political integration, the abolition of deep-rooted stratification within the social network and the resulting discriminations.

In the United States, unlike Europe, there has been a growing concern with social studies over the past ten years. The words with which two American research workers started their articles published within five years of each other clearly testify to the changes that have occurred in this brief period. Charles R. Keller, in an article written in 1961 entitled *Needed: Revolution in the Social Studies*, stated that "social studies are in the educational doldrums. In mathematics, science, English and the foreign languages, the curriculum is being revised, improved and brought up to date, but things are relatively quiet on the social studies front, where perhaps the need for revision is greatest".[1]

In his contribution to the book entitled *New Frontiers in Education*, 1966, William H. Hartley wrote in an entirely different vein. "Social studies are at war... to date the skirmishes have been largely local, with considerable guerrilla activity. There are signs, however, that the war is about to break out on a national scale".[2] Hartley believes the cause of the revival in interest and increase in experimental programmes in the field of social studies to be the action taken by the Department of Health, Education and Welfare in financing the social studies project in 1962, which was sponsored by the universities and the State Departments of Education. Later, in 1964, a larger budget appropriation was voted under the National Defence Education Act, the Act that had previously allocated funds to improving the teaching of mathematics, science and foreign languages. It is not for financial reasons alone, however, that there has been a sudden outcrop of action and discussion on the teaching of social studies in American schools. A decisive contribution has been the more widespread movement to review curricula, especially following the Woods Hole Conference findings in 1959 and Bruner's critical pedagogical thought, as well as the indirect (or perhaps less openly declared) effects of the aggravation of social tension, racial conflict, internal imbalance and international political events, forms of tension which have affected even the school and the cultural world. It would be oversimplifying matters to separate

---

[1] C. R. Keller, "Needed: Revolution in the Social Studies", in *Saturday Review*, Sept. 16, 1961, reprinted in B. G. Massialas and A. M. Kazamias (eds.), *Crucial Issues in the Teaching of Social Studies*, Prentice Hall, Englewood Cliffs, N.J., 1964, p. 38.

[2] W. H. Hartley, "Social Studies", in F. and C. L. Guggenheim (eds.), *New Frontiers in Education*, Grune and Stratton, New York, 1966, p. 104.

the two factors by saying that the general movement towards curricular reform has brought about changes which emphasise the development of knowledge and the processes of learning, while the tensions have had a greater effect on social education, in other words have influenced the educational practice concerning the social behaviour and the development of social attitudes. In fact, the two trends often merge and integrate. In many cases, it is because of the need to alter subjects of study and methods of learning that we are forced to criticise the traditional concept of social education, which is considered to be "sentimental, contrived, self-conscious and ineffective"[3], and to define new outlooks based upon a more realistic attitude towards current social problems, on greater readiness for change, on receptiveness towards the society and culture of other countries and other social groups.

The new trends in social studies in the United States, and in particular the experimental projects being conducted there, can be summarised as follows[4]:

1. Most studies begin with an analysis and description of the generalisations and concepts relating to the various social sciences.
2. The new curricula are evolved jointly by university research workers, methods specialists, teachers and evaluation experts.
3. When planning the social studies curriculum for the school of the future, the aim is continuity and smooth progress from the pre-primary to the senior high school.
4. Whereas history, geography and civic education used to predominate in the social studies curriculum, proper emphasis is now being placed on economy, anthropology, sociology and social psychology.
5. Thought is being given not only to continuity of the subjects studied, as described in 3 above, but to the sequence in which skills, attitudes and critical ability are developed.
6. The "finding out" method, by which the pupils consider the facts and try to draw their own conclusions, using the same techniques as those employed by social science research workers, is considered to be one of the best ways of assimilating knowledge, learning methods and appreciating the significance of social studies.
7. The combined use of various teaching aids is suggested: textual material, audio-visual aids and source materials.

---

[3] R. C. Preston, "The Social Studies: Nature, Purpose and Signs of Change", in *The National Elementary School Principal*, XLII, April 1963, reprinted in H. Hillson (ed.), *Elementary Education*, The Free Press, New York, 1967, p. 91.
[4] See W. H. Hartley, *op. cit.*, pp. 110-111.

8. The new social studies curricula will require careful research, thorough planning, testing in the classroom, subsequent review of the findings and amendment before they can be put into practice in the school. An essential part of the process is evaluation, using the best instruments that are available.
9. The content of the curriculum is being extended to Asiatic and African cultures, which have formally been neglected in social studies.
10. In former curricula, children were first introduced to what was close to them and then their knowledge was gradually extended. Today, selected subjects are replacing this system as they are better able to develop the power of generalisation and the acquisition of basic value concepts. Instead of narrow-minded nationalism, children are being given a broad view of the world.

In 1967, there were more than 50 major projects in the field of social studies in the United States. As observed by Edwin Fenton, most of these projects related to a fairly narrow sector and were almost exclusively concerned with objectives, teaching strategies, materials, ways of grouping pupils and the training of teachers. Nonetheless, this meant that "within a few years these elements will fuse into coherent programmes which will stake the entire educational system".[5] One consequence of the sectorial nature of these projects was that teaching and learning activities did not reflect progressive thought on the organisation of teaching. "Despite all the experiments with team teaching and other patterns of flexible pupil deployment, most social studies education takes place in a self-contained classroom".[6]

Notwithstanding these limitations and the over-optimistic use of the term "revolution" when referring to current innovations in the social studies curriculum, innovations that are far less revolutionary than those achieved in the first half of the twentieth century in America and Europe, we must admit that the debate and action in the United States over the past ten years have been highly stimulating. We shall refer to the situation in America several times, even though the subject of our report is the future of the elementary school in Europe.

In discussing the European school situation in general and that of West Germany in particular, Wolfgang Mitter[7] observes that "current

---

[5] F. Fenton, *The New Social Studies*, Rinehart and Winston, New York, 1967, p. 120.
[6] *Ibid.*, p. 93.
[7] W. Mitter, "'Social Studies' in der amerikanischen Elementarschule", in *Die Grundschule*, I, 4, October 1969, pp. 35-46.

developments in the social studies curriculum and the pedagogical debate accompanying those developments in the United States should be thoroughly analysed and we should give careful consideration to whether the American findings can be transferred to Europe and whether they are applicable". He lists three basic factors on which light could be thrown by such an analysis. Firstly, man and his social relationships. This may become the principal theme of education in the primary school, overcoming the danger of lack of interest in social and political subjects among the children, rendering them susceptible to the preconceived ideas imparted by extra-scholastic influences which will prove difficult to uproot in later phases of their education. The second aspect is whether the content of education can be transmitted sincerely. Experiments conducted on the teaching of social studies in the United States appear to show that the primary school child has a greater ability to form concepts than has generally been recognised and that it is of little value to use examples (Mitter even calls it irresponsible) which conceal very specific ideologies: for instance to depict the state as a father figure, the family as the root of society, etc. The third aspect finally, is the image of society which is outlined in the experimental programmes in America. The reformers, Mitter states, refuse to idealise the values of the American way of life. They adopt Bruner's concept that the function of the school is not merely to provide a link with outside society but to enable children to explore alternative ideas and reinforce their desire to seek those ideas. Nevertheless, the image of society projected by the new social studies curricula does not differ greatly from the traditional concept, even when these studies deal with situations of conflict and the problems to which social change has given rise. "In consequence, they are essentially *affirmative* despite the fact that emancipatory prospects... can be discerned at many points". In discussing the objective limitations imposed by the pupils' level of psychological maturity, Mitter concludes that "nor can we evade this problem, if we take seriously the concept of a political education in the service of man's self-determination. The degree to which emancipatory goals can be inserted into the curriculum at elementary level is more difficult to establish than at the higher levels of education, since by neglecting the affirmative element we prevent the child from achieving a rational understanding of the present, with all its conflict and its compromises, and the attempt at emancipation is doomed to failure from the start".

BROADENING THE FIELD OF SOCIAL STUDIES

As we observed at the beginning of this chapter, the introduction of the term "social studies" implied that the subjects and methods were being extended beyond the subjects and methods inherent in the disciplines that had previously dominated the study of man and his environment. Even Dewey and the other advocates of educational reform in the first half of our century accepted the predominance of those subjects.

Today, while some authors still consider history and geography to be the main components of the social studies curriculum, placing other subjects such as anthropology, economy and sociology in a secondary position[8], others underline the significance of introducing the more recent social sciences even at elementary school level, and not in a secondary role. One of the advocates of this second point of view was Hilda Taba, working in the field of social psychology and learning, who directed an experimental programme on social studies. She deplored the fact that the contribution of more recent disciplines was ignored in school education, for she affirmed that they could "offer important needed insights to understanding and interpreting the world today. Anthropologists, for example, point out that anthropology, the only science which specialises in the 'whole' culture and the 'whole' man, is conspicuously absent both in the content of curriculum and among the concepts with which social phenomena are explained and interpreted".[9]

In an article which appeared in 1965, discussing trends taking shape in the field of social studies, James M. Becker summarised the educational significance of the broader field of social studies as follows: "Such study has value not merely for its own sake, but for the sake of understanding the rich resources of pertinent wisdom available for dealing with contemporary problems. It is important, therefore, that attention be directed to the nature of recent developments in the social sciences, the influence of these developments upon current efforts to strengthen social studies instruction, and the emerging trends which stem from these efforts... Such disciplines as anthropology and social psychology have not only evolved but are demanding that their techniques and findings be brought into play along with the insight provided by older fields such as history and geography. Political science in-

---

[8] See, for example J. Jarolimek, *Social Studies in Elementary School*, Macmillan, New York, 1963 (2), p. 318.

[9] H. Taba, *Curriculum Development, Theory and Practice*, Harcourt, Brace and World, New York, 1962, p. 269.

creasingly turns its attention from descriptions of institutions to analysis of process and to theory. Scholars are trying to adapt cybernetics and communications theory to the requirements of the social sciences. The search for common principles of human behaviour and the increased possibilities of prediction are concerns of prominent social scientists. These impressive developments in the social sciences bring within the range of elementary and secondary schools opportunities to create new and improved curricula which in turn will help students to build a framework of basic ideas about human behaviour and the nature of our complex world".[10]

In extending the range of the study of social life, the main goal is to acquire greater understanding of our contemporary world. One of the chief contributions that social sciences can make is to shed light upon the processes of change which, while they create doubts and difficulties and uncertainties in our present situation, forshadow its possible developments in the future. It has been stated that the content of educational curricula "is too strongly oriented toward the past to provide a realistic understanding of the current social science" and that "we depend too much on the 'lessons of history' which no longer suffice to give proper perspectives toward the forces of the future or even to develop a facility to apply them to future contingencies".[11] If the individual is to be prepared for the problems of change, Bruner sustains, the educational stress must be upon studying the possible rather than the achieved. He believes that the study of history should be enriched by the incorporation of the social and the behavioural sciences so that we can make generalisations with respect to variations in the human condition.[12] Obviously this does not mean that we should no longer study the past. On another occasion, Bruner defined history as an extension of those needs which drive man to seek and find the remote reasons for his actions and his dilemmas, the precedents for his attitude towards the future, and he noted paradoxically the affinity between the knowledge of history on the social level and the sense of one's own identity on the personal level.[13]

In the United States, while it is intended to revise the history and

---

[10] J. M. Becker, "Emerging Trends in the Social Studies", in *Educational Leadership*, 22 Feb. 1965, reprinted in H. Hillson (ed.), *op. cit.*, pp. 95-96.
[11] H. Taba, *op. cit.*, p. 275.
[12] J. S. Bruner, *Toward a Theory of Instruction*, The Belknap Press of Harvard University Press, Cambridge, Mass., 1966, p. 36.
[13] J. S. Bruner, *On Knowing, Essays for the Left Hand*, The Belknap Press of Harvard University Press, Cambridge, Mass., 1964.

geography curriculum, there are also many plans to introduce elementary economy, anthropology, sociology and psycho-sociology to the primary school. The projects being introduced differ widely, one of the reasons being the decentralised school system in America, and it is difficult to identify features common to all schools apart from the more general trends which we have already described. Nevertheless, two alternative methodologies are emerging from the major experimental projects: the first is the rational development of one individual discipline, as in the experiment in economic education conducted by Lawrence Senesh in schools in Elkhart, Indiana, one of the first curricula whose aim was to extend the field of social studies, or in the *Sequential Curriculum in Anthropology for Grades 1-7*, directed by Wilfred Bailey of the University of Georgia. The second trend is the introduction of basic concepts of various social sciences into courses organised around a series of themes – the home, family, school, work in the community, the state, etc. – as for example in the *Contra Costa County Social Studies Curriculum* launched under the guidance of Hilda Taba, or the curriculum drawn up by Joseph C. Grannis and teachers in Lexington, Mass., public schools.[14] These two alternatives are related to the differing schools of thought which have grown up over the past decade in the United States, one favouring the subject approach, the other opting for the coordinated approach.

There is a certain tendency in the European primary school to broaden the range of social studies. Certain experiments have been conducted in Italy by groups of teachers, for instance.[15] In the curricula for the Swedish *Grundskola* (1969), there is a clear intention from

[14] Periodical news on the projects relative to social studies is given in the publications issued by the National Council of Social Studies, in particular in *Social Education*. R. C. Preston provides a detailed summary of certain projects in *Teaching Social Studies in Elementary School* (Holt, Rinehard and Winston, New York, 1968³). See also L. S. Kenworthy, *Social Studies for the Seventies*, Blaisdell, Waltham, Mass., 1969, pp. 73-75. H. Taba, in *Curriculum Development*, *op. cit.*, gives ample illustrations of the *Contra Costa County Social Studies Curriculum*, particularly in Chapters 20 and 22. In the production of new social studies curricula, of special note is the Educational Development Center (EDC) to which the Educational Services Inc. (ESI) and the Institute for Educational Innovation (IEI) belonged in 1967. *Man: a Course of Study*, in which J. S. Bruner collaborated, is published by the EDC (see J. S. Bruner, *Toward a Theory of Instruction*, *op. cit.*, chap. 4).

[15] An example is in the Pestalozzi School, Florence. It originated in the exchange of correspondence between fifth grade children (10 year olds) and pupils of the same age in a Turin school, mainly children of emigrants from other regions. The different make-up of the two groups was the starting point for research on the theme of emigration and of its geographical, economic and social aspects. For this purpose, pupils found out data through a questionnaire, worked out statistics, and consulted various documentary sources with regard to income, population distribution in different areas of production, and the morphology and climate of the Italian regions. (See A. M. Brizzi Caputi and B. Chiesa, "Una nuova ricerca d'ambiente in quinta elementare", in *Cooperazione Educativa*, XIX, 11, pp. 8-24).

the very first grade not to restrict "knowledge of the environment" (*Hembygdskunskap*) to a purely descriptive and fragmentary approach. Instead, the children are given a broad knowledge of sociology, anthropology and economy, observing the diversity of family life, criticising the traditional discriminations in the roles of the sexes, analysing significant aspects of production and trade, comparing family, school and community situations that differ from the environment in which they themselves live.[16]

There is a similar and even more marked trend in the Nordrhein-Westfalen curricula, also dating from 1969. The three basic themes recommended for this area of education are: man the producer and man the consumer; man and time; the individual within society.[17]

Through study of the first theme, it is hoped that children will become aware of the problems of economic life (supply and demand, the production of goods, trade and barter, etc.) so that the basic principles governing this field of research become clear and "idyllic" concepts can be avoided. Aspects of human activity (home, family life, food, production, commerce, education, recreation, etc.), studied individually in the first two grades of the *Grundschule*, are taken up again and coordinated in the third grade in developing the theme "let's build a city". The second theme is based upon the need to foster a sense of time and an awareness of "becoming" in the child. Building on the foundations of the children's immediate experience, by the third and fourth grade they are introduced to periods of time remote from their direct personal experience. In the fifth grade, children study the history, local geography and local economy of their own *Land* so that they have an overall view to use as a point of reference when contrasting the differences between their life today and life in the past. The third theme considers social relationships in a more specific sense, both from the institutional viewpoint and as an area in which the children will be called upon to show a sense of personal responsibility. Special emphasis is placed upon situations that arise out of their school life, viewing these in a wider social context. In so doing, specific subjects such as relationships between racial groups, emigration or class distinctions are used to introduce the children to wider considerations of an economic, legal and political nature.

---

[16] *Läroplan för Grundskolan, Orienteringsämnen*, Svenska Utbildningsförlaget, Stockholm, 1969, pp. 14-22.
[17] *Richtlinien und Lehrpläne für die Grundschule, Schulversuch in Nordrhein-Westfalen*, A. Henn Verlag, Wuppertal, 1969, pp. 250-252 and 274-344.

We believe the following conclusion can be drawn from the above. One of the features of the school of tomorrow will probably be an extension of social studies, which are becoming a focal point in the debate on education, the subject of research and a trend clearly visible in recent curricular reforms. The educational significance is obviously not merely that more social studies subjects will be included in the future. It is not a question of increasing the amount of information (and this is a point to which we shall refer in a subsequent paragraph), but rather that the child's conceptual approach to society will be rendered more effective, rich and flexible and that the contributions of social and behavioural sciences will be used to this end. In the curricular reform which we have delineated, special attention should be paid to the principles governing the selection of subjects and the experiences through which the concepts and methods of social science can be assimilated by primary school children.

SUBJECT APPROACH VERSUS COORDINATED APPROACH

One of the central themes of the movement for the reform of social studies curricula in the United States is the debate on alternative methods of teaching: should rigid partitions between subjects be removed to introduce a "wholistic" concept of education, or should subjects be separated to emphasise the specific methods and contents peculiar to each?[18] The fact that research workers in different fields of social sciences have been active participants in this movement, sometimes taking a leading role in the planning and testing of new curricula, has helped to focus attention upon the specific content of individual subjects, sometimes comprising the comprehensive concept of social studies which has gained wide acceptance in American schools, at least at the elementary level.

The objection to the "wholistic approach" has been raised that "the social sciences are not a single, ordered body of facts and theories, operating through an internally consistent and generally accepted uniform methodology. In so far as the social studies are derived from the social sciences, it has been most difficult to identify a coherent and unified core of concept and factual contents".[19]

[18] The two positions are compared in *Focus on the Social Studies*, NEA Department of Elementary School Principals, Washington, 1965, which reproduces the general session speeches and the final panel discussion at the DESP annual meeting.
[19] P. E. James, "Geography", in *The Social Studies and the Social Sciences*, Harcourt, New York, 1962, p. 44.

Today, in fact, there is keen criticism not so much of the attempt to integrate the different disciplines but of what is currently known as the "scrambled approach", the generic syncretism, the attempt to reconcile different subjects without due attention to the scientific ordering of principles. Even those who advocate the integration of social studies prefer to use the expression "coordinated approach" rather than "wholistic" teaching, justifying their position on the grounds that while contemporary scientific research accentuates the need for certain forms of specialisation, scientific progress is made by cooperation between research workers and by integrating contributions from different disciplines.[20]

The more advanced trend in curricular reorganisation seems to be the elimination of rigid partitions between subjects (compartmentalisation), in furtherance of the principle that learning should lead to the acquisition of structures inherent in each individual subject, a principle upon which the movement for curricular reform over the past ten years has been based. The emphasis is now being placed upon the acquisition of interdisciplinary structures and this, it has been observed, seems to highlight the need to "base education on the 'unitary' world of the child's experience".[21] Even in this general trend, however, there are differing schools of thought. On the one hand, the multi-disciplinary approach is favoured as it is recognised that each of the social sciences is independent in itself, representing a specific point of view and considering one aspect of human behaviour, although it is admitted that "no subject in the entire social studies curriculum is devoid of contamination by each other subject", and that distinctions are not "between subjects that are rigidly separated, but between subjects that merge".[22] Others favour a "process-centered curriculum" characterised by "inter-disciplinary learning", to avoid the artificiality of compartmentalisation that takes no account of the "duplication, overlap and cross-application" between the disciplines. "If the child's study is based on the ordered activity of a discipline's practitioners instead of on its epistemological confines, a more functional course of study for the school may be achieved".[23]

---

[20] See P. H. Odegard, "Fragmentation vs. Coordination", in *Focus on the Social Studies, op. cit.*, pp. 16-20.
[21] W. Mitter, *op. cit.*, p. 41.
[22] M. Scriven, "The Structure of Social Studies", in G. W. Ford and L. Pugno (eds.), *The Structure of Knowledge and the Curriculum*, Rand McNally, Chicago, 1964, p. 92.
[23] J. C. Parker and L. J. Rubin, *Process as Content: Curriculum Design and the Application of Knowledge*, Rand McNally, Chicago, 1969 (3), p. 61.

This is the line of thought that seems to have inspired the most progressive trends in the teaching of social studies in Europe. In England, the Plowden Report states that sterling educational work is being done by those schools that are moving away from the traditional compartmentalisation of subjects and are concentrating pupils' work upon multi-disciplinary themes, availing themselves of experts in various branches of learning on the school staff. This working method, which involves the use of textual source materials, study of the environment and the conduct of scientific investigations, is not usually applied before the age of 10 or 11.[24]

Also the social studies curriculum for the Nordrhein-Westfalen *Grundschule* is based on the inter-disciplinary approach. The recent curricula for the *Grundskola* in Sweden, on the other hand, is structured so as gradually to emphasise differences between subjects. In the first three grades of the elementary school, children are introduced to their environment through the study of a series of themes. In the fourth to sixth grades, they move on to a differential study of history, geography and civic education, while the approach to natural sciences is still integrated. It is not until they reach the senior level, in the seventh to the ninth grades, that they study natural sciences separately. Nevertheless, teachers are advised to link the various disciplines in the stages during which they are gradually being separated.

The concept of *activités d'éveil*, which is being applied to the primary school in France, emphasises not only the integration of the social subjects but also the links between social studies and natural sciences. An example of this integration is the connection between the concept of the balance of nature and the social implications of the conservation of the environment.[25]

The relationships between the components of social studies still raise many questions and constitute a stimulating field of investigation for research workers. Nonetheless, we believe that the solution to these questions will depend not only – and not so much – on attempts at epistemological organisation of sciences but rather by research upon the mental operations involved when we are faced with the need to solve a problem or to broaden our knowledge of a specific subject and we have to go beyond one specific sector of research, combining the views and information of different sectors. Scientific research has not

---

[24] *Children and their Primary School*, HMSO, London, 1967, Vol. I, p. 226.
[25] *Le Tiers-temps pédagogique*, Cahiers de documentation, série pédagogique, Institut Pédagogique National, Paris, 1970, p. 64.

yet provided sufficiently reliable information on this subject to assist with organising the curriculum and with teaching. However, in intellectual activity in general and in the field of social sciences in particular, the rigid "division of labour" is clearly proving to be inadequate; there is a need for flexibility so that we can adopt differing points of view and synthetise the contributions of each. We must not wait until children reach the upper levels of education before attempting to form this mental attitude, an attitude that is fundamental not only for intellectual development but also for social maturation. It is a specific task of education at the elementary level. For this reason, we believe that the trend towards inter-disciplinary study will be reinforced in the education of the future, discarding generic solutions that diverge from a true scientific approach to social reality, such as those which are often camouflaged behind the term "study of the environment".

CRITICISM OF THE "EXPANDING ENVIRONMENT APPROACH"

Another problem relating to social sciences teaching is the sequence of teaching that should be adopted when planning the curriculum. Here again we shall refer to the current debate in the United States as it may throw light on the situation in Europe.

The stress laid upon the community, traditionally believed to be the basic structural element of American society, and the belief that learning in the elementary school should be directly linked with the child's own environment and then gradually be extended in space and in time, are the reasons for the general adoption of the "widening horizons approach" or the "expanding environment approach" in the curriculum. One of the advantages of this approach was that different subjects could be built up around a common central theme.[26]

This criterion is adopted in the framework recommended by the report of the State Central Committee on Social Studies to the California State Curriculum Commission (1961).[27] Between 1954 and 1959, institutes, associations and experts in education and other sub-

---

[26] M. Dunfee and H. Sagl (*Social Studies through Problem Solving*, Holt, Rinehart and Winston, New York, 1966, pp. 311-312) trace back the widening-horizons approach to the Virginia Course of Study (1934) which organised study material around "social functions", i.e. "common activities in which cultural groups of the world have engaged for a long time": home, school, community life, adaptation of life to varied natural environments and to advancing physical frontiers, effects of inventions and discoveries on daily life, effects of machine production on living.

[27] *Report of the State Central Committee on Social Studies to the California State Curriculum Commission*, California State Department of Education, Sacramento, 1961.

jects worked on this report. There are many references to the report in the literature on the subject and it undoubtedly represents a milestone in the reform of teaching curricula for the whole cycle of education, from kindergarten to the 14th grade. The broad scientific framework for the basic concepts of some of the disciplines and the tentative approach towards a "world-wide viewpoint" in the theoretical part of the report do not, however, seem to be reflected in the subjects of study recommended for individual grades: the purely descriptive seems to predominate, the focal point being the local community and the American way of life.

One of the most forceful advocates of the gradual broadening of environmental knowledge is Paul R. Hanna of Stanford University. He suggests a complex two-dimensional outline of social studies: a "sequence" plan covering 11 communities, seen as a sequence of concentric circles extending from the family to the world community; and the "scope" plan covering 9 basic human activities – production, transportation, communication, education, recreation, protection, government, creation, expression. Each community sphere is studied in the light of each of these 9 activities, emphasising the complementary relationships between communities.[28]

Objections to the "expanding environment approach" are based on the belief that children today have far more frequent opportunities than before to break out from their immediate neighbourhood, their small local community or their town. A contributory factor has been the growth in communications, especially the mass media coverage. It is objected that the "expanding environment approach" is in practice superseded by the child's everyday experiences in his life outside the school and that this approach does not provide sufficient incentive to clarify his ideas and to broaden his knowledge. This theory is supported by research showing that, even at elementary school level, interest in social studies is elastic and can be extended from the local community to the world with as much ease in the first grade as in the sixth.[29] Although there are obviously limitations upon a child's ability to organise his knowledge in the light of space and time relationships, it is

---

[28] P. R. Hanna, "Design for a Social Studies Program", in *Focus on the Social Studies, op. cit.*, pp. 28-45.

[29] R. Ellsworth, "Trends in Organisation of the Social Studies", in J. U. Michaelis (ed.), *Social Studies in Elementary Education*, 32nd Yearbook of the National Council for the Social Studies, Washington, 1962, p. 124. The author quotes the survey by J. D. McAuley of a sample of 715 elementary school pupils in Pennsylvania, published in *Social Education*, 8 December 1961.

believed that these limitations should not prevent elementary school children from comparing different ways of life with their direct experience in their immediate environment, even though they may not truly understand the topological and chronological differences between these ways of life.[30] Of relevance to this point are Dewey's remarks upon the stimulus to learning provided by what is distant and remote and, on the contrary, the sense of mental constriction and waste of time felt by children when asked to consider things that are too familiar to them.[31]

Discussing the well known project, *Man: A Course of Study*, Jerome Bruner explains how this course differs from the teaching methods which start by presenting the child's everyday world, his home and his neighbourhood, since it is difficult to generalise about an over-familiar reality. Bruner replaces the gradual "expanding environment approach" by the comparative method, which he believes to be more productive on the conceptual level as it stimulates curiosity and can be used to help children discover common principles or generalisations that extend beyond the dissimilarities of the various situations under study.

A "half-way solution" may be the *Contra Costa County Social Study* proposal: although the sequence of themes is very close to the sequence adopted by the expanding environment approach (home, family, school; work in the community; comparative study of communities; the State of California today and in the past; life in the United States; the Western Hemisphere; international trade; the United Nations), it is suggested that each subject be studied by comparing different situations, so that children discover for themselves basic concepts in the fields of sociology, anthropology, history, geography and economics.

Several of the latest recommendations on the organisation of the social studies curriculum have been based on this study. For example, L. S. Kenworthy outlines a curriculum covering the kindergarten to the 12th grade, in which "the old concentric circle theory of the curriculum" is replaced "with a dual curriculum which emphasises the United States and the world, usually in alternative years".[32] B. R. Joyce, on the other hand, suggests a pilot curriculum in which each elementary school grade is given a limited number of themes which it

---

[30] See B. R. Joyce, *Strategies for Elementary Social Sciences Education*, Science Research Associates, Chicago, 1965, p. 10.
[31] J. Dewey, *How we think*, Heath, Boston, 1933.
[32] L. S. Kenworthy, *op. cit.*, pp. 76-77.

examines through a "cross-cultural depth study" so that children can make comparisons of their own and other societies.[33]

This criterion for the organisation of study material, which in some respects is reflected in the curricula for the Swedish Grundskola, appears to be most in line with the educational goals of social studies and to be the best solution for the school of the future. This method may in fact "extend the child's horizons" (and there is no reason why his horizons should be extended by a pedantic and gradual process), due allowance being made for the stimulus of things that are not too ordinary or familiar, while at the same time we avoid the risk of social studies becoming a mere exercise in the acquisition of knowledge, devaluing the society in which the child lives and by-passing the problems of his own society.

THE COGNITIVE ASPECT OF SOCIAL STUDIES

The problem of the acquisition of knowledge is today a focal point in educational thought and a recurring theme in research on the reform of teaching programmes. The problem has also been applied to social studies; in this field, too, stress is laid upon the learning of "structures", on the concepts of "discovery" and "enquiry", on the "process-centered approach", on acquisition of the ability to "transfer". All these subjects have been discussed at length in other sections of this report, but we think it opportune to review them briefly, if only to underline their significance in the framework of social studies, both in the inherent goals of this branch of education and in the educational prospects that have for the most part been developing outside the field of teaching.

Social studies are commonly known as "informational subjects". Dewey himself accepted this definition when he made a distinction between the informational study of history and geography and the type of activity whose purpose is the acquisition of specific practical skills (such as reading, writing, drawing and music) and also between history and geography and the "disciplinary" subjects in which the ability to reason is more important (such as mathematics and formal grammar). Nevertheless, Dewey warned against the risks of imposing overrigid distinctions, since the acquisition of information must continue to be an integral part of teaching the child to think.[34]

---

[33] B. R. Joyce, *op. cit.*, pp. 157-161.
[34] J. Dewey, *How we think, op. cit.*, pp. 128 and 131-132.

In practice, when the term "informational" is used in the educational field in describing certain subjects of study or a certain type of knowledge, some of its connotations are negative. It is used, in substance, to refer to "parrot learning" of facts and ideas and to a lack of conceptual involvement. In this sense of the word, it has also been attributed to social studies in general, on the assumption that the specific function of social studies, especially at elementary school level, should be to provide citizens with the basic knowledge that will enable them to find their bearings in their own social and cultural environment and to enter into the life of society. This function might be sufficient were society and culture static and conservative, but it is entirely inadequate if society and culture are conceived in dynamic terms, if the man is expected to participate in a continuous process of innovation and experimentation. If this is so, intensification of the experience of socialisation and the growth of channels of information other than the traditional channel of the school must be offset by stimulating the child's capacity for reflective thinking if he is later to take an active part in changing society. If this is to be the goal, the quality of knowledge imparted in this field of social studies must be raised from the very earliest levels of education.

The need for change in this direction is clear even today. First of all, with the general trend towards extending the period of compulsory schooling, the elementary school need no longer concentrate on cramming "basic information" into the child in the space of a few years. L. Legrand, Director of the Research Department at the French National Pedagogical Institute, discussing the educational goals of the *activités d'éveil* in the primary school, which include social studies, has remarked "...in the time when most children went to school until the age of 11 and schooling took place in the primary school, it seemed essential that the child be equiped with mental baggage, consisting of a given number of facts and a given number of attitudes that it was believed he needed to take his place in society at a later date... The main objective today is no longer to acquire this basic knowledge, but, through educational action, to help him to shed the preconceived ideas he has formed for himself, to bring his concepts up to date and to construct new concepts and attitudes which will help him to attain the level of true scientific thought".[35]

Another factor has contributed to change: the ever-growing in-

---

[35] L. Legrand, "Les activités d'éveil au cycle élémentaire", in *Le Tiers-temps pédagogique*, *op. cit.*, p. 58.

fluence of channels of information other than the school. The Plowden Report (discussing geography teaching, although its remarks are applicable to the whole area of information) states: "the cinema, the press, and most of all television have made available to everyone a general visual knowledge of the world such as was impossible for adults, let alone children, before their invention... Such knowledge may be superficial but it bears the ring of authenticity. This makes the task of the school at once easier and more difficult; easier because the sources of knowledge are greater than school geography alone, and more difficult because the wealth of impression possessed by children will be incomplete, confused and often coloured by the selection and purposes of the programme observed".[36]

In one of the conclusions reached by the International Seminar for Directors of Educational Research Institutes and Professors of Education organised by the UNESCO Institute of Education, stress was placed upon the implications for the future of education of the transfer of informational tasks from the school to communication circuits outside the school. The seminar stated the need for educational research to be based mainly upon the prospects for change – upon themes which are *porteurs d'avenir* or "harbingers for the future" – and affirmed that "the school is less involved in the transmission of knowledge (which is provided to the pupils in abundance by the mass media) and more directed towards helping the pupils to organise their knowledge. For this reason, it is vital that research be conducted in the following domains: quantitative and qualitative evaluation of what is supplied by the mass media and what is supplied by the school; the study of preconceived ideas as obstacles to the reception of knowledge from the extra-scholastic world; children's attitudes towards non-school information; the role of social factors in the acquisition of structures that can be used to organise knowledge".

The concern of educators, now or in the future, may not be lack of information but rather that the child is unable, critically, to absorb and organise that information. There is a risk that he will become submerged and disorientated by the mass of fragmentary information. This problem is highly relevant to our field of investigation, because the extensive coverage of the mass media has become a significant social factor, because the content of the information teaching the child and the adult through the mass media is mainly concerned with aspects

---

[36] *Children and their Primary School, op. cit.*, p. 234.

of social life and finally, because – quite apart from the specific content of the messages, which may have been intentionally selected by those who operate the channels of information – the mass media have an enormous influence upon the attitudes of the individual towards society and its problems. The individual at the receiving end may be content merely to absorb that information passively but in fact be alienated so that he does not bother to take decisions or concrete action.[37]

For all these reasons, social studies should undoubtedly take on specific new educational tasks. It is difficult to define these tasks, however, on the basis of a clear cut separation between the "informational" process and the process which emphasises the "organisation of knowledge". While the former consists merely of absorbing predigested knowledge through modern communications techniques, the latter tends to exercise subsequent external control over the knowledge acquired through these techniques, without allowing for the true potential of these techniques as tools for the construction and organisation of knowledge. The concept and use now being made of audio-visual aids in the teaching of social studies, in other words their sole or prevalent employment for fruition rather than for production, as dispensers of information rather than as the instruments of investigation, place a serious limitation upon the constructive use of modern communications techniques in the process of learning. New prospects will open up to the school in its function as the organiser of knowledge once it reconciles the instaneity and extensiveness of communications circuits with wider access to these circuits not only to receive but also to transmit information, using modern communications techniques to state and analyse the problem and to structure the lessons of experience.

The application of the problem-solving approach to social studies is of special relevance in the educational concept according to which this form of teaching does not impart "a congeries of facts" but a "study more rational, more amenable to the use of mind".[38] By this Bruner

---

[37] See P. F. Lazarsfeld and R. K. Merton, "Mass Communication, Popular Taste and Organized Social Action", in B. Rosenberg and D. M. White (eds.), *Mass Culture*, The Free Press of Glencoe, New York, 1960.

[38] J. S. Bruner, *Toward a Theory of Instruction, op. cit.*, p. 96. A detailed demonstration of the problem-solving approach to social studies is given by M. Dunfee and H. Sagl in the above-mentioned work. They agree with Bruner as to the role of the structure of disciplines in learning, but differ in other aspects from his programme of social studies. They believe that the subject of enquiry should arise from pupils' everyday experience, rather than from the facts that contrast with it. As an example, they quote the subject of the effects of communication on community living. Investigation starts with an initiation phase which introduces pupils to the specific subject to be studied, and continues through cooperative planning of a set of activities (reading, community experiences, construction and processing, audio-

implies that children cannot be provided with a ready-packaged body of knowledge but that they themselves must be involved in the process of organising that knowledge. This point will be reached when social experience acquired at first hand can be used to supply the motivations for, and the subject of, research, laying emphasis upon situations of tension and the need for changes in the existing situation; or when, through second-hand experience, children are asked to examine selected materials drawn from social life from which certain aspects have been omitted, filling in the gaps for themselves, or problematical situations that arouse the wish to explain or supplement. The emotional response and participation that this approach tends to arouse will stimulate thought so that the child goes beyond the bare bones of the problem and establishes links between the facts and figures at his disposal, seeking further information, formulating conjectures and hypotheses on the theoretical and practical outcomes of the situation which he is considering, exploring alternatives and testing their validity.

This process harmonises with the pupil's approach to the "structures" of social sciences (in the sense in which the term is used by Bruner and Schwab), considered separately and on the inter-disciplinary level as a whole. In the context of a problem situation, "psychology" and the "way of thinking" peculiar to each become instruments in the search for a solution (according to Bruner, "there is nothing more central to a discipline than its way of thinking. There is nothing more important in its teaching than to provide the child the earliest opportunity to learn that way of thinking".[39] In the same way, the discovery by the pupil of "generalisations" through investigation

---

visual experiences, experimenting) that help the child to establish concepts and generalisations. One example of the problem-solving approach to real life situations and to topical questions is the approach mentioned in note 24 concerning the enquiry on emigration carried out by 5th grade pupils; others are experiments conducted by the "Scuola e Quartiere" (School and Quarter) movement in Florence. The "Plowden Report" hints at the problem-solving approach to history and geography on the basis of local study (pp. 228-234), while extending the enquiry to facts and situations which are not immediately observed. There are similar trends in the Swedish *Grundskola* emphasising the development of pupils' skills in identifying problems, cooperative work-planning, use of various sources of documentation and of mathematics, statistics and graphs to represent and compare social phenomena. In an article, L. V. Nemčenko deals with the problem-solving approach to the teaching of history and social subjects in third and fourth grades of the Soviet school. He considers this method of teaching as an adequate means to stimulate an emotional and intellectual disposition in pupils which reinforces the teacher's approach to the argument presented. In this case, the problem is raised mainly by asking pupils questions and letting them arrive at their own conclusions. (L. V. Nemčenko, "Problemnae izučenie obščestvenno-istoričescogo materiala v III-IV klassach" (Problem teaching of historic-social material in 3rd and 4th grades), in *Načalnaja Škola*, 4, 1968).

[39] J. S. Bruner, *Toward a theory of Instruction, op. cit.*, p. 155.

Social Studies

in the field of social sciences is the conclusion of a process which, originating in the search for a solution to a specific problem, is extended so that the findings can be applied to a variety of similar situations.

In recent educational literature, there is general approval of the move away from the original definition of the contents of various disciplines in terms of "generalisation" (in other words in the terms of the conclusions to a complex series of investigations at the highest level of abstraction, a typical example being the report of the State Central Committee on Social Studies in California) towards a definition in terms of "concepts", for example the concept of social class, leadership, culture, etc. It is recognised that concepts – rather than a synthesis of the conclusions reached by research workers – can play a central and dynamic part in promoting the process of enquiry among children, as "concepts" are the elements of the hypothetical relations in a given research context and provide guidance in the classification, selection and organisation of facts.[40] B. R. Joyce adopts the same principle when he declares that he prefers to use the term "organising concepts" rather than "structure", "in order to avoid any possible misconception that these ideas which explore and define consequences and relations are static or purely formal in nature; they are, instead, working concepts – concepts which... one may use daily to encounter and organise reality".[41] According to this view, the formation of knowledge is broken down into a sequence of levels, each one characterised by a different degree of abstraction and generalisation, corresponding to a different degree of structuring the study materials.[42]

---

[40] E. Fenton, *op. cit.*, p. 14. Hilda Taba considered that many social science generalisations "lack universality and dependability: some are little more than hypotheses, others involve value judgements and belief. These types of generalisations must be applied and used in a different manner from those of physical science, and their application needs to be surrounded with different sets of qualifying conditions". (H. Taba, *Curriculum Development, op. cit.*, p. 217). B. R. Joyce, on the same subject, points out that "the child should learn to make inferences and generalisations as he finds more data that necessitate revisions. In fact, information should be presented to the child in a sequence that requires him to revise and restate general concepts and causes him to learn that the present state of anyone's knowledge is tentative. This aspect of our teaching strategy is necessitated by two factors. The first... is that knowledge of society is tentative and shifting. The second is that the shifting, changing nature of social life itself demand of us flexible modes of coping with and managing problems". (B. R. Joyce, *Strategies for Elementary Social Sciences Education, op. cit.*, pp. 36-37).

[41] B. R. Joyce, *op. cit.*, p. 20, note 6, and pp. 48-51.

[42] B. R. Joyce distinguishes three levels of "organising concepts" (*op. cit.*, chap. 4, and pp. 154-155): *observed concepts*, "formed by noting similarities, differences or relations between objects that can be apprehended directly by senses, such as verbal statements or physical action", i.e. concepts of a descriptive nature (for example, those of the conjugal family and extended family); *inferred concepts*, resulting from a comparison between observed concepts, such as the God-fearing concept and in general those concepts that define values and belief; *ideal-type concepts*, which refer "to such complex or large-scale phenomena that they are

The emphasis on the operational function of concepts and generalisation is typical of a trend towards dissociating the learning of social studies from exclusively inductive-descriptive processes (which still predominate in this field), and towards the introduction of forms of learning which rely on intuition, the construction of models and the hypothetical-deductive technique. This means that learning can be directed towards structural investigation of social reality, an investigation based upon the testing of models used to depict the laws governing the component parts of a given system which operate at deeper seated levels than immediately observable reality. "The basic principle", as Lévi-Strauss declares, "is that the concept of social structure does not refer to empirical reality but to models constructed on the foundation of that reality. This clarifies the difference between two concepts that are so similar that they have often been confused, in other words the concept of *social structure* and the concept of *social relationships*. Social relationships provide the raw material for the building of models which help us to understand *social structure*. In no case, therefore, can the latter be identified with the set of social relationships that can be observed in a given society".[43]

'ideals' that have no perfect representatives in reality", such as the concepts of technological development and underdevelopment or the various denominations of political movements, forms of government, economic systems etc. In the lower grades of the primary school, the more accessible concepts of social sciences would seem to be those of the first type; at the middle level the formation of ideal-type concepts could be reached, while only at the senior level could the process of inference for the formation of the second type of concepts be introduced. H. Taba makes a distinction between *specific facts and processes, basic ideas, concepts*, and *thought systems*: these are four levels of knowledge, a different grade of difficulty in the organisation of study material corresponding to each. The first is limited to pure fact-finding and description; the "basic ideas" explain facts at a higher level of generalisation, establishing relations between them, such as the idea of the causal relationship between culture and natural environment; the "concepts" concern complex systems of highly abstract ideas resulting from study of an interdisciplinary nature, such as the concepts of democracy, interdependence, or social change; finally, the "thought systems" include the aggregation of concepts and of methods of thinking and of enquiry proper to each single subject. The term "structure", in the meaning accepted by Bruner, corresponds here to the second level in the organisation of knowledge: "the basic ideas", searching analysis of which leads finally to the "thought system". The objective of intellectual education should be to provide the opportunity for significant experiences that aim at "organising the kaleidoscope of concrete facts and events in the basic ideas, concepts and modes of thought". In this process, ideas that "cut across many disciplines and are supported by the study of facts combined from various subjects" are of greatest importance in social studies. (H. Taba, *Curriculum Development, op. cit.*, pp. 174-181).

[43] C. Lévi-Strauss, *Anthropologie structurale*, Plon, Paris, 1958, Ital. transl., Il Saggiatore, Milano, 1966, p. 311. The use of the notion of structure in different contexts of human sciences is analysed by R. Boudon (*A quoi sert la notion de "structure"?*, Gallimard, Paris, 1968). He demonstrates how this term is commonly used with two meanings referring to two successive moments in the analysis of a datum: in the first case the term "structure" indicates the presence of regularities and relationships of interdependence between the elements that make up the datum, in the second case the term is used to describe the theory of these

A stimulating contribution to the subject of the formation of knowledge in the field of social studies is, in our opinion, the concept of sociological imagination worked out by C. Wright Mills.[44] The educational implications of the principle underlying Mills' social investigation – in other words, the linking of intimate individual reality and the wider social realities – have until now been considered mainly to demonstrate the social conditioning of education; they have not, however, received the attention they deserve as a criterion which should guide teaching. In addition to Mills' suggestion regarding training in the use of imaginative ability in the study of social problems, a new guideline for education may emerge from the basic concepts of his sociology: the connection between biography, history and social sciences as a means of understanding one's own and other people's existence, the structure of society reflected at the level of the individual's everyday experience.

The fact that most of the above considerations have not yet been translated into practical terms, that as yet no approach has been evolved appropriate to the intellectual level of elementary school children, should not detract from their value as guidance on future trends in the teaching of social studies. A great step will have been taken in this direction when we go beyond the type of education whose sole aim is to instill information, when we adopt the problem-solving approach and the enquiry method, "the experience of what it is to use a theoretical model, with some sense of what is involved in being aware that one is trying out a theory"[45], while at the same time we develop a sense of sharing in human problems, in the living conditions of other communities, so that we can understand the connections with broader social situations.

SOCIAL STUDIES AND SOCIAL EDUCATION

The concept of sociological imagination, when applied to education, establishes a close link between social studies and social education – two aspects of the educational process that have often deliberately and

regularities and interdependent relationships. This distinction and the different types of hypothetic-deductive procedure that the structural analysis implies undoubtedly offer interesting suggestions for social studies teaching, apart from the difficulty of reducing them to terms of experience suitable for primary school children. On the other hand, as structuralism at present refers to many and various concepts, it is difficult to transfer it into a single-orientated teaching practice.

[44] C. Wright Mills, *The Sociological Imagination*, Oxford University Press, New York, 1959.
[45] J. S. Bruner, *Toward a Theory of Instruction*, p. 96.

inappropriately been kept apart on the grounds that social studies are basically cognitive in nature while the task of social education is to promote social and emotional development, the formation of attitudes and social behaviour. In practice, the need to forge a close link between social studies and social education, a need that has been so clearly stated by Dewey, has been taken up by contemporary educational schools of thought. One of the tasks of education, they believe, is to tackle the problem tearing our world apart, problems in which the individual must feel himself to be totally involved, for they influence his social attitudes and his social conduct. This is the reason for devoting special thought to the social and emotional aspects of personality, both by concentrating some of the experience gained in the teaching of social studies upon these aspects and by allowing for these aspects when adapting the curriculum to the psychological and social characteristics of the pupils.

Of special significance in this respect are experiments whose aim is to bring social sciences home to the child by making him aware of the dynamic forces in his personal relationships and within the group of which he is a member. For example, Lippitt organised group dynamics activities in the second and third grades of the elementary school, the subject being the pupil-teacher relationship. Another experiment was carried out in the Valley Winds Elementary School in Riverview Gardens, Miss., in which the T-group techniques were made accessible to the children after they had been tried out by the teachers.[46]

Nonetheless, it must be admitted that in social studies, perhaps to a greater extent than in any other area of education, the acquisition of knowledge is strongly conditioned by the process of socialisation (social learning) in which the social-emotional component plays a determining role. In teaching social studies, the fact must not be neglected that "children start with some quite definite social learnings which have already shaped some of their meanings, attitudes and thought patterns". In consequence, "if there are differences in social learning, there must also be differences in what the social studies programme emphasises". In organising the curriculum in the light of the criteria of differentiation and articulation suggested by the different social and emotional backgrounds of the children, the educational effectiveness of this teaching can be increased to promote "a cumulative growth

---

[46] M. Scriven (*cit.*, p. 93) quotes Lippitt's experiment, while B. R. Joyce (*cit.*, p. 276) quotes that of Valley Winds Elementary School.

in thinking and social attitudes and insights".[47] Further contribution towards the integration of social studies and social education are the experimental projects conducted by the Institute of Educational Research of the School of Education, Malmö, Sweden, under Professor Å. Bjerstedt. In one of these projects, on the subject of "social development and social training at school", an attempt was made to investigate the following three factors:

1. *Capacity to cooperate* (adequate inter-group communication and techniques for dealing with conflict), resulting from systematic group training.
2. *Optimum resistance to authority and propaganda* (the capacity to make up one's own mind independently, the power to resist irrelevant attempts to exert influence), resulting from, among other things, special exercises in the critical reading of newspaper texts and specially prepared propaganda-tainted material.
3. *World citizenship* (understanding of, and feeling for, development in other countries, less thoughtless dismissal of the unfamiliar, foreign, strange etc.) resulting from special educational material about international activities and the problems of foreign cultures, for example.[48]

The last of these three points brings us to one of the central themes in the reform of the social studies curriculum. To borrow an expression from Hilda Taba, the need for a "balance between intellectual proficiency and intelligent social perspective" is not satisfied by the provincialism and racialism that is still characteristic of much of this teaching. The opening of a child's cultural horizons to international fields should be considered an essential feature of elementary education. This was a point dear to the hearts of the advocates of progressive education. Today, the same cause is taken up, in some cases even more forcefully, when we survey the international scene with its conflicting trends and phenomena: the enlargement and intensification of relationships between different countries, the gathering momentum of economic and political integration, the emergence of peoples who have only recently acquired their independence but who still manifest a feeling of national pride even to the point of Chauvinism, continual wars and situations of grave tension and new forms of colonialism. We might be

---

[47] H. Taba, "An articulated Social Studies Curriculum in the Elementary School", in J. Jarolimek and H. M. Walsh (eds.), *Readings for Social Studies in Elementary Education*, Macmillan, New York, 1965, pp. 104 et seq.
[48] See *School Research*, Newsletter of the National Board of Education, Current Projects 1969/15, Stockholm, December 1969.

accused of excessive pessimism were we to say that in reality the education of today is still far more greatly influenced by the second set of phenomena than by the first. Nevertheless, we must not underestimate the risk that, despite an apparently far more cosmopolitan outlook, far from cosmopolitan concepts and attitudes in fact still prevail. In his introduction to the work upon which he cooperated, *The Social Studies and the Social Sciences*, Bernard Berelson, summarising the contributions of workers in different branches of learning, noted that the first thing that a student of social studies should learn "has to do with cultural diversity: explicit attention to differences among human ways of life". He quotes from an essay by M. B. Petrovich: "if the subject is taught primarily as a vehicle for drawing comparisons favourable to our own way of life, this is bound to be to a didactic tone, an air of selfrighteousness, and an almost unavoidable tendency to stack the facts".[49]

Today, when we speak of educational windows opening onto the world and "cross-cultural sensitivity" we refer to the trends and outlook for the education of tomorrow rather than actual observations on education today. Many projects initiated by international bodies such as UNESCO have contributed greatly to accelerating developments towards this end. Of special significance, however, are certain experiments conducted in various countries on curricular reorganisation.

In the United States, the tendency towards international or intercultural (cross-cultural) education has been brought to a head by experiments in many social study curricula based upon anthropology, to some of which we have already referred, or dealing with "world affairs". In the British elementary school, the Plowden Report states, the role of geography has become the broadening of children's knowledge of the local and national environment. In the course of primary education, the anthropological emphasis gradually becomes more marked. It is believed that this branch of learning has an educational purpose not only in the cognitive sense but also in the formation of attitudes. The really important factor, the Plowden Report observes, is that "people should understand people, and in the primary school a significant contribution may be made to this end".[50] Of special value in the future of international social education are the projects introducing foreign languages into the elementary school as a subject in the curriculum or as an extra-curricular activity. These projects, in some cases promoted as a result of international cultural exchange

---

[49] B. Berelson's Introduction to *The Social Studies and the Social Sciences, op. cit.*, p. 10.
[50] *Children and their Primary School, op. cit.*, pp. 234-235.

agreements, have been introduced in many European states. They will certainly multiply in the future when the process of integration has gained momentum in Europe and the learning of languages and appreciation of other peoples' cultures are considered essential from early childhood.

In the Soviet Union, there have been very significant experiments in the special schools, most lessons being given in a foreign language and the whole school environment reflecting the life and culture of the country whose language the children are studying. Even in ordinary Soviet schools, however, great stress is placed upon international education and special projects and clubs devoted to the theme of friendship between peoples are encouraged.

Looking towards the future, we can envisage that education in internationalism will undoubtedly benefit greatly from the use of modern communications techniques, especially if these are used in the school not so much to transmit programmes predigested in the production centres but rather to produce material that can be exchanged between schools in different countries.

Another trend current in the field of social studies that is worthy of consideration because of its obvious implications for the development of attitudes and conduct is the introduction of highly topical subjects into education, particularly those which are causing profound unrest in society and which most clearly reveal the tensions caused by society in a state of flux. Education must not neglect those areas of culture which, due to the effects of the social context within which the school operates, are usually considered to be taboo. B. R. Joyce, repeating the opinion of other workers who have tackled the same subject, specifies a wide range of themes for which social studies should provide the most suitable terrain: economic problems; racial conflicts and relationships with minority groups; social distinctions; sex, courting and marriage; religion and morality; nationalism and patriotism. Each of these taboo areas conceal prejudice and preconceptions which make them difficult to investigate and openly to discuss in the school.[51]

The subject was taken up in a recent publication by Joe L. Frost and G. Thomas Rowland, who described future developments in this sector of education in the following words: "The child in the social studies curriculum of the future will find new exciting fields to explore. The taboo topics – sex, drugs, racial relations, violence – and many

---

[51] B. R. Joyce, *op. cit.*, p. 10.

others previously believed to be too difficult for young minds – psychology, politics, economic systems, pollution, war – will be among the fields of enquiry. The key concepts and generalisations of the social sciences, with relevance across cultures, will replace the 'quiz show' content of the past, and the logic of conceptual structure in building curricula will become obvious. As humanistic, social and intellectual objectives become relevant to our times, the effects will be observed in the miniature society of the classroom, for behavioural change must be evident if its presence is to be assumed. Such change should deeply affect ghetto-area classroom behaviours because decades of deceit and discrimination have had their effects in the production of harsh human relations".[52]

The community aspect of education has in a sense been "rediscovered" and given new force by allowing children to study the most urgent problems of our time and developing their sense of personal commitment to society. By this means, the close connections between the reality of school and the far wider reality of society are clearly shown. For example, it is generally recognised that if the school attempts to perpetuate a "child-sized world", if it teaches no more than "verbalism" and "language skills and general language development", it will be ineffectual in a world whose institutions and traditional values are in a period of crisis. The suggested alternative is an education on which the main emphasis is upon "the affective goals, so that the resulting activities do not become ends in themselves but serve only as means to positive emotional involvement". Social action on a child scale which includes "activities to improve the school environment" and "activities for the betterment of the wider community outside the school", may help to restore the integration of affective relationships both on the personal level and on the community level.[53]

When, however, it is shown that community problems to a great extent reflect a given social structure and that the attempt to overcome these problems must not be confined to the emotional life, social action will be seen as political action. The study of social problems will become a component of political education. With this purpose in mind, in recent years in certain European countries (although we believe mainly in Italy) educational experiments at primary school level have

[52] J. L. Frost and G. T. Rowland, *Curricula for the Seventies: Early Childhood through Early Adolescence*, Houghton Mifflin, Boston, 1969, reprinted in part in *Childhood Education*, Sept./Oct. 1969, p. 10.
[53] B. R. Joyce, "Social Action for the Primary School", in *Childhood Education*, February 1970, pp. 254-258.

been conducted outside – and generally in open conflict with – the official school system. The "School and Neighbourhood" (*Scuole e Quartiere*) movement originating in Florence advocates a type of school "which enables the participants to judge the reality surrounding them and thereby to acquire a permanent critical capacity", and which "will teach the duty of political participation".[54] The working methods adopted in this type of alternative school can be summarised as follows: group work, seen as the antithesis of authoritarianism and as a means of counteracting the competitive nature of the middle class school; insertion of the group in the life and problems of the neighbourhood; breaking down the barriers between intellectual work and manual work; links with the factory, which is seen as the site of workers' organisation; the application of non-repressive and non-authoritarian educational methods; analysis of the subjects and methods adopted by the bourgeois school so that, knowing them better, they can be counteracted.[55]

The contribution that these experiments can make to the subject of our enquiry is, in our opinion, not only the attempt to establish a closer link between social studies, the social experience of the pupils and the problems of the community, but also, and above all, a rejection of the patterns which prevail in this field of education; in other words it is a refusal to look at society through rose-coloured glasses. This throws light upon the contradictions that exist in our society and emphasises the subjects at the core of the burning political struggle: it can be interpreted as a clear symptom of the radical changes already taking place in the structure of society and of the far from easy quest for re-adjustment.

This does not mean that we cannot foresee subsequent developments in the teaching of social studies in a society which, having eradicated the deep-rooted causes of social contradiction and conflicts that exist today, can tackle the problems of its own survival and change in a far calmer atmosphere, making greater use of creative imagination and thought in solving those problems. Society itself would be considered an open field of experiment for new forms of community life and social change, for new types of productive and cultural organisation and for new educational processes. The teaching of social studies would receive continual impetus from community life inside and outside the school

[54] *Scuola e Quartiere*, La Stamperia, Florence, 1969, pp. 17-18.
[55] From the final report of the 1st Meeting of "Scuola e Quartiere" (Florence, June 27-29, 1970), published in *Scuola e Città*, XXI, 6-7, June-July 1970, pp. 327-332.

and from the relations with other communities. The formation of knowledge would acquire practical relevance and in itself would represent a phase in social education, being applied on the many occasions afforded by the organisation and implementation of the school's own activities or the life of society.

In the year 2000, education will probably be considered inadequate not only if it is confined to transmitting the heritage of the past but also if its sole aim is to develop a critical awareness of social and cultural reality. The truly important goal may be to develop the child's capacity to look into the future and, with others, to plan new developments in social and cultural life. Knowledge of the past and investigation of the present will be related to this forward-looking goal.

7. ARTISTIC AND CREATIVE ACTIVITY

BY

ANTONIO SANTONI RUGIU

AESTHETIC ACTIVITY AS PLAY

Herbert Spencer maintained that the factor common to play and the arts is that they make no direct useful contribution to life.[1] The British thinker's words reflect a view still widely held in the 19th century, a view whose educational implications (especially in "pedagogy of effort") were later disputed by the new Progressive Education movement ushered in by Dewey. Dewey emphasised the ideological roots of that view which, knowingly or unknowingly, reflected Schiller's intuitive thought that man is truly human only when he is at play.

Spencer's observation that play is a manifestation of "superfluous energy" in young mammals, who do not have to fight against their instincts or work because they are protected and fed by their parents or groups of adults, confirms the long held idea that expressive and "aesthetic" activities – especially the motor and mime activities – constitute pure enjoyment. They are seen as a tolerated "holiday", a legitimate and sometimes useful holiday provided that it is confined to a given period. The educators used to believe that "fine games last little".

Erikson writes that "even the most strenuous and dangerous game is by definition not work; it does not produce commodities. Where it does, it 'goes professional'. But this fact, from the start, makes the comparison between adult and child play somewhat senseless, for the adult is a commodity-producing and commodity-changing being, whereas the child is only preparing to become one". The pattern is in fact identical. Free expressive activity is a form of recreation and escape for society, the purpose of which is to restore the optimum con-

---

[1] H. Spencer, *Principles of Psychology*, vol. II, New York, 1897, p. 628.

ditions for human productive activity and programmed effort as quickly as possible. The child's training closely follows this model purpose and in method. Even when the assumption that education is a preparation for life is finally abandoned in favour of the idea that education is life itself, the logic that governs adult life being reproduced in an education situation, the activities generally referred to as play or enjoyment – which by common consent include the arts – are considered to be no more than an ingredient or an accessory.

Since man is expected "to have a definite role in society, playboys and gamblers are both envied and resented by the working man. We like to see them exposed or ridiculed, or we put them to worse than work by forcing them to live in luxurious golden cages". We could add that the same applies to art and artists. "The playing child, then", continues Erikson, "poses a problem: whoever does not work shall not play. Therefore, to be tolerant of the child's play the adult must invent theories which show either that childhood play is really work, or that it does not count. The most popular theory and the easiest on the observer is that the child is *nobody yet*, and that the nonsense of his play reflects it".[2]

Once we are drawn into a discussion of children's play, we risk being swamped by a rising sea of literature. Here we shall merely emphasise the true equivalence between play and aesthetic activity (it is no mere semantic coincidence that in the main Western languages the words *to play, jouer, spielen* refer both to games and to artistic performance). The educational status and role ascribed to play correspond in every way to those ascribed to the arts. In this respect the pedagogic and social levels also coincide, that is, the educational patterns and cultural patterns still prevailing.

Since the specific function of each factor or group of factors derives from and is related to the function of other factors, which become more and more "structural" as we trace them back in time, this situation may have originated from the capitalist division of labour or from the imperative demands of production inherent in the reign of technology, with no substantial distinction between capitalist and collectivist ideologies and régimes. We could also explain the contradictions in the efforts to reform education as arising from structural economic contradictions in our society. These relationships, too, are widely discussed and written about today, although few clear conclusions have yet been reached.

[2] Erik Erikson, *Childhood and Society*, Penguin Books, Middlesex (England) 1965, p. 207.

CREATIVITY, A SOCIAL NECESSITY OF TOMORROW?

One of these contradictions, reflected in the educational field, is the tendency to emphasise both individual creativity and the productivity of the systems to which the individual belongs. In other words, there is a contradiction between the desire to encourage the ability to adjust to and appreciate values, "divergence" or "field-independence", and other skills considered as essential for creativity (the reader is referred to the list drawn up by De Bartolomeis in his contribution to this study), and the contrasting tendency in work to foster "convergence" or "field-dependence", even at managerial level.

What we have not yet achieved is a reconciliation of the attitudes called for when arriving at a decision or when reversing a previous decision, and the attitude that we should adopt when implementing the decision. A skilled worker, a technician and an executive must be trained to adapt their learning and behaviour to any job they have to tackle; they are not trained merely for one specific job. This decreases or eliminates the need for periodical basic retraining. Nevertheless, once a man has adapted to a change in his work, that work itself may require little capacity for divergence or fluidity. In practice, a job consists of rigid functions. As soon as a choice is made, the capacity for freedom and inventiveness is immediately repressed and becomes a source of daily frustration.

This contradiction in the attitude to work produces an ambiguous feed-back in scholastic education, which is modelled simultaneously on two opposing patterns. The ambiguity makes the feed-back even weaker, especially in the education of young children, where there is insufficient impetus for a radical reorganisation of the curriculum or educational aims.

Creativity in the school of tomorrow will depend on the extent to which changes in education reflect social research and greater understanding of the demands being made.

Let us take a look at the situation from a strictly "scholastic" point of view. An ideological and political discussion would no doubt lead us into fascinating territory, but it would only increase the uncertainty surrounding our forecast of future developments. En passant, we note that as a result of the ambiguity and the varying pressures in the school, nothing noteworthy has yet been achieved in promoting creativity in general and artistic creativity in particular.

THE MARGINAL ROLE OF ART EDUCATION

It is an undisputed fact that the arts still enjoy only a marginal role in the elementary school (from the age of 5-7 to 11-13 in the school systems of various countries). None of the experts or educators interviewed was satisfied with the role of creative activities in primary school education in his own country.

In the scale of values still held dear at the elementary level of education, artistic and creative activities are increasing in prestige but have not yet achieved a sufficiently high status to be considered as fundamental to the structural logic of the type of education provided for this age group.

Nonetheless, the school which the child attends from infancy to early adolescence still pays more attention to the arts and creativity than do subsequent levels of education, at which these activities tend to die out except in schools specialising in the arts.

The concept of "education through art" has not yet penetrated the structure of general education. This is true not only of the Utopian concept of Herbert Read, who saw art as the mainspring of education for a civilised and peaceful future, but also of the more realistic desire to see the arts take a leading part alongside other components of education.

The fact that the younger child is given greater scope for artistic activities is due to pressure at the end of the 19th century and the beginning of the 20th from the Progressive Education Movement. This movement advocated free, spontaneous expression on the part of the child, especially through drawing and modelling. Another reason for the greater emphasis at the elementary stage is the fact that the products of the child's creative expression were used in tests to evaluate the development of certain aspects of the child's personality and social behaviour.

The concept that the child is "all feeling and imagination", possessing a treasure of inner riches which he should be allowed to express without inhibition or interruption, was one of the main points of the movements for reform that started up about 70 years ago, especially the schools run on free lines.[3] This concept is now reflected in the curricula of more formal schools, although not to the extent originally advocated. In the

---

[3] Particularly the schools of Bremen, Hamburg and Kearsley on the principle of the *Gemeinschaftsschule* (Ludwig Gurlitt), *Gemeinschaftserziehung* (Berthold Otto), *Gesamtunterricht* etc., as also the movements of the *Wandervögel*, the *Pfadfinder* and the better-known attempt of the *Landeserziehungsheime* of Lietz.

Artistic and Creative Activity

course of time, despite a long series of events[4], it still occupies only a marginal role in the current processes of education.

The proof that, in traditional school ideology, the role of art has long been considered to be merely recreation and relaxation is the sometimes ruthless suppression of art in post-primary schools. A survey recently conducted by Ursula Springer has shown that even in "classic" education, art in the junior and senior secondary schools has not only not increased over recent years, but in some cases has been curtailed. In the syllabus for European school institutions, "music and art education have become optional subjects, an astonishing fact when we consider the strong national pride of most countries in their artistic creations. Besides, the greater emphasis being placed upon the use of free time could be a reason not only for maintaining but for promoting the introduction of drawing and music. In reality, however, neither in official statements of school policy nor in general guidance on study curricula is much stress apparently laid upon these subjects, with the exception of West Germany... (where) according to tradition every student in the junior secondary school continues to be offered at least two hours' artistic and musical education a week. The total number of hours in the Berlin Gymnasium course is 21, almost double that in East Germany (one of the countries devoting most time to these subjects) and more than three times that of many other nations such as France and Italy. Obviously, at present all countries give priority to intellectual education over aesthetic education".[5]

The writer's final comment stresses the known fact that the main aim of schools is to "educate" in the sense of developing and organising knowledge and concepts. Since education at the elementary level is less concerned with this aim, it is believed that more time can be devoted to activities that stimulate the imagination and the power of inventiveness, rather than making the children learn by rote and drilling them in intellectual agility, emphasising manipulation rather than abstraction.

In this respect, the elementary school enjoys a status of privilege, even if it is the status of the one-eyed man in the kingdom of the blind. There is a slot for art in the elementary school, but there ceases to be room for art at higher levels. From the very start the educational ideal

---

[4] I. Wojnar, *Estetyka y Wychowanie*, Italian Translation, *Estetica e Pedagogia*, La Nuova Italia, Florence, 1970.
[5] U. K. Springer, "Curricoli europei nella scuola secondaria", *Scuola e Città*, 10, 1969, pp. 493-494.

is an intellectual one, but development of the intellect is seen as an end goal which children achieve through intuition and self-expression, especially in the first few years of school. This means, however, that intuition and self-expression are seen as means to an end and as purely transitional in nature; sooner or later they will have to give way to a more rational approach, unrelieved by such compensations or "distractions".

The belief that still prevails in every country is that the onset of puberty marks a milestone in the process of institutional education, that it is the time at which the child develops his intellectual faculties. It is believed that a "loss of creativity", especially in the field of art, occurs in puberty and the years leading up to puberty; this is still considered inevitable rather than something to be circumvented or mitigated. No serious consideration seems to have been given to the idea that this loss of creativity is in fact induced by the society in which the child grows up, a society whose values the school reflects, and that, in consequence, if society's cultural preconceptions and the conditioning implicit in the process of schooling were altered, the crisis could be avoided or attenuated.

LOSS OF CREATIVITY IN THE TEN TO TWELVE AGE GROUP

The future of creativity in general and artistic expression in particular depends to a great extent upon whether this idea is proved to be true. For the time being, the hypothesis appears to be confirmed to a certain extent by certain school situations in the years of puberty – for example the new comprehensive middle school in Italy for 11-14 year olds which has adopted methods that appear to be successful in helping the child to retain the richness and inventiveness of expression typical of his earlier years. If, however, it is found that the loss of creativity that occurs at the onset of puberty is an inherent part of development for anthropological or auxiological reasons, and is therefore irreversible and unavoidable, there will be little prospect for expanding creativity in the school system of the future, not only in the secondary school but even at primary level.

"It is well known that the passage from childhood to adolescence marks a crisis in aesthetic creativity. The child who can express himself freely up to the age of 10 or 12, giving his own picture of the world and depicting his creative links with that world in different ways (graphic, plastic, mime, etc.), is subsequently inhibited by the advent

Artistic and Creative Activity

of rationalistic, intellectual, realistic and even 'grammatical' patterns. Our pedagogical systems are still planned in the light of evolution... In any case, the problem originates in the junior school, when free and 'diverging' perceptions and representations connected with artistic creativity are considered 'dangerous' and non-productive for the purpose of academic achievement and must give way to 'converging' procedures and aims, to set performance. The problem lies in the connection between the development of artistic, scientific and literary-linguistic creativity: if these elements continue to be associated, we would find that the crisis is not a natural but an artificially induced and therefore avoidable crisis".[6]

If it is proved that the loss of creativity on the threshold of puberty is not inevitable (and it should be remembered that specialists in child development sustain that puberty is slowly but gradually starting at an earlier age) one of the effects may be a reassessment of artistic activity throughout the primary school, so that emphasis upon the arts will not gradually fade as the children move up from the infant school to the adolescent classes. If the aims and values of the secondary school cease to represent a shift of emphasis to the traditional types of learning and work, in short if there is a continuity of goals and methods between the primary and the subsequent levels of education, the forms by which versatile creativity is expressed (artistic, of course, but also scientific, technological and linguistic) will no longer face the threat of being "killed off" but be reinforced by the confidence of their continued existence.

We must admit, however, that it will not be easy to reverse the trend. In the cultural field, strong objections will be raised on the grounds of philogenetic evolutionism, the belief that man in his development reproduces the same laws that govern the development of mankind as a whole, that he progresses from pre-logical and intuitive forms of thought to rational concepts and deductive processes. This is a belief that has pervaded all the schools of thought on educational innovation over the past century and in the first half of this century. Paradoxically it has often been used to legitimise the logic of the old education systems for the post-puberty age. The firmly-held preconception of the primacy of reason, the belief that the instrument of reason cannot be reconciled with the inventive and imaginative processes inherent in early childhood, can be overcome only if the illusory nature of this

---

[6] A. Santoni Rugiu, *The problem of the crisis in Aesthetic Creativity*, report to INSEA Congress, Coventry (England), 15 August 1970.

non-reconciliability is demonstrated. There must be a proven need for dynamic links between the development of reason from early childhood and the development of factors grouped under the name of "creativity". A child deprived of the sensory, emotional and intuitive elements is gravely handicapped in forming intelligence in the modern sense of the word. In the same way, when intellectual development is pursued even in the primary school using outdated educational techniques, it prejudices the development of a personality that can make productive use of several dimensions.

THE PRECARIOUS NATURE OF PRIMARY EDUCATION

The possibility of reconciling two patterns hitherto considered as opposed to each other in the education process, of combining the two potentials for the development of the human personality (sharply contrasted in traditional models of education) is vital when making basic decisions upon the school of tomorrow. "It is a link of the maximum pedagogical importance: the moment of choice between the normal patterns founded upon pairs of opposites (art and feeling versus science and reason, in this case) and the more recent approach which analyses these opposites into more detailed breakdowns, revealing the connections between each set of pairs. In principle, there is a tendency today not to accept that science makes no use of intuition or imagination, that art does not profit by the use of rational processes". (Although, unfortunately, we have little concrete knowledge of the "functioning of the actual processes" and before we can resolve the problem, theoretical and experimental research projects must be conducted to examine the two processes both in isolation and in combination from the first year of infant school.)[7]

Attention should also be paid to the problems associated with another crisis, the one that takes place on moving up from the nursery school to the elementary school, particularly where this move occurs at the age of five or six. It is the first occasion on which the subjects that develop the child's creativity are reduced for the first time, especially when the child goes on to elementary schools that do not help the newcomer to bridge the gap. The impact of the child's first encounter with traditional learning goals, the modern version of the three R's, the different sense of purpose which the child perceives in new and

---

[7] A. Bassi and A. Santoni Rugiu, *Creatività e deprivazione artistica*, La Nuova Italia, Florence, 1969, p. 123.

Artistic and Creative Activity

unexpected demands from his environment (a new interaction with his teacher, in many cases new ways of arranging space and furnishing, new methods of evaluation, lack of individual attention, etc.) still today bring about a "school starter crisis", a crisis that is less obvious and less widely investigated but no less serious than the crisis upon moving up to higher levels at puberty.

In this way, the elementary school is in the grip of two crises, one at the beginning and one at the end. The area that suffers most is artistic activity, not only because it gradually fades into the background faced with competition from "formal" subjects, but especially because the basic motivation for artistic activity, considered to be legitimate and to have priority in the pre-school and the first few years of elementary school, is gradually but inevitably pushed to one side (although this may cause great stress to certain children). Achievements believed to be vital in the educational experience of the three to five year olds are little by little displaced towards the edge of the educational pattern; at first crucial, they become subsidiary and finally are discarded altogether, being considered almost detrimental to the traditional goals of learning.

The movements for educational reform in our century go right to the heart of the problem when they claim the child's right to a non-restrictive educational approach "tailored to fit the child". They emphasise the value of activities, in Dewey's words, as ideal instruments for concentrating or correlating the pupils' development as a whole, the acquisition of knowledge being dependent upon relationships with the outside and inside environment, thus stimulating the development of ability to "reconstruct" knowledge and the environment itself.

However, no clear theory was evolved or effective action taken on the basis of this fundamental and as yet little explored intuitive understanding gained by the progressive education movement. The reasons were many: the wide range of arguments and goals of the various schools of thought; the fact that the time was not yet ripe, as the scientific instruments were not yet available to translate that intuitive understanding into practical terms; and finally cultural, ideological and political resistance to the shelving of the "glorious" models of education dating from the pre-industrial and neo-industrial societies (it should not be forgotten that these models of education had brought about mass elementary education, abolishing general illiteracy in the 19th century).

The great dream of allowing the child to be free in a school made to his measure was to a certain extent realised by the partial "liberalisation" of the schools themselves. While the previous century's goal – universal education – was unaffected, the child was no longer denied the right to free development. One of the effects of this process of liberalisation of the elementary school curriculum was greater stress upon artistic activity, in practice drawing and modelling – here again, based upon the successful experiments in the kindergarten at the end of the 19th century and early in the 20th. In this way, the child gained the right to express himself and the benefit of being able to develop graphic and plastic skills.

The tendency to view childhood as an oasis of legitimate but temporary, limited aesthetic expression, of "guarded liberty", is not, however, irreversible. For decades, new educational principles have been advocated, from infancy onward, including the goal of permanent education. Educational reform, which began last century in the pre-school, has gradually crept up to the elementary school and the pre-adolescent level, although there have been limitations and distortions. Radical revision has now begun of educational and methodological concepts at the secondary school and university level. At the same time, there is greater realisation of the fact that education does not end with the bodies of higher education but continues throughout life in all man's social relationships. This rethinking of the educational process is leading towards greater realisation of the value of optional activities whose purpose is mainly creative.

If emphasis upon art – in the many forms that aesthetic activity may take – is to be included without reservation among the basic aims of reform, it will be of benefit not only to those levels of education directly involved in the reform but also to the whole field of child education, pre-primary and primary, for the practice of the arts will be freed of the limitations to which it has been subject. The child would be able to engage upon artistic activity without this activity being arbitrarily suspended at a certain point, and the conflict between expressive activities and "compulsory" subjects, in other words between desirable but in fact marginal behaviour patterns and educational behaviour, would be resolved. Once artistic experience in the broad sense of the word becomes one of the main ingredients of education at later ages, it can flourish in the primary school not as a short-lived "extra" but as a true "educational" subject which will promote behaviour patterns that will continue to be central in more advanced forms even at higher and more permanent levels of education.

ART AND ART EDUCATION: INFLUENCES AND AUTONOMY

The impulse towards "vertical" reform, however, will not succeed merely by extending the privileges now accorded to infancy to later childhood and adulthood. Two important and interacting factors will help to achieve this aim:

a) the status of the arts in society and their actual role (up to now there has been a wide gap between the social prestige of art and its actual bearing upon the concrete life of society);

b) the development of art forms that are no longer "pure" but "synaesthetic", which are derived from many branches of the arts and are breaking down the traditional distinctions and hierarchies between the Fine Arts and what are known as the "minor arts", and between the Fine Arts and drama, spectacle, etc.

If these cause a crisis in the internal hierarchies of the traditional groupings – for example, the primacy of design over manual production, of the theatre over the cinema – so that every form of aesthetic creation is placed on an equal footing, promoting forms and languages which, for instance, combine graphic elements with phonic, scenodynamic, mimic, verbal elements and so on, this will be all to the better.

The forms of art that have gained acceptance in the school up to this time have been based upon the traditional distinctions between general artistic production, with the emphasis upon drawing and painting on the one hand and musical activities (above all singing, individual and choral) on the other, in other words, the essential components of the Fine Arts and Music, the Arts with a capital "A". There has been a growing trend in recent times to place a little more emphasis upon other forms of the arts, such as handicrafts and dramatic play.

In the same way, an attempt has been made, almost solely on the theoretical level, to prove that the artistic type of production by children – in general education, not only education for future specialists – should to the extent possible not reflect the set adult patterns in its classifications and priorities. "It is here that the philosophy in Art Education distinctly differs from the so-called Fine Arts. Whereas the emphasis in art education is on the effect which creative processes have on individuals, the sensitivity derived from aesthetic experiences, it is the aesthetic product which is of importance in Fine Arts", says Lowenfeld.[8] Artistic activity in the school is one of several aspects of creativity

---

[8] V. Lowenfeld, *Creative and Mental Growth*, Macmillan, New York, 1957, p. 4.

and should be more closely linked to and provide more opportunities for communication with technical and scientific activities than with the "advanced" activities of Art as conventionally defined. The internal homogeneity of the apparently disparate components of a free educational activity (inventiveness, the search for "surprising" solutions, etc.) should in the long run prevail over the extrinsic forms of homogeneity of each of these components with the corresponding adult activities.

This theory is undoubtedly stimulating, but whether it can be put into practice depends on whether the functions of creativity in the educational process are in fact complementary, forming a homogeneous structure. The "pigeon-hole" view of the Arts still current, the distinction between graphic activities and constructive activities, between musical forms and poetic forms and so on, is the cause for the attempt to relate each of these components to their "wholes", in other words to the corresponding activities on the formal adult level, so that the interactions established (although the influence has for long been one-sided, the "whole" influencing the component, not vice versa) are still more manifest than the long desired interactions within the range of educational activities. These activities should in fact be viewed as autonomous and interdependent factors in the development of creativity.

Nevertheless, one step has been taken in the direction of independence: the child is allowed to express himself freely and is no longer made to conform with the dictates of "beauty" and to comply with the established rules or art. This is not a great step forward towards the conquest of independence, since the search for the "beautiful" in the product of the arts was already losing ground in the field of aesthetics – at least in avant-garde circles – at the same time as the traditional canons of art were being rejected. Divergencies were looked on with greater favour and "academic grammar" of all types was criticised. On the whole, however, it should be recognised that the school system has for once been a follower of new trends, if not a pioneer. For once, the school has sided with the reformers rather than with the conservatives, breaking with its tradition in other fields. The fact that it has adopted a more progressive line – and this is also true of more general cultural influences such as the changing role of the artist in the industrial society – does not mean, however, that the school has acted independently of adult culture.

For some years the influence of developments in adult art could have profitably been used in the implementation of those changes so long desired by the new education movement and the pioneers of creativity.

Following the rejection of the canons of all branches of the arts in the second half of the 19th century and the early years of the 20th, taking the path of primitivism and the irrational (and therefore, in the light of the philogenetic theory, of the child's view of the world) and then following the various "informal" trends, the aesthetic revolution is now not merely questioning style but tackling culture and ideology and in consequence education itself.

THE INTERACTION BETWEEN ART AND SCHOOL

We believe that three factors are basically responsible for the fact that contemporary "adult" art has come closer to the aims of reformers in child art education:

a) the opportunities for artistic production have become universal or more "popular". Everyone is now considered capable of expressing himself. As early as 1919, the Bauhaus movement asserted that "our objective is to form a new type of artistic creator, sensitive to every sort of need, not because he is a prodigy but because he is able to respond systematically to human demands. We desire to make him aware of his creative potential, not frightened of its novelty, through an activity not governed by rules... The fundamental pedagogical error of the Academies has been to focus upon the genius, not upon the average man". This also implies that the ability to "depict" does not require a long apprenticeship of rule learning and the acquisition of technical skill, but rather a refinement of sensitivity and receptiveness to stimuli and to the processes of thought and communication which may be (and often is better) achieved through non-artistic experience.

b) a devaluation in the "professional" status of the artist, of artists as a caste, of the distinction between the professional and amateur. Aesthetic activity becomes a specific "way of living", open to anybody who is prepared to live in that way no matter how great his skill or personal training.

c) the greater stress laid upon the concept of fruition, of personal or group fulfilment, compared with the traditional emphasis upon goals, upon the objectively measurable value of the product. The process is more important than the product, a factor that has a special affinity with the trends of modern art education. There is also opposition to "commercialisation" of the product of process, exposing it to the vagaries of changing taste and rendering it susceptible, sometimes unwittingly, to market "manoeuvres". This has led to the popularity of products "with no tomorrow" that cannot be reproduced in any form (for example, happenings), which do not lend themselves to marketing. Sculptures, for instance, are made of junk or technological waste, or materials as ephemeral as sand, water or light. In essence, art is now being seen as play, as a delight in the obsolescence of its products.

d) the confines between the creator and the spectator are becoming blurred and the spectator is in a sense becoming the creator. The ideal public is the creator himself, or at least the people involved in the creative process. The concept of participation is a tacit or overt acceptance of an emotional experience, even if there is no end product. Here again, there is a strong analogy with the trends in art education, in its objections that "showing off" has an adverse effect upon creative activity (exhibitions of drawings, musical recitals, theatrical performances, etc.) as the desire for public appreciation interferes with the process of self fulfilment desired by the creator.

The general aim, therefore, is that artistic performance should benefit the personality of the creator himself, even in the case of group creativity used solely or secondarily for therapeutic purposes. This throws light on educational goals, although the discussion may refer to adults or "professionals". Even where no visible influence has yet been proved, there are undoubtedly parallel tendencies in art education and in art forms in general. It will perhaps not be arbitrary to borrow a comment by R. Arnheim on this subject: "In reality I cannot think of any factor essential to art or to any artistic creation the source of which cannot be recognised in the work of children".[9]

Nevertheless, the analogies and influences – even though, as we have said, the influences are as yet unexplored or only partially explained by reference to the common matrices of different schools of perceptive, dynamic or social psychology – are not confined to analyses of overall trends. Let us consider certain details: action painting, kinetic art, the art of materials and gestures, abstraction, concrete art, concrete-abstract art, mobiles, the art of signs, neo-dadaism and even pop art, op art and conceptual art (the list is endless) provide a range of art experience in our time that has striking affinities with the child's artistic activity. There are affinities in its motivations, in its techniques and in

[9] R. Arnheim, *Arte e percezione visiva*, Feltrinelli, Milano, 1962, p. 118; original: *Art and Visual Perception*, 1954.

its goals. All these trends share a stress upon the "non-canonical", on what was formerly considered random, haphazard or vulgar. They all share the desire to break through the time-hallowed boundaries between the various forms of art and to "steal" concepts and techniques from over those confines, often promoting them to a dignity not theirs in their original form.

A closer and certainly more conscious analogy is to be found more in the field of revolutionary developments in the fine arts or music than in the domain of what are generally thought of as "grammatical" activities. Here again, there has been a shift in emphasis away from professional execution, following accepted rules and based upon written texts, to improvisation (this may sometimes be more simulated than real, as with the Living Theatre, symptomatic though this group may be), towards a dramatic "slice of life" as unpredictable as a happening. There is an analogy with the various forms of dramatic play engaged in by groups of children, to such an extent that the new forms of theatre introduced by young people and adults seem to be a carbon copy of the models already tried out upon children.

Although at first this close affinity was not apparent, for some time now there has been a growing popularity of the trends in the adult world in education, a rediscovery of the primal impulses of dramatic play, a belief in its value as a release, as a debunking and implicitly therapeutic force. In essence, to create art is seen as the living of significant experience, or rather as the attribution of meaning to what is experienced within the group by means of a specific strategy of immediate perception and emotion. The establishing of communication with others, spectators and non-participants, has become secondary or in certain cases completely irrelevant. To traditional communication with the person observing a painting or a sculpture, listening to music, etc., is now preferred the involvement of that person, who thus becomes a participant. It does not matter whether or not he actually takes part but he must be inside the process, not outside looking in.

In practice, this breaks down the barriers between the role of the spectator and the role of the creator, and sets off a search for a new integrating role in which, in the final analysis, everyone is a creator or at least a catalyser of the creative process. An illustration is the description of a dramatic "happening" engineered by elementary school children in Turin in an adventure playground. The purpose of the experiment was to foster their powers of free expression. The only suggestion thrown out to the children was a theme that might act as a stimulus:

"Hippopotami and crocodiles in the adventure playgrounds... or anything else you like". The children waved placards with slogans such as "I am a theatre" – "Hippopotami not at home, in the jungle" – "an amateur actor today is better than an ignorant audience tomorrow" – "our teacher is an actress employed by the State". The organisers of this experiment (which they said was inspired by American "street" theatre) describe their attempt as "an entertainment which, by trying out a different concept of the space that can be used for theatre, is played out in an actable area where the children can come on, go off, move up or down, invent or construct their own space with materials that help them make the best possible use of their dynamic and creative freedom. For our part, we were given the opportunity of studying the status and function of theatrical technique in a setting allowing active, creative participation in the show by the actor and technician on an equal footing, integrating both in a new role – operators and agents provocateurs of action which still remains theatrical action".[10]

Such examples of inter-personal creation restricted to the players go beyond dramatic play, whether in childhood or in adult life. The same thing is to be found in kinetic art, which presupposes perceptive integration and that the person looking at the art will re-create his own art; and in the newest forms of music hall in which the spectators mingle with the actors and there is no space between the stage and the audience; and even among the chansonniers who ask the audience to "sing along with me". Attempts to achieve audience participation in the theatre, were made as far back as the early years of this century, as for example, in the theatre of spontaneity and improvisation, *Stegreif-theater*, founded by Moreno in the 1920's in Vienna, as well as other experiments subsequently formalised by Pirandello and his imitators. In essence, the aim was to restore to theatre its original nature of a collective ceremony in which all the participants were the consumers of the artistic products that they themselves created. Even the *café-chantant* was, in its period, a popular version of a "play without a stage" or "audience participation". The striking thing today is that small avant-garde groups have introduced such radical changes that the centuries-old concept of the theatre has now become decadent.

What is completely new is the attempt to apply the same trend to the figurative and similar arts which have never from their very beginnings invited participation but, on the contrary, have jealously

---

[10] "Il lavoro teatrale nella scuola", "Quaderni di *Cooperazione Educativa*", no. 5-6, 1970, p. 17.

defended the individual nature of their inspiration, concept and production. The poet and the writer, for instance, admitted the existence of the outside world only once their work was complete and others were called upon to appreciate (and buy) it.

The general trend, therefore, is to bring the spectator into art, even to the point of considering that nobody but the participant in the process of art can enjoy that process or product. There is no place for the onlooker, for the outsider, for the person who does not "live" the artistic process. The type of communication possible inside the circle of participants, of the people "involved", obeys dictates of emotion that would not be understood by a spectator, even if it were possible for a spectator to exist. Moreno asserted that Aristotle's error was to believe in the catharsis of the spectator. Only the actor can undergo catharsis, only the person who lives through a process, suffers and creates it. In the future there will be no virtue in aesthetic contemplation. This is a subject to which we shall return, for our theme includes an examination, however summary, of all the forms of "passive artistic experience" so amply provided by the mass media today, probably even more so tomorrow.

THE TENDENCY TO SYN-AESTHETIC FORMS

Another factor in the evolution of current artistic forms is the tendency to incorporate concepts and methods typical not only of related forms (for example, when a material, or plastic, dimension is added to graphic art), but also of quite different forms. Kinetic art uses gesture and mime. The mobiles of Calder, Martin and Munari have demolished the concept of stable sculpture by contrasting the acquisition of form of a moving object to the immobility inherent in a statue, inspired by film techniques. There are many other instances, including psychedelic music in which sound is inseparable from the play of light.

In short, there is a trend towards "syn-aesthetism", merging the concepts and expressions formerly characteristic of different art forms or incorporating completely new concepts in a continuous search for new and surprising inter-aesthetic or syn-aesthetic idiom. This search is obviously easier in the "composite" arts such as the theatre, whose equivalent on the educational level is dramatic play. Drama has always used many resources to achieve its goals: mime, words, sound, the plastic and decorative arts, etc.: what is new to today's trend is that the formerly predominant method of expression in a given form of spectacle is being combined with other aspects. For instance, dialogue (the verbal instrument) is becoming less important in comedy and tragedy, music and singing in opera, mime and dance in the ballet and pantomime, etc. The search for integrating idioms also helps to abolish the traditional hierarchies in each genre, a hierarchy which was the result of conventional rules, achieving an equality of opportunity for each of the elements making up the new idiomatic language.

From this viewpoint, too, the interaction – whether conscious or sub-conscious is of little importance – between evolving forms of the arts and the corresponding solutions on the educational level is undoubtedly beneficial and will lead to many future developments. In the first place, this syn-aesthetic trend and its "revolutionary" objective have started to make a breach in the high wall of privilege surrounding verbal expression compared with artistic expression, even at the level of the child.

The supremacy of the word has generated forms of discrimination in the school among educational subjects. These accentuate similar tangible discriminations in adult culture to such a point that, for example, "poetry" is still kept separate from the arts in general and occupies a leading role in the elementary school of almost every country (certainly in every European country), since poetry is a citizen of the privileged realm of verbal language.

This is not the time to embark upon a historical analysis of the reasons for that position of privilege and for its perpetuation in educational curricula, despite the declared aim of keeping abreast of the times, although this would be an extremely interesting and enlightening analysis. It is certain that no true progress in scholastic education can be achieved in the future unless, starting in the infant school, these anachronistic hierarchies which favour certain forms of language over others are abolished. There is no longer any valid reason for training the child for a future dominated solely by verbal forms of language based on the narrow semantics of the past which implied that the only form of language is written and spoken language, while there are many good reasons for making use of the integrated structures and functions in the personality of the child.

It is obvious that the child does not share the same overwhelming preference for verbal rather than graphic or technical expression. He probably does not perceive any functional difference between these forms of expression, at least until he is induced to do so by his educator, until he becomes conditioned to accept a scale of "scholastic" values,

Artistic and Creative Activity 231

each with its formal, artificial, distinction. Since the first goal of education is to teach the child to read and write, a child's mother tongue is in fact being forced to observe the rules of spelling, grammar and finally, syntax. In other words, even though most teachers have liberalised their techniques, the verbal activity of the elementary school child is still governed by a preoccupation with the assimilation of rules and functions of correct oral and written expression. This preoccupation has been made less obsessive by modern methods so that learning has become faster and the evaluation of learning more indulgent, or at least more patient. Nonetheless, the tacit logic underlying the verbal activity of the child is still that of the "hunt for mistakes". Accuracy may become an end in itself, although the child may escape from this duty in his own jottings, stories and diary, etc. Nevertheless, although he may pay less heed to accuracy in these, he will necessarily repeat the prevalent attitude. The precious instrument of language and verbalisation, despite or perhaps because of its privileged position, is almost never suited for creative purposes, so that the child is deprived of his natural capacity for using this "instrument" with inventiveness, drawing upon the rich resources of expression that it could provide. This causes inhibitions which may reappear in other forms through the process of transfer and subconscious dynamism, forming a spontaneous strategy of verbal creativity even more marked in pupils of social classes with a low level of culture.

The learning of language is obviously not the only or even the main source of inhibition and deprivation. Stereotyped learning which soon becomes stereotyped performance on the part of the child is unfortunately all too common, although less than in the past, in arithmetic for example. Lowenfeld states that text books for arithmetic and language (and, despite progress, the text books are still basically the same) all too often indulge in the illusion that to repeat a concept will help the child to learn. "Add six birds to the three – how many are there?" If a "number concept" is promoted by the use of clichés, the child may become creatively inhibited. The author of one such text book once defended his method to me by saying: "I am only interested in promoting better arithmetic – I don't know anything about art". I replied that my concern was with the child, not with art or arithmetic. There is a confusion between a subject-centered and a child-centered method of teaching. Experimental research has shown that imitative methods have adverse effects upon the child's creativeness.[11]

[11] Lowenfeld, *op. cit.*, pp. 15-16.

ART EDUCATION AS A MULTILATERAL PROCESS

A child-centered school presupposes a radical revision of the concept of the child who is to be the focal point of the educational experience, a recognition that the child, like the adult, is a complex of factors in a process of development, usually not definable or distinguishable. It is no longer possible to ignore the adverse effects which repetitive methods used in one sector (or one subject matter) may have on other sectors. As Lowenfeld rightly notes, "If the child becomes inhibited in one area it may be felt in another".[12]

In the future, therefore, the sphere of aesthetic activities of a creative type – and we emphasise the word creative, since we have not yet seen the last of certain "repetitive" practices such as asking the child to colour in ready-drawn figures, to copy objects or to make tracings – must once again include *verbal* creative activities, either by themselves or preferably as components of syn-aesthetic activities having equal weight. At the same time, language as a formal subject of learning and the exercises traditionally connected with the study of language will be dropped. The same also applies to arithmetic and to elementary science in general. There is no sense in preparing the way for creative activities if the methods adopted in those fields run counter to the process of creativity and force the pupil to follow cognitive paths placing rigid barriers between possible mental and operational links, reducing the inventive factor to the minimum by accepting only one answer to a problem and no others.

Nor is it to be conceived that a given subject matter, traditionally unified, should be broken down into two or more parts for the purpose of different or even opposing goals. Language cannot continue to be a subject that is learned through the assimilation of a set body of rules and at the same time be a component of creative activity. One of the two methods would inhibit or cancel out the other and it is almost certain that, as in the past, the creative aspect would be the one to suffer. In the long run, there would be no real change.

CREATIVE TECHNOLOGY

Another factor of great importance in the sphere of creative activities within the primary school of tomorrow will be technology, still known under its former names (crafts, technique, slöjd, etc., i.e. manual activi-

---

[12] *Ibid.*

Artistic and Creative Activity

ties having a constructive purpose), which only partly satisfied the needs of education in a rapidly expanding technology.[13] Here again, even more obviously than in language and arithmetic and similar subjects, application and repetition still predominate. Present day technical activities are in an even worse plight than the arts; the objections that we have already raised to teaching practice in the field of the arts are even more applicable to technical exercises, where the copying of models, the implementation of other people's projects and the outside conditioning of the child when handling various materials mean that this type of work is preplanned and rigid. Evaluation of the child's "talent" is based mainly on the skill, speed and accuracy with which he arrives at the end product. Although every elementary school now decries the professional approach, the pupil is in fact made to tackle technical activities like a miniature workman. His concern to meet all the specifications for the products that he has been set to make (or the components of that product assigned to him) usually makes it impossible for him to diverge from the instructions he has been given. He is not allowed to add anything new to the process or to the end result.

Another disadvantage of technical and manual activities as they are often practised today, unlike artistic activities, is the pressure of time. Full attention is focused upon the product. If the pupil is slow or if his end product is incomplete or if he fails to produce an end product, the child's "technical" ability is negatively assessed. This is the result of the transfer to education of those rules that govern adult work, where each operation has its time limit.

This conditioning, which is based both upon a specific aptitude towards manual activity and to long standing prejudice underlying the view of manual work as servile and non-skilled, prevents the change in outlook that will be necessary if technical activities are to be reformed to bring them into line with the true significance of technology: the development of inventive skills, allowing children to develop at their own rate even – and perhaps especially – when these processes do not follow the prescribed or foreseeable pattern.

From this point of view, technical activities are closer in spirit to the artistic activities that we have been discussing than any other kind of subject. In technology, as in the arts, there is a need for the broad individual freedom in invention and execution, especially as the value of technological experience, like aesthetic experience, lies in the inner

---

[13] See the brochure illustrating the official curricula of compulsory schools in Sweden: *Läroplan för grundskolan: Teknik, Slöjd, och Konst.*

process that it stimulates rather than the fact that it improves performance (although performance may be significant for the feedback that it provides with those processes).

"It is extremely important that future education in technology be as much concerned with the aesthetic aspect of the problem as with the functional (in fact, it would be better to think simply of one problem – the aesthetic-functional one), but I do not mean producing the art-craft product, or machine product plus art overlay... Too much education is concerned with processes and subjects, not enough with ideas. I generally find the reverse is more productive: if the ideas are meaningful and personally exciting, then the processes evolve in a more fruitful way". The author of these comments, Tom Hudson[14], goes on to say that even in the child of 4-5, the idea "is the dominant factor in creative production: a box became a 'house' by an act of preference and selection, but it could also be a ship, a basket or any other container, for the child has understood the basic structure and simple function of the form".

It is clear that insight into structure and function develops in line with the technical ability of the child and vice versa. An older child of 7 or more can think and work with more sophisticated forms because he has a more definite and concrete sense of "inherent structures". Technological performance is a very valid way for the child, and later for the adolescent, to approach and interpret his environment, besides being a far more interesting goal than the traditional production of objects of greater or less beauty or value. The dividing line between technological activities as such and aesthetic activities becomes very blurred, often disappearing altogether.[15] Creative technology also provides an excellent link with scientific development, especially in the field of geometry and in what is known as "creative" geometry (devising problems of relationships, variations of standard joints and all types of topological solutions and "games" with two-dimensional and solid structures, etc.). One exercise, for instance, is to apply a solid tube to a plane

[14] T. Hudson, *Creative technology*, report presented to the INSEA Congress, Coventry (England), 1970.

[15] An example of functionality of this type can be found in the following experiment by the group who organised the dramatic activity described above, this time in the "Hammer Game", an imaginative-mimetic-constructive game. "Everyone was invited to grip the hammer and imagine it becoming other things. The hammer became a pendulum, a guitar, a microphone, a vacuum cleaner, depending on the mimetic actions of the child. This imaginative game was then transferred to the (scenic) structure, thus giving dramatic significance to what the children had spontaneously constructed. The structure could be a sky-scraper, a mountain or a swimming pool, and the children as a group used the structure according to these suggestions". (*Il lavoro teatrale nella scuola, op. cit.*, p. 27).

tune and to allow the former to move freely on the latter, observing the forms that are produced with different materials, temperatures, lights and so on, emphasising the plastic engineering or aesthetic output aspects, the functional or non-functional nature of a given product, in the light of individual taste. In the child, the concept of function tends to differ from the concept of utility or use of the product. A product that is non-functional in itself may be seen by him as a functional structure, just as a system that is irregular and symmetric in itself may be perceived by the child as regular and symmetric for the purpose of future projects.

ARTISTIC AND SCIENTIFIC CREATIVITY

The hypothesis – and it is a hypothesis that has been tested in a growing number of similar experiments over the past few years – is that once the child manages to devise and check his own technological solutions that are functional in their own way, he also rejects conformist solutions at the level of perception and ideation. His ability for problem-setting and problem-solving develops more satisfactorily and rapidly than with the standard forms of manipulation and production, whether these are guided or whether they are spontaneous. If the school of tomorrow can make good use of this hypothesis, it is almost certain that the power of abstract thought can be acquired at a far earlier point in the child's development and will be seen as not following on, but virtually contemporary with, concrete thought.

Technological activities, however, do not merely affect creative geometry – seen not as a subject but as a wide field in which the child can devise new forms and new relationships, no longer hidebound by mathematical and numerical convention, but using his imagination to develop a rich constructive idiom. From a slightly different point of view, technological experience may contribute to aesthetic development; for instance, activities using colour, light and other "apparent" qualities that affect structures both artistically and technologically.

Along these lines, lines that the traditional technical educators considered to be secondary or decorative, aesthetic, technological and scientific creative activities will develop. The criterion unifying all these activities will be that they develop inventive and productive abilities, still closely linked in the child but all too separate and isolated in the adult world due to the division of labour and the resulting cultural and educational prejudices. One of the tasks of the education of tomorrow will be to ensure that they continue to develop in unison or in close inter-relation.

It must be the goal of the future educational system to identify, stimulate and develop the many psychological and practical potentialities of the child, many of which are still ignored or starved from the very first. Even if these potentialities are better understood, they will develop only when the burdensome set patterns of education, the fragmentation of perception, ideas and production and hierarchical classifications are abolished.

All research on creativity points to the conclusion that creativity is an existential and functional whole, both in theory and in ascertained behaviour. Creativity is an overall function of the personality, not subject to fragmentation or hierarchical classification of its components. Lowenfeld, in the third edition of his best known work, was able to state that "recent experimentations in finding attributes which are responsible for *general* creativeness in individuals have revealed that they are the same attributes as found in any creative process".[16] He cited research conducted by Guilford and Brittain on people working in the arts and in the sciences. Their conclusions, he said, were the same: creativity always follows the same functional rules. Nor has this been disproved by subsequent research. Visalberghi observes that any distinction between definable aspects of creativity based on the traditional categories of culture and education is arbitrary. It is no longer possible to sustain that there is a dichotomy between "art and science; between aesthetic education and the initiation to logical and scientific thought"[17], as Montessori and Dewey asserted with reference to early childhood.

THE ROLE OF EMOTIVITY

To the extent that creative activity of an aesthetic type is a form of behaviour whose aim is to solve a problem, and that scientific or technological activity is nothing without imagination, to distinguish between the faculties typical of creativity or technology is as useless as the old-fashioned distinction between reason and feeling, between logic and sensitivity. Rational processes are intimately linked with emotional processes; even emotions are incorporated in structures which could

---

[16] Lowenfeld, *op. cit.*, p. 4.
[17] A. Visalberghi, "Arte e scienze nei programmi di studio dell'istruzione obbligatoria", in *Vita dell'Infanzia*, Rome, 1968, p. 5.

Artistic and Creative Activity

not exist without them, just as thought could not take form were there no emotion. As Chesterton so truly said, the madman is not the man who has lost his reason, but the man who has lost everything but his reason.

Education over the next few decades can certainly no longer ignore the importance of the sphere, far wider and more vivid during early childhood, which we can place under the general heading of the sphere of emotion, or at least those emotional components implicit in the processes described as non-artistic. In his major work on art, Dewey remarked that to think directly in colours, tones and images is a technically different operation from thinking in words. The fact, however, that the meaning of paintings or symphonies cannot be translated into words or the meaning of poetry into prose does not imply that thought is the monopoly of the latter.

One aspect of creativity that has gradually come to light in more recent research, an aspect that has repeatedly been pointed out by Lowenfeld, is that it provides a link with reality. Creativity, in the modern sense of the term, should be distinguished from apparently similar concepts which define it as essentially escapist, the attitude of the dreamer or the rebel who opposes all that is reasonable and normal. The "divergent" should not be seen as being in direct opposition to the "convergent", whatever the direction it may take and the fruit it may bear. In essence, a creative attitude is something more than mere inventiveness as opposed to repetitiveness. It is a capacity for reorganising stimuli into a new structure so that they produce an equally new result but one that is consonant with psychological or environmental reality, not with a dream world.

In other words, creativity is a form of re-living, with slight changes, one's relationship with the internal and external environment. Whatever the language it uses and whatever the method, it is always based upon reality.

This is why, in addition to the forms of artistic, scientific and technological creative activity already discussed, we should include what we may call "creativity in social studies", in other words an analysis of the environment around us, the search for unconventional viewpoints, for detail and for the link between them. Let us suppose for example that we give a group of pupils a camera (or a movie camera or any instrument that may be invented in the future) and set it a theme of this kind: "in X number of shots, record your family life or your father's or your mother's working problems, or an excursion with your friends or scenes from the life of your district, etc.". The theme can be illustrated verbally or in writing; instead of photographs, the pupils could make drawings or sketches or a tape recording, and so on. Every aspect of a child's life, or preferably the life of a group, can be documented creatively, illustrated and discussed by the children and the educators. There are so many methods and techniques available today; tomorrow they will be virtually unlimited.

In the final analysis, however, this activity forms part of those already described. Artistic, scientific and technological observation and the use of instruments which make the child's ability for analysis more acute are in themselves a valuable and as yet almost unexplored method of interpreting the world around him and of comprehending and changing that world. At the same time, the mass media of the future and their growing use in schools will extend the child's horizons to the whole world.

THE FORMATION OF AESTHETIC TASTE

This topic leads to two other subjects: the formation of "artistic taste" and the employment of new means of communication. The traditional motivation for the teaching and practice of art was to help children to appreciate works of art, either artificial or natural, to impart a liking for the things of this life that can be seen as expressive of beauty by assimilating certain rules. The belief of the New Education Movement that the purpose of any educational activity is not to prepare the child specifically for the equivalent activity in adult life but to develop general personality attitudes has unintentionally reinforced that traditional goal. The inevitable "crisis of puberty" has accomplished the rest. Unless the purpose of the child's artistic activity is to train him to be a painter or an actor, etc., and if his creative abilities are destined to end at puberty, then the only way in which his painting, modelling or acting will benefit him will be to provide a grounding in receptive sensitivity, a capacity for artistic appreciation in his adult life.

In short, the school has produced no more than consumers of cultural products, products similar to those that the child has handled for so many years on his school desk. A child studies the works of great authors for years for the sole purpose of becoming a more appreciative and cultured reader. For some decades now, it has been easier to reproduce works of art and this has increased the consumer attitude far beyond the period of school and in a very different way from the conventions established by the school. Much has already been spoken and written about this social phenomenon and we need not dwell upon it here.

The point with which we are concerned here is this: as the communications media improve and their coverage becomes wider, will they accentuate the consumer attitude? Will the educational system be affected and will the school itself provide an early incentive in the same direction? The temptation to do so will be strong, as the use of the mass media appears to ensure a faster and more efficient learning process, in the same way as programmed learning. The use of ever more comprehensive, economic and functional means of communicating works of art (which may be reduced into the form of programmed sequences and brought down to the level considered to be acceptable to the pupils) will become increasingly attractive. This may be strongly supported by the traditional assumption that the function of the school is to transmit predetermined units of learning and values and instruments from one generation to the next. As the technical methods of reproducing works of art multiply, the idea may once more gain acceptance that art education should be imparted by providing contact with "great works". It will be asserted that the reason why this contact was neglected and the role of artistic education devalued was a lack of opportunity for establishing contact between the school and masterpieces. On the day when the teacher can press a button and reproduce the whole of Raphael or the whole of Brunelleschi in the classroom, or a montage of the great performances of Toscanini or Abrasov, or passages from Goethe or Shakespeare read by well-known actors, the old concept of education by "contact" will find a formidable ally.

There is a risk, therefore, that even at primary level the school will become a permanent audio-visual centre; the risk is greatest in those areas of learning in which such a development would destroy creativity and the many motivations for creativity. We must reach a decision now whose repercussions will be felt in ten, twenty or perhaps thirty years. The children themselves must use the growing mass of information and teaching facilities as tools to enlarge and refine their perceptive, imaginative and expressive potential. It does not mean that they cannot use the same instruments for documentary and analytic purposes, provided that this promotes creative activity. The students will be able to use the same media for communicating their own methods or the results of their work to companions in the same school or in other schools or even in other cities – and, dare we hope, in other nations. The important factor is that they should not merely be at the receiving end but should have the opportunity to discuss, participate in and enrich the content of what they receive.

The vast technological apparatus which is bound to be available in the year 2000 will surely allow two-way communication in the school, communication between one group of pupils and another, between pupils and the outside world. It is to be hoped that the same pattern will be achieved by the mass media outside the school system, so that the mass media will no longer manipulate the public but become an instrument of communication, the content diffused by the mass media being provided by the users, so that they become channels of communication as is the telephone and the postal service today. We emphasise this point, because it would be Utopian to predict such a revolutionary use of the communication and reproduction media in the educational process were these media to be used otherwise in society at large. For ideological reasons, for reasons of economy (industry could adapt communication facilities to the needs of education but could not produce two different types of facilities) and cultural politics, it is unlikely that the schools will operate independently in the future, especially if in its independence it runs counter to the patterns that prevail in society.

We shall presume, then, that today, on the threshold of the 21st century, the formation of taste is no longer an objective. The objective at which we should aim is to develop overall creative abilities which may – as methods become more individual – take "artistic" forms in John, the form of "technological ability" in Mary, and so on. It is vital, however, that the different manifestations are not separated at the root. There should not be a different logic and different opportunities for the two cultures, for they both satisfy a comprehensive need and their goal is indivisible. "Taste", artistic and scientific and any other form, will acquire shape and meaning when it is viewed as the ability to meet the needs of creativity.

These requirements begin at the level of perception, selection and organisation of internal and external stimuli. A creative personality reacts in an unpredictable way to stimuli from his surroundings, but his response will incorporate the qualities of freedom, inventiveness and individualisation inherent in the creative processes. In this sense, the most convincing definition of the creative factor is that it is the factor found in a *field-independent* personality. Aesthetic taste and appreciation thus become the ability to re-create, an open-mindedness not susceptible to indiscriminate influences, attributing its own set of meanings rather than accepting them ready-made, restructuring information and levels of aspiration in the light of practical projects, even when the internal processing does not necessarily culminate in a product. Indeed, in the most creative personalities, such activities may merely take the form of planning or hypothetical exploration not apparent to the outsider nor producing a tangible product. No conventional evaluation can be made of these processes; they cannot be dismissed because of the absence of an objective result for in fact they are valuable processes of accumulation, clarification, *tâtonnement*, without which no creative product could materialise.

CONTEMPLATION AND ITS RELATIONSHIP TO REALITY

These re-creative processes are to be found in many fields of activity. In the aesthetic sphere, the analogy with the old stereotype of "contemplation" is only partial. The object of contemplation was not the work of art but the "beauty" that it might reveal. The contemplative attitude is to be found more in field-dependent than in field-independent personalities.[18] The reason is obvious; contemplation has in a sense been used as an educational and behavioural method and implies faith in structured and predetermined values, identifying uncritically with set models. It implies induced choices and provides no stimulus for personal choice.

Recent literature on human behaviour in the presence of art, even at the level of child education, has often stressed the identificational and projective value of contemplation, especially of phenomena based on the organisation of images in dynamic forms that act as substitutes for perception, such as the cinema or television whose cameras select and give shape to the image. This is true and a positive factor, provided that contemplation does not replace and suppress the process of re-creation. Whether this occurs does not depend upon the language or situation of the artistic entertainment, but rather upon whether the spectator himself abdicates his powers of selection and imagination.

In conclusion, perception itself, as M. Milner maintains[19], is an act of the imagination. We almost always use unconsciously conformist codes which do not acknowledge perceptive "divergence", but we

[18] H. A. Witkin et al., *Personality through Perception*, Harper, New York, 1954.
[19] M. Milner, *On not being able to paint*, Heinemann, London, 1962.

could create our own personal codes, even to the extent of seeing the "invisible part of a chair or a carrot" to quote Milner's own example, or of perceiving the outlines of separate objects as one continuous line constituting a single object. Modern painting from the Impressionists on, for example, has been motivated by the search for new methods of perceiving reality and of imaginatively transfiguring that reality.

The powers that should be developed in the child of the future are those which help him to establish a perceptual relationship with reality, so that he can accept communicated codes in a flexible manner while at the same time he is able to construct "aberrant" codes. In other words, we should endow the child with a far wider ability for intuitive analysis than the ability afforded him at present by the normal processes of education and culture formation. We must be aware of the need to promote the child's development of intuition, to stimulate and enrich it, not let it blossom spontaneously and then smother it on the pretext that the child is going through a period of crisis. This objective obviously depends on educational criteria which:

a) devote the same energy to the formation of powers of imagination and reprocessing as is today dedicated to teaching the child to assimilate facts and to organise those facts intellectually;
b) do not accept that these powers disappear with the onset of puberty;
c) see the act of production as being merely the conclusion of a process that has been "creative" from the moment of conception.

The act of creation and the receptive act of re-creation (although this distinction is fictitious and is used merely for convenience) must be seen as the two ends of a same thread, or rather the two poles of a dielectric element. In future taste, contemplation, etc., should be regarded as no more than an important aspect of creativity.

ARTISTIC CREATIVITY AND THE TEACHER

The emphasis placed upon an artistic or creative education in the training of future primary school teachers will obviously reflect the value placed upon this type of education in the curriculum of the schools in which they are to teach. It should be no surprise to us that this aspect of their training has almost universally been neglected, both quantitatively and qualitatively: it has been superficial and sketchy and has not provided the instruments that a teacher needs if he is to carry out goals defined several decades ago. The defect is even more glaring in systems where elementary school teachers are trained at no higher than secondary level themselves; but even where they are trained at higher level, despite the substantial progress already made, especially in Great Britain and Sweden, it is the universal opinion that a satisfactory standard has not yet been achieved.

According to Lowenfeld, it is vital that artistic activity and creative activity in general be a "dynamic, ever changing process" and that it should fulfil all the requirements we have been discussing, "not only for the student, but even more so for the teacher who needs this flexibility both to understand and motivate the individual and to shift and adapt his thinking from individual to individual".[20]

Academic or technical mastery of the subject being taught is less important than a capacity to identify with the child in his creative work, for if there is no empathy the teacher will be unable to help the child to produce and develop his projects in a creative manner. In a book written for parents, Lowenfeld stressed that to teach children's art a teacher needs psychological understanding more than technical knowledge and skill. He specifies that the main requisite for the educator (and we should like to see this term in current use instead of the anachronistic word "teacher") is that he should be concerned with the creative process and himself be a creator.[21]

This point is of the utmost importance. The question is: how can we ensure that the attitude of our future educators will be sufficiently creative to stimulate corresponding attitudes in their pupils? How can this objective be achieved when the training methods and the educational system producing these teachers of tomorrow are still based upon the study of subjects in isolation, imparted by passive and repetitive methods? How can art education, or any other type of creative activity, be conceived as no more than the subject of a lesson?

It is always difficult to break out of a vicious circle and we are here faced with the vicious circle of attempting to reform an educational system but being unable to do so because the teachers who are to implement that reform have been trained under the old system. The only way to solve the problem will be to embark upon far more advanced training techniques than at present, as soon as possible, with a more advanced concept of education than is now current in the schools where the teachers are to work. Only by this means will we provide a sufficiently large body of educators in twenty or thirty years time who are trained for the model of education that we hope to see.

[20] V. Lowenfeld, *op. cit.*, p. 80.
[21] V. Lowenfeld, *Your Child and his Art*.

There is now a fairly widespread belief that the basic feature of the educator of tomorrow must be his ability to behave creatively, to organise the environment and his pupils' activities in coherent ways. If the educator is to be a creative personality in this sense, he must achieve and maintain a balance between emotion and intellect so that his powers of creativity are not handicapped by the usual inhibitions. We can verify the truth of the hypothesis that anybody can be creative and produce creatively if they can overcome their inhibitions, especially those of subconscious origin. To achieve such an equilibrium does not mean that all internal conflict will be resolved. On the contrary, a person who aspires to be a creator, beginning in the educational sphere, must be prepared to accept conflict without being so disturbed by it that he becomes inhibited. Those who study the process of creativity and psychodynamic development agree that self-realisation, the freedom from the anxiety of being unable to cope with conflict, is a prerequisite for creativity (Moreno, Rogers, Maslow, etc.).

This is one of the main problems in psycho-pedagogical research on the training of educators for the future. We could not hope to introduce a school based upon the principles of creativity unless we first concentrate upon those who are to act as mediators and guides in the creative activities. The problem of training educators to assume new roles does not concern the province of art alone (especially at the elementary level), although it has special significance in this field because artistic activities should provide the guidelines for the curricula of the future. (De Bartolomeis has provided a clear outline of the psychological problems involved in the training of future teachers.)

But the teacher does not work in isolation, nor is the teacher-pupil relationship considered any more to be the only relationship of importance in the educational process. The need for group activity in the teaching and training of children is widely appreciated. Team teching is increasingly common and should be encouraged at the elementary level. The view of a school founded upon laboratories (as described by De Bartolomeis) suggests two solutions for the future:
a) there will no longer be a single teacher for a single class, but specialised teachers who, combined or in turn, help groups or subgroups of pupils with various types of activity;
b) the "class" teacher will remain but will provide a "home base" for each group of pupils, guiding them in the basic steps of each activity; he will be assisted by specialised educators once the activities become more complex.

Artistic and Creative Activity

A third solution could apply to both (a) and (b): the teaching team could include specialists in psychology, physical and mental hygiene, educational technology, community life, etc.

It would be a pointless exercise at this juncture to decide which of the two solutions is preferable. Only experimentation, both general and adapted to local changing situations, can help to guide the choice of models for twenty or thirty years hence. The important factor is that team teaching, however it is organised and however it operates, should in fact materialise and that it should provide an example of creative behaviour, that it should be flexible, versatile and practical, that it should not allow the resurgence of hierarchies of knowledge and status, that it should prevent the crystallisation of attitudes which would counteract creativity.

BIOGRAPHICAL NOTES

ORNELLA ANDREANI DENTICI has for many years been researching into cognition processes and doing experimental studies into memory and intelligence. She has recently been in charge of an extensive investigation, for the IARD Programme (*Individuazione e Arricchimento dei Ragazzi Dotati*), on socio-cultural conditions of intelligence, of speech, of motivation and attitudes.

She is Director of the Institute of Psychology and the University Counselling Centre of the University of Pavia.

FRANCESCO DE BARTOLOMEIS is Professor of Education and Director of the Institute of Pedagogy of the Faculty of Education of the University of Turin. At this university he directs the school which specializes in psychology, education and the psychology of education.

He has carried out a great number of studies on educational methods and the psychological and sociological aspects of education and he has broadened his interests recently in the field of the psychology of art and of aesthetical criticism.

Among his main publications are: *Introduzione alla didattica della scuola attiva; La pedagogia come scienza; La psicologia dell'adolescente; Formazione tecnico-professionale e pedagogia dell'industria; Cultura, lavoro, tempo libero; La ricerca come antipedagogia; Metodi e nuova cultura nella pedagogia d'oggi; Orientamenti attuali per la scuola primaria; Scuola a tempo pieno.*

LAMBERTO BORGHI is Professor of Pedagogy and Director of the Institute of Pedagogy at the University of Florence.

After obtaining his doctorate in Philosophy at the University of Pisa he was a professor of history and philosophy. From 1941 to 1948 he was professor of philosophy, Italian and history at several American universities. In 1948 he obtained his doctorate in Social Sciences at the Graduate Faculty of Political and Social Science, New School for Social Research, NYC.

Since 1949 he has been a professor of education at several Italian universities; in 1952 he was a visiting professor of philosophy at the Graduate Faculty of Political and Social Science, New School for Social Research, NYC. In 1955 he took up his present position.

He is a member of the international committee of The World Education Fellowship and of the Steering Committee of the Italian Pedagogical Association. He is also Vice-President of the Comparative Education Society in Europe and President of the Italian Federation of CEMEA (*Centres d'entrainement aux méthodes de l'éducation active*).

He has published a great number of articles in various magazines, e.g. "*Scuola e Città*", and several books among which are: Education and Authority in Modern Italy (Florence, 1951); John Dewey and Contemporary Educational Thought in USA (Florence, 1951); Education and its Problems (Florence, 1952); Education and School in Italy Today (Florence, 1958); Education and Social Growth (Florence, 1963); School and Community (Florence, 1964); School and Environment (Bari, 1964); and Sex Education (Florence, 1968) of which he was co-author.

ANTONIO SANTONI RUGIU is Professor of Pedagogy at the Faculty of Education at the University of Florence. He is Director of the revue on educational problems and policy "*Scuola e Città*".

He is particularly interested in socio-political conditions which influence the role of the teacher and education in general. More recently he has developed his studies in the field of creativity.

Among his main publications are: *Il professore nella scuola italiana* (1959); *Educatori oggi e domani* (1966); *Creatività e deprivazione artistica* (1969); and *Gruppi e didattica universitaria* (1973).

GASTONE TASSINARI is Lecturer at the Institute of Pedagogy of the Faculty of Education at the University of Florence. Since 1972 he teaches Comparative Education at the same Faculty. From 1960 to 1967 he directed the schools of the "*Società Umanitaria di Milano*" and attended the experiments of the "*Scuola media*" full time.

He collaborated in several investigations: in 1962-63 in the investigation into the level of literacy of the Milanese people, instigated by the Municipality of Milan; in 1963-64 in the investigation on the methodology of professional teaching in Europe, instigated by the EEC; in 1967-68 in the research on communication processes and on social attitudes of young people, under the auspices of the CNR (*Consiglio Nazionale delle Ricerche*) and under the direction of Prof. Lamberto Borghi.

LYDIA TORNATORE is Professor of Pedagogy at the Faculty of Letters and Philosophy at the University of Florence and is Director of the "Pestalozzi" School in Florence.

Her studies have been particularly concerned with the psychological problems of learning and organisation of the curriculum, and she has dedicated special attention to the didactics of science and mathematics.

INDEX

Adorno, Th., 12, 19
Ahlstrom, K. G., 40
Allan, D. W., 85
Allport, G. W., 12
Andreani Dentici, O., 36, 247
Anthony, E. J., 100
Arnheim, R., 226
Bailey, W., 190
Baldi, 126
Barbieri, 125
Bartlett, 95
Battegay, R., 100
Becker, J. M., 188
Benjamin, J., 24, 25
Berelson, B., 208
Bereiter, C., 53
Bernstein, B., 34, 36, 54, 57, 62, 63, 127, 128
Bion, R., 100
Bjerstedt, A., 207
Borghi, L., 247
Bourbaki, N., 150, 156, 163
Brittain, 236
Bronfenbrenner, U., 87
Bruner, J. S., 6, 9, 10, 30
Cabassi, 136
Calegari, 136
Cassirer, E., 29
Cattell, B., (test), 125, 129, 131
Cavallini, 124
Chesterton, 237
Chomsky, C., 92, 94
Cruchfield, 95
Davis, R. B., 164
De Bartolomeis, F., 215, 244, 247

Deutsch, M., 34, 36, 62, 65, 138
Dewey, J., 6, 7, 8, 9, 15, 22, 23, 26, 29, 32, 34, 72, 92, 188, 197, 198, 206, 213, 221, 236, 237
Dienes, Z. P., 149, 150, 156, 160, 162, 164
Duse, 126
Engelmann, S., 53
Erikson, E., 25
Fantini, M. D., 55
Fenton, E., 186
Foulkes, S. H., 100
Frech, H. W., 85
Freire, P., 31
Frenkel-Brunswick, E., 12, 13
Freud, S., 98, 100
Freudenthal, H., 167, 168
Frost, J. L., 209
Gille, (test), 125, 129
Goldman, S., 85
Goodman, P., 7, 20
Grannis, J. C., 190
Guilford, 95, 236
Guthrie, 92
Hanna, P. R., 196
Harding, J., 11
Hartley, W. H., 184
Havighurst, R., 130
Hay, L., 102
Hegel, E., 23
Hendrick, I., 25
Heziel, H., 100
Hilgard, E. R., 80
Horkheimer, M., 12, 19
Hudson, T., 234

Hull, 92
Husén, T., 81
Hutchins, R. M., 4, 5
Jespersen, O., 29
Johnson, O., 52
Joyce, B. R., 85, 197, 203, 209
Kallen, H., 15, 55
Keller, Ch. R., 184
Kenworthy, L. S., 197
Kilpatrick, W. H., 15
King, E. J., 74, 75, 77, 78
Kneller, 95
Krasno, R. M., 85
Lawton, D., 127
Legrand, L., 199
Lévi-Strauss, C., 93, 94, 204
Lewin, K., 16, 98, 102
Lichnérowicz, J., 155, 156
Lippitt, 206
Lobau, 127
Lowenfeld, V., 223, 231, 232, 237, 243
Lutte, 140
Magaret, A., 30
Marcuse, H., 3, 4, 23, 24
Markuschewich, A., 158
Marx, K., 26
Mattioli, 140
Maslova, G. G., 159
Maslow, 244
Milani, D., 31
Miller, R. I., 65, 103
Mills, C. Wright, 20, 205
Milner, M., 241, 242
Mitter, W., 186, 187
Moreno, J. L., 102, 228, 244
Montessori, M., 10, 236
Olds, Jr., H. F., 70
Osborn, A. F., 97
Papy, 149
Pavlov, E., 92
Petrovich, M. B., 208

Piaget, J., 10, 17, 18, 30, 93, 125, 126, 150, 151, 152
Picard, N., 155
Pollock, H. O., 167
Postman, N., 6
Proverbio, 140
Read, H., 23, 216
Reading, (test), 131
Riesman, D., 20
Robinsohn, S. B., 83
Rogers, C. R., 5, 14, 95, 244
Rokeach, M., 13
Rowland, G. Th., 209
Russell, B., 18, 19
Santoni Rugiu, A., 248
Sarti, 140
Schwab, 202
Senesh, L., 190
Shaplin, J. T., 68
Skinner, B., 92
Slavson, S. R., 100
Spencer, H., 213
Stukat, K. G., 79
Sudman, 126
Sullivan, H. S., 98
Taba, H., 188, 190, 207
Tassinari, G., 248
Taylor, W., 95
Thorndike, R. L., 92
Titone, R., 41
Tolman, 92, 93
Tornatore, L., 248
Torrance, 95
Tumin, M. M., 11
Vegetti, 125, 134, 139
Visalberghi, A., 236
Vygotsky, L. S., 9
Watson, 92
Wertheimer, M., 93
Weingartner, Ch., 6

I'